CARING
discipline

Practical Tools
for Nurturing
Happy Families
& Classrooms

"**This class, along with the well-written book**, has brought harmony back into our home."
— *Lori Mendoza, mother*

"**This is the single best book on parenting I have read** … I don't know of any parent who would not get something of enormous value from this book. The techniques are practical and effective, and ever mindful of building and respecting the child's self-esteem … the book is great beyond words, because if you practice what is in its pages, it will transform your life and your household … I do not think it is exaggeration to say that our world would be completely transformed if *Caring Discipline* were required reading for all parents."
— *Review from confirmed purchaser on Amazon.com*

"**I have taught the sixth grade for twenty-one years** and thought I had a good handle on discipline, but after reading JoAnne's material, I found out how little I knew about understanding children's misbehaviors … I highly recommend this material to all educators and parents."
— *Ronald R. Schoeler, elementary school teacher*

"**The *Caring Discipline* material is the only course** on parenting that I have ever taken that helped me understand the reality of a child … The ideas are practical and simple, very easy to implement. I have had great success with my children, and my children have had a mother who is a lot more fun!"
— *Joyce A. Humble, mother*

"***Caring Discipline* is the best parenting book out there**. I have recommended it to a ton of friends over the years, as it gave us the tools and knowledge to become better parents and to create a family environment of cooperation, good communication, and mutual respect. I was involved with a group of parents that would read the book and meet weekly to discuss the material and exercises - moderated by a friend who started and ran a Montessori school … Those few weeks in the parenting group and the discussions from the book were invaluable to my husband and I … This book is a must read for all parents!!!"
— *Nancy Smorch, parent*

"**Your book has been our bible** … thank you!"
— *Janet Gillman, mother*

"**What I have learned** has permitted me to nearly completely resolve the behavior issues that I had been struggling with … I am so grateful!"
— *Courtney Acostarates, mother*

"**Now in a thoroughly updated and expanded** edition, JoAnne Nordling's *Caring Discipline* continues to provide a model for classroom educators of a step-by-step process for successfully managing the misbehavior of children and teens, whether in the home setting or at school … highly recommended for classroom and home schooling."
— *Midwest Book Review*

"**This book has changed how my wife and I parent** … Ms. Nordling has written a book which offers parents a complete toolbox of actions and approaches to help kids be joyous and free while learning how to behave in respectful and non-indulgent ways. I have friends who balk at the word discipline, but I think of this as a toolbox in a book. I have learned about how I sabotage my own parenting, how to determine what is misbehavior and what is age-appropriate in my kids, as well as how to decrease self-indulgent behavior such as whining, complaining and holding the family up. I highly recommend this to parents of kids ages 3.5 through adolescence."
— *Brian Mayer, father and high school teacher*

"**This book has given me the tools** I need to discipline my 7-year-old daughter without damaging her self-esteem. It gives you EASY, practical steps that … are easy to remember! My daughter's attitude has changed considerably since I began to incorporate this book into our everyday routine. Even if you don't feel like you have time to try something new, you do have time for this! It's an easy read, and your life will be better for it!"
— *Carey Johnson, parent*

"**Some of the issues our teachers, parents, and children** are dealing with today are unlike any other issues I have run into in my thirty years at our school. We all often find ourselves in 'uncharted territory' and have repeatedly looked to *Caring Discipline* to find solutions to the challenges we face. It has never let us down … "
— *Sue Husband, founder and director, Montessori Children's House (Pre-school-sixth grade), Lansing, Michigan*

"*Caring Discipline* **is a book for the ages ... thank you!**"
— *Vicki Skellcerf, mother*

"**I would HIGHLY recommend this book** to any parent, teacher, or anyone who comes in contact with another human being ... We got the honor of taking a class from the author of this book. Although it is geared for parents, it is truly a great book for how we should treat any other person we come into contact with. It takes a different approach than anything I've seen/heard/read in other books/classes (and I have a degree in early childhood/elementary education!)"
— *Review from verified purchaser on Amazon.com*

"**I don't need to tell you** what an amazing difference you helped make in my relationship with my daughter, because you saw me (and all the other attending parents) glowing with success from our new understanding of our children. Our children thank you and we all thank you, again and again and again ... I know that I speak for all the parents in our class. The results are priceless ... and infinite!"
— *J.D. Bruinier, mother*

"**JoAnne Nordling has written a truly insightful text** which will be of great value to all who care for children. A powerful book, I highly recommend it!"
— *Donna Medenma, elementary school teacher*

COMMENTS from *Caring Discipline* Parenting classes evaluation forms:

"**I used to just yell** and hit the kids when they did something wrong. Now I find it amazingly easy to do these other things instead. And when I started the class I never thought it was possible."

"**Our kids are as grateful** as we are!"

"**It changed my whole life** for the better."

"**I just want to let you know** the class was amazing ... I hope to pass this information on to friends and family."

"**It works! It works! It works!**"

CARING
discipline

**Practical Tools
for Nurturing
Happy Families
& Classrooms**

FIFTH EDITION

JoANNE NordliNq, m.s., m.ed.

Caring Discipline is an expanded and revised
edition of *Taking Charge: Caring Discipline That
Works at Home and at School*

Parent
Support Center

Portland, Oregon

Published by Parent Support Center, Inc., www.parentsupportcenter.org,
503-796-9665

ISBN 9780988518421

This book is sold with the understanding that the subject matter covered herein is of a general
nature and does not constitute legal, counseling, medical or other professional advice for any
specific individual or situation.

Graphic Design: Design Studio Selby

All photographs used by permission

Printed in the United States of America

"Discipline is the slow, bit by bit, time-consuming task of helping children to see the sense of acting in a certain way."
— *James Hymes*, *a founder of the Head Start program*

"Never break a child's spirit."
— *Ellen Berggren Swenston*, *eighty-four-year-old great-grandmother*

"I'm holding on with my heart."
— *Ricky*, *age four, swinging high at Fanno Creek Children's Center*

To my sons, Dirk, Eric, Chris, and Craig,

my husband, George,

my parents, Dora and Verle,

and my sister, Carla

Acknowledgments

There are so many people responsible for the development of this successful approach to child discipline I cannot list them all, but here are some of the people I am especially indebted to:

The parents and teachers who used the material and asked so many productive questions throughout the development of this text.

Dr. Morris Tiktin, family counselor, who introduced me to the consequence and democracy concepts of Rudolf Dreikurs.

Jean Lawrence, founder of Fanno Creek Children's Center of Portland, Oregon, for her many sensitive insights into the behavior of children.

Sue Edmiston, parenting teacher and family counselor, whose teachings sent me on the fruitful search for completing her idea of an appropriate correction for each misbehavior. I have elaborated and refined Sue's idea but the basic Adlerian core came from her.

Lorraine Heller, my partner at the Parent Support Center of Portland, Oregon, whose dedication and compassion has been an inspiration, and whose constant encouragement to complete this manuscript has been invaluable.

My teachers in the graduate counseling program of Lewis and Clark College, Portland, Oregon: Dr. Bob McIlroy, Dr. Jerry McCubbin, and Dr. Gordon Lindbloom. I would especially like to thank Dr. Don Nickerson, who helped me come to terms with some of the difficult experiences of my own childhood.

Sean, Lisa, Sharon, Ted, and all the children I worked with in play therapy, who revealed to me the awesome integrity and strength of every child's inner self.

I am especially grateful to Jewel Lansing and Miriam Selby for their invaluable editing advice. (It is no exaggeration to say that without Miriam's help, the fourth and fifth editions might never have seen the light of day.) I would also like to thank Ron Olisar, Louise Waitt, Linda Williamson, Lorraine Heller, Derene Meurisse, and Betty Daggett who gave so generously of their time and talents in preparation of the early manuscript.

And finally, a very special thank you to the many people who have supported Parent Support Center and the *Caring Discipline* program throughout the past 26 years. Teachers: Lorraine Heller, Sarah Lauer, Denise Meurisse, Marilyn Mays, Vanessa Timmons, June Howell, Joanne Delmonico, Michele Miller, Karen Bissonette, Kristin Lasher, Cheri Shea, Jane and Brian Mayer. Board Members: Helen Platt, Nancy Mitchell, Lorraine Heller, Barbara Blakesly, Joanne Delmonico, Louise Waitt, Emily House, Karen Bissonette, Sue Alperin, Alexandria Gamboa. And Advisory Contributors who have given so generously of their time and talents, Loretta Culbert, Gloria Jacobs, Chris Nordling, Craig Nordling, Randall Kester, Ron Olisar, Angela Nordling, George Taylor, Annie Nordling, Steve Tower, Charmaine Lindsay, Teresa Guierre, Karina Salom, George Vigileos, Bob Griggs, Paul Lyons, Fran Germany-Griggs, Shawna Elliott, Matt Bissonette, Robert Selby, and Marge Columbus.

All the caring teachers, counselors, and parents I have encountered over the past sixty years. I learned from each one of them something of the astonishing capacity that exists in adults for loving commitment to their own, and to other people's, children. Many of these experiences are included in this book. Names of the adults and children involved have been changed to protect their privacy.

Contents

Preface

As a multicultural and increasingly multiclass society, we have not developed a unified approach to child rearing. Fortunately, there are widespread attempts to overthrow the often cruel and repressive child-rearing practices of our Victorian ancestors, but we cannot agree on what should replace the old "spare the rod and spoil the child" philosophy. We are in transition from what the Swiss psychiatrist Alice Miller calls the "poisonous pedagogy" to something new, but we are not sure what. The media illuminate first one point of view and then another. As a young parent who had four children in five years, and later as a beginning teacher, I myself experienced the confusion of trying to sort out these many "expert" voices. Each new book I read, each new workshop I attended promised the answer. And while each was helpful in some way, no one approach seemed to be enough. I would go home or back into the classroom, prepared to do what I had just learned, and discover that real life constantly presented me with new misbehaviors that did not seem to fit the current philosophy.

In particular, I remember my early immersion in the teachings of Rudolf Dreikurs. Dr. Dreikurs had the keen insight that children must be allowed to experience the consequences of their own behaviors if they are to grow into responsible adults. He was right, but my dilemma came when I tried using his ignoring and consequence approach for all misbehaviors. I discovered that logical consequences and ignoring do not work for every situation.

Then came my introduction to the insights of people like Carl Rogers and Thomas Gordon, who taught the importance of listening to the child's feelings. This, I was positive, was the answer. I am still convinced that acceptance of a child's feelings is one of the most powerful positive influences we can bring to a healthy shaping of a child's life. But listening to feelings did not solve all the problems in the child/adult relationship. I once saw a mother trying to hold her eight-year-old boy at arm's length while he kicked her repeatedly in the shins. She kept saying in a solicitous

tone of voice, "Now, now. You must be really upset about something."
He kept right on yelling and kicking her. Obviously, some other response
was needed. I could not figure out how logical consequences or ignoring
applied to this kind of situation. The only logical consequence I could
think of at the time was for her to hit him back. But I was as positive then
as I am now that hurting a child does not work either.

Many people still believe in hitting children for misbehaving. Some
even believe that hitting kids is somehow good for them. Yet recent studies
have repeatedly shown that aside from the deeper ethical consideration
of whether it is right to deliberately hurt another human being, hitting
children seems to create an escalating cycle of more misbehaviors. Often
the very child who adults advise "needs a good spanking" is most frequently
spanked at home. Children who are spanked on a regular basis do not
develop adequate inner controls to regulate their own behaviors. These
children often misbehave in school settings where there is no spanking
allowed, and many continue the pattern into adulthood of always needing
powerful forces outside themselves to set limits on their behavior.

Next I discovered the writings of Abraham Maslow. Dr. Maslow's
philosophy of how human beings develop into emotionally healthy persons struck me as being absolutely true, but it took many years before I
grasped how to specifically translate his hierarchy of needs concept into a
concrete, everyday approach to parenting and teaching.

Haim Ginott's insights into the use of descriptive versus evaluating
language and Eric Berne's concepts of the importance of early scripting
were beacons of light for me as I struggled to develop a unified and specific
approach to child discipline.

I did not like B.F. Skinner and the other Behaviorists. I was opposed
to the manipulation of people of any age. It took me many years in the
private and public school of hard knocks before I finally accepted that the
Behaviorists, too, had some legitimate insights into child rearing, that you
did not have to treat a child as though you were training an animal for a
circus act in order to apply some basic Behaviorist principles.

The idea, put forward by Alice Miller and John Bradshaw, that the
fuel driving a violent society is the repressed feelings and humiliations

we suffer as children, came too late to help shape my early thinking, but it is welcome corroboration as to the validity of this loving approach to child discipline.

Through thirty-nine years of parenting, teaching, and counseling, I became increasingly aware that although children have a right to grow up as independent people in control of their own lives without being demeaned and humiliated by adults in the name of good discipline, adults have an equal right to expect certain kinds of behavior from children. An outcome of my personal struggle to balance the needs of both adults and children has been the gradual development of an approach to child discipline that allows adults to initiate specific action to change the disruptive behaviors exhibited by so many children in this culture, while still respecting the dignity of the child. It is a unified pattern that incorporates all common childhood behaviors. The pattern can be learned and applied selectively to each unique adult/child situation. It is a pattern that works for me and for the vast majority of the parents and teachers in the *Caring Discipline* parenting classes.

This is not to say that *Caring Discipline* is the answer for all the problems that arise in the adult/child relationship. There are many extreme situations, for example, family members who are incestuous, drug addicted, or who have chemical imbalances in their brains. This book does not attempt to address these circumstances. But most adults who demean children with physical punishment or who humiliate children in nonverbal and verbal ways do so either out of a mistaken belief that this is how adults are *supposed* to discipline children, or out of a sense of helplessness and frustration at having lost control of their home or classroom.

A family or classroom in which the adult feels out of control, and in which many of the children feel unappreciated and unloved, can change to one in which the adult feels in charge and is able to direct children's lives with respect and concern for their individual needs. Of course the changes cannot become permanent after reading once through a book, watching some video tapes, or attending a few weeks of class meetings. It takes time to change old habit patterns so that under stress we do not revert back to our old ways. Most of us need at least one other person with whom to share ideas and feelings as we try to change old, ingrained attitudes and habits of human relationships.

Many of the parents in my parenting groups report that things go much better at home for three or four days after the most recent class meeting. But if there is stress at home, they begin to slip into the old patterns with their children. For this reason, the Parent Support Center of Portland, Oregon encourages parents who have completed our five-week *Caring Discipline* course to organize their own ongoing discussion groups to help each other through the times they feel the need for emotional support or help in solving specific situations at home. Teachers and school support personnel have organized similar informal groups within their school buildings.

In this same way, I hope that readers of this book will form their own groups so that each reader can join with at least one other person and continue to build on the foundation begun here. If even a small discussion group or class is not possible, you can always view a six session presentation of the *Caring Discipline* parenting program with myself as teacher produced in 1997 on YouTube at www.YouTube.com, and then enter "Parent Support Center" into the search window.

The *Caring Discipline* approach shows the adult how to take charge of the adult/child relationship so that both adult and child can feel respected, secure, and loved. Most parents and teachers can use the basic principles set out here. There is no magic to the process. The pattern can be taught. It can be learned. It takes hard work, but the way is open.

JoAnne Swenston Nordling
Portland, Oregon

Preface to the Fifth Revised Edition

This 5th edition of *Taking Charge: Caring Discipline That Works at Home and at School* has been given a new title in response to repeated requests for a more accurate description of the nurturing component of the *Caring Discipline* approach. Hence the new title, *Caring Discipline: Practical Tools for Nurturing Happy Families and Classrooms*.

The most gratifying aspect of publishing this book has been the feedback from parents and teachers who tell me about the unique ways they have used the *Caring Discipline* philosophy to improve discipline and deepen their relationships with children. Sometimes their stories make me laugh, sometimes I am on the verge of tears, but always I am touched by these storytellers' insight, creativity, and obvious love for the children in their care.

It is my hope that with the addition of more ideas on how to apply the *Caring Discipline* principles to individual problem situations as they arise in the family or classroom, this edition will be even more helpful to you. You can also view a six session presentation of the *Caring Discipline* parenting program with myself as teacher produced in 1997 at www.YouTube.com, and then enter "Parent Support Center" into the search window.

With the increasing concern over the dramatic incidents of violent teenage behavior at school and in the home, the *Caring Discipline* principles are ever more necessary. They are a clear-cut, directly applicable answer to questions raised by administrators, school counselors, teachers, and parents. I believe that if schools adopted this approach to discipline, violence at school would greatly diminish. At home, parents would once again be in control of the relationship with their children. All would benefit from the nurturing atmosphere of increased respect for learning and for one another.

JoAnne Swenston Nordling

Special Foreword
to School Counselors

This book is a direct outcome of parenting four sons, being a teacher at all grade levels, and, finally, working as a counselor in elementary schools. In all these areas I am indebted to not only my own children for all they taught me about human relationships, but to the many teachers, children, and parents who gave me continual feedback throughout the years. Gradually, I learned more and more about how to provide caring, effective discipline for children. The ideas presented here took even clearer shape when I became a school counselor. It was then I realized it wasn't enough just for the school counselor to befriend and counsel a child. I also had to figure out how to teach parents and teachers what I knew, because teachers and parents are far more important to a child's life than I could ever be. As I gradually learned how to teach parents and teachers what I had learned, the *Caring Discipline* philosophy took shape, bit by bit, idea by idea, experience by experience.

I am convinced that school counselors can be the catalyst uniting teachers and parents in that "whole village" it takes to raise a child, a village that needs to come together in a partnership geared towards achieving the common goal of raising and educating strong, responsible, and caring kids of every race, ethnic group, and creed. When parents and teachers distrust one another, the school counselor is often the only person who can step in to find ways to reduce suspicion, and to help forge a partnership between parent and teacher. Much of the reason for suspicion and lack of trust between adults at school and at home is that we lack a common vocabulary for even discussing discipline without becoming defensive and emotional. It is my hope that school counselors will use this book as a tool offering a common vocabulary and discipline approach uniting home and school to the benefit of all our children.

JoAnne Swenston Nordling

CHAPTER ONE
Getting Started

Our culture has many different ways of disciplining children. As parents and teachers, we are a collection of individuals, each independently pursuing our own parenting or teaching style. We often disagree with our best friends about how to discipline kids. We have different rules for toilet training, weaning from the bottle, off-limit items, bedtime, diet, schoolwork, clothing, hair styles, curfew. The list is endless. Teachers within the same school building often disagree on how to discipline their students. Usually, even one's own spouse was reared in an entirely different family setting and sometimes has almost an alien concept from ours on how to handle discipline.

Everyone agrees that children need to be loved before they can become responsible, strong, and caring adults, but we differ widely on just how to express that love as we guide them throughout the early years of their lives. Some parents and teachers believe in the old adage, "Spare

1

the rod and spoil the child," while others insist that the rod referred to in the Bible is a shepherd's crook that was used not to beat the sheep but to guide them. Other parents and teachers believe that adults should get out of the way, just "stand back and watch them grow."

If you are an elementary school teacher or a day care provider, you are well aware of how often you act as a parent for other people's children. As a surrogate parent, working with very young children who have been removed from their parents for six to ten hours a day, you are asked to provide for many of their emotional needs during the time they spend with you. In fact, you probably spend more time with the children in your charge each weekday than most of their parents are able to do. The demands of earning a living mean that many parents have only a precious three or four hours each working day to spend with their children, and much of that time must be taken up in doing household chores.

Classroom teachers interact with the children in their classrooms much as they interact with their own children. Especially in the area of discipline, teaching style and parenting style are inseparable. Most school teachers agree that as they parent, so do they teach. It is clear that as teachers, day care providers, and parents, we all begin at the same place—the way we were parented when we were children.

We either parent in the same way as our parents did, or we consciously bend over backwards trying not to parent as they did. If we try not to imitate our parents, we are left in a vacuum, not having experienced any other kind of child-raising methods. After all, you learn to be a parent by watching your own parents. Consequently, under stress, we tend either to fall back into our own parents' behavior patterns or withdraw from the scene altogether. Which of us has not been horrified at least once at our own behavior towards our children, "And I said I would never act that way with my kids!"

How can so many caring, concerned parents and teachers have so much trouble with children? Parents who are responsible people in their own lives often have children who grow up to be irresponsible. Their children do not mind, they avoid chores, they misbehave at school. When they become teenagers, they are among those who smoke and drink, experiment with harder drugs, have exploitive sexual experiences. They are often involved in stealing and lying. Increasingly these teenagers are involved in incidents of school violence. Many of these kids follow along with any peer group who will have them, no matter what the value system of the peer group and how opposite it is to that of their parents. It is such a paradox. Parent after parent expresses the wish to just quit and walk away. "Sometimes I wish we could give that kid away and start over." But of course, caring adults are too loving and too responsible to walk away. Most of them stick it out and suffer, totally bewildered and suspecting that maybe it is something inherited, something "in the genes."

Teachers, too, go through similar kinds of misery in their relationships with their students. Many young teachers start out in their profession buoyed up by the anticipation of how satisfying it will be, to make a difference in the world, and to leave the world a little better than they found it. The reality they experience is that there are large numbers of resistant, even hostile, students who refuse to do their schoolwork, who will not even extend basic courtesies to their teachers. In some situations, there is even a threat or actual incident of physical violence. All this combines to create a growing bewilderment in the young teacher, culminating in resentment and anger. Teachers are freer to walk away from their profession than parents are. Still, many teachers keep at it, even though they feel betrayed and wounded by the behavior of many of the kids in their classes.

Most parents and teachers fall into two general groups. The first group, the adult-oriented parent/teacher "A", believes that adults know best what children need to do, that children are too inexperienced and too young to make their own decisions. There is no doubt in the A-adult's mind that children should not be allowed to annoy adults and that children should know their place. Parent/teacher A experiences very little inner struggle over when to correct the child. It seldom, if ever, occurs to A-adults that the child might not love them if they make too many demands on the child. The belief that adults know best enables A-adults to feel comfortable as disciplinarians.

In spite of feeling comfortable with the act of disciplining a child, however, A-adults can still find themselves in a situation where the child does not do what the adult wants to have done. This is the classic power struggle: If the adult says YES, the child says, or quietly does, NO. Some children are afraid to openly refuse adults. They may agree with whatever the adult insists on, but they go underground with their opposition by passively resisting and doing exactly the opposite of whatever the adult says whenever they get the chance.

This power struggle becomes especially intense as the child grows into puberty. As children's minds and bodies mature, they become more and more convinced that they are capable of running their own lives. A-adults, on the other hand, regard the child as a dependent who ought to conform to the rules and values of the household that feeds and clothes him, or the school system that educates her. In spite of the fact that these A-adults are loving, dedicated, and comfortable with the idea of discipline, they often find themselves in a bewildering state of perpetual conflict with the child. Other people say the child is spoiled and needs a good spanking, even though sometimes the child has often been spanked. The A-adult comes to think of the child as irresponsible, ungrateful, and uncaring, a disappointment to the family and to all school personnel who work with him or her. The child in turn feels misunderstood, picked on, and un-loved. The child's behavior consequently worsens as the downward spiral of defiance and punishment continues. Both adult and child feel deeply wounded by the other's apparent lack of love and respect.

The child-oriented parent/teacher "C," on the other hand, experiences a tremendous amount of inner struggle over when and how to correct the child's behavior. C-adults wonder whether they are allowing children enough room to express themselves. They wonder whether the child will still love them if they make too many demands. C-adults often ask themselves, "Do adults have the right, just because they are older, to tell another human being what to do?" Consequently, parent/teacher C suspects that children have just as much right to decide how to live their lives as the adult does. C-adults also have a strong belief that if they are kind, understanding, and fair, children will respond by behaving in a simi-lar fashion. C-adults tend to think that adults only need to love children and then stand back and watch them blossom.

Parent/teacher C is bewildered if the child begins to show signs of developing into a self-centered "me first" person who expects to always get his or her own way. No matter how often C-adults defer to the child, the child seems to demand more and more. "Give that kid an inch and he takes a mile." Parent/teacher C is confused and hurt when the child avoids doing a fair share of routine chores, including schoolwork, demands a disproportionate share of attention in any situation, constantly interrupts adult conversations, expects others to always play by his or her rules, and frequently has difficulty forming friendships with peers. As before, other people often advise that this child is spoiled and needs a good spanking. Parent/teacher C usually does not spank unless pushed to the extreme. Instead the C-adult has intense heart-to-heart talks with the child about becoming more responsible, more generous, more ambitious, and more considerate of others. But the more the C-adult reasons and cajoles, the more the child refuses to change. Here again, a power struggle between adult and child emerges, although this time it is disguised by the unwillingness of parent/teacher C to make direct demands on the child.

Of course, no one individual parent or teacher falls absolutely into either the "A" or the "C" category. People are too complex. There are always too many variables. Still, most parents and teachers can place themselves somewhere along this continuum line. *Think of it as your default position, the place you snap into, without conscious thought, during that first second you are confronted with a child's misbehavior.* Where would you place yourself? Your spouse or partner? Your co-workers? Your parents?

Parent/Teacher A _____ Parent/Teacher C
(Adult has absolute authority)   (Child has at least equal authority)

There is nothing intrinsically wrong with having the basic assumptions of a parent/teacher A or a parent/teacher C. Each style has strengths. Each can learn from the other. One Head Start teacher who calls herself a C-adult, says she is always grateful when she has an A-adult working in her classroom as a teaching assistant, because she knows the A-adult will keep reminding her that adults need to provide the security of routines, predictable rules, and firm consequences. An A-type teacher says he is grateful that the C-type counselor in his school is available to talk to his students, because the A-teacher cannot get his students to share personal problems with him. It is hard for this A-teacher to listen to his students because he is convinced if the kids would just do what he tells them to do, all their problems would be solved.

It is interesting how often couples turn out to have opposite parenting styles. Perhaps, when we choose a mate, we recognize at some nonverbal level our need for an opposite, complementary point of view. It should not surprise you if your spouse tends to parent differently than you do. Unfortunately, the temptation for both spouses is to criticize and try to change the other's parenting style. Try not to re-sculpture your spouse. You will not be able to do it anyway. All you will accomplish is to get your spouse upset and uncooperative. Besides, *fighting among adults over how to discipline children is guaranteed to cause even more misbehavior on the part of the children.*

Talk over your parenting style with your spouse or partner. It does not matter whether or not your present spouse is the biological parent of the children. If he or she is living in your home and acting as a surrogate parent, he or she needs to be an equal partner in raising the kids. Try to respect and understand the other person's default position. Talk together about the strengths and weaknesses of your respective styles. Neither of you needs to change your basic personality. Try to accept, at least in some measure, one another's differences. If you can do this, you will be able to work together to adapt the methods in this book to your own situation, thereby creating new and effective parenting skills for yourselves.

It would be helpful if you and your partner could have a weekly discussion meeting while you work your way through this book. Or maybe you can find one or two friends who would like to get together once a week. If you are a school teacher, try to find two or three fellow teachers to meet with you on a weekly basis. It is difficult to learn about one's own parenting/teaching mindset without having another adult around to give you feedback, to offer ideas, and especially to be there to listen while you think out loud. Trying to learn about yourself all alone is like an eye trying to see itself or a tongue trying to taste itself. We are too close to get ourselves in clear focus.

However, if your partner does not want to participate, and your friends are too busy, or if none of the other teachers are interested, try to accept their decisions and do the best you can on your own. As Rudolf Dreikurs advised, "Do what you can do."

Whether you tend towards the A or the C end of the continuum line, take heart. It is the aim of this book to help you learn some ways to stop the power struggles you may now be involved in with your children at home or school. Hundreds of parents and teachers, both A and C-adults, have found that the concepts and processes described in this book have not only eased the pain of parenting or teaching, but have also brought them a sense of true joy in their family and classroom relationships.

You are a conscientious and loving parent or teacher, or else you would not have bothered to read this far. Loving adults, no matter how different their parenting philosophies, hold in common basic values and goals for their children and students. Every parent and teacher wants the kids in his or her life to grow up to be responsible, loving, creative, confident, and courageous adults. No one wants their children to grow up either bullies or door mats. We want our kids to be able to take on leadership roles as well as to be willing to cooperate. We want them to be confident in their own abilities. We want them to be willing to risk. We want our kids to hold themselves in high self-esteem while, at the same time, respecting the worth of other human beings. The *Caring Discipline* parenting program will help you guide the children you love toward those goals.

Your values are important. *To change your parenting approach, whether you are an A or a C-parent, you do not have to change your values. You have only to change the way in which you teach those values.* Parents are the primary teachers of their children's behavior and value systems. Teachers run a close second. If your children's behaviors and attitudes are presently a worry to you and indicate that they are not learning what you want them to learn, then it is time to change your parenting and teaching approach. This book is designed to help you do that. The principles and methods described in these chapters work. They have worked for others over and over again and they will work for you.

Guidelines for Weekly Group Discussions

1. Read chapters One and Two before your first meeting. After that, the book is organized for your group to read and discuss one chapter a week, but it is possible to do two chapters a week if you feel the need to go faster.

2. Read each chapter assignment at least five days before your discussion group meets. This will allow you enough time to do the exercise given at the end of each chapter before your next meeting.

3. Participants in the group can be from two to eight people.

4. Choose a regularly scheduled time, once a week, when you can relax and enjoy one another's company.

5. Rotate leadership of the group each week.

6. Each group member is to share his or her thoughts and feelings only to the degree he or she wants. *If anyone does share private experiences, it is important to keep that information confidential.*

7. Help other group members to think out loud by listening to them. *Do not argue with them because they perceive the world differently from you. Do not give advice unless someone asks you for it.* There will be time for advice later on when you begin to do problem-solving together.

8. Take turns talking. Decide on a way to insure that each person gets an equal amount of time to think out loud. You may need to use a timer or a "talking stick" (an object to hold as each person takes a turn talking) in order to give each person equal time to speak. This tends to be more of a problem as the group gets larger, but it is not uncommon that even two people need some such means of distributing time fairly.

9. Ten minutes before your regular closing time, go around the group and give everyone the chance to talk, just in case they have something on their minds but have not had the opportunity to say it.

Chapter 1 Discussion: GETTING STARTED

1. Tell about a time you were disciplined when you were a child.

2. What kind of family did you grow up in? Tell what you most admired about the way your parents raised you and what you most disliked.

3. In what ways are you raising or teaching your children differently from the way your parents raised you? In what ways are you doing things the same?

4. Write a description of the kind of adult you want your child (or children you teach) to become. Take a turn sharing this with the rest of the group.

5. Make two lists: List 1—the things about your child (or the kids in your classroom) you feel happiest about. List 2—the things about your child that worry or anger you. Share these lists with the other members of the group.

6. Do you consider yourself an A or a C-parent or teacher? Create a continuum line by sticking a long strip of masking tape on the floor. Mark A at one end and C at the other. Move to the location along the tape you consider to be your default position. Take a turn explaining to the group your reasons for placing yourself in a particular spot on the continuum line. Where do you place your spouse? Your parents?

7. Using two large sheets of paper, make a list of what you think are the strengths and weaknesses of both the A and C-parenting/teaching styles.

from *Caring Discipline: Practical Tools for Nurturing Happy Families & Classrooms*

Chapter TWO
Paying Attention

To be totally ignored is a painful experience. Children will go to any lengths to be noticed. Children can sometimes use words and ask to be noticed. Think of the times your own child has called to you, "Look at me, Mommy," or "See what I can do, Daddy." Or, how many times has one of your students run up to you on the playground yelling, "Watch this. Watch this." But when children, of any age, do not know how to verbalize their need to be noticed, they act it out. One of the things I used to do whenever I wanted attention was to clean the bathroom. I knew my mother would always stop whatever she was doing and praise me if I scrubbed that bathroom. My brother used a different method for attracting my mother's attention. He broke things. Each of us, in our own way, was saying, "Come pay attention to me."

This process of interacting with other human beings by paying attention to them and having them pay attention to you is called social reinforcement. Social reinforcement is the most powerful tool available to you for changing the behavior of your child, yet very few adults understand how to use it effectively. Social reinforcement is widely misunderstood and misused, sometimes even by professional educators and counselors. In order to understand the basic concepts of social reinforcement and how to effectively use social reinforcement to improve children's behavior, we need to examine three broad categories of behavior.

The Three Basic Behaviors

First, there is negative behavior. **Negative behavior** means the child is doing something the adult does not like. The child may be rude or continually bring home a poor report card even though he or she is capable of average work. The child may whine, steal, fight with siblings, avoid doing chores, and on and on. The adult feels irritation or anger at the behavior.

The second category of behavior is positive. **Positive behavior** means that the child is doing something that pleases the adult. The child may be a hard-working student, be responsible about changing school clothes, or clean his or her room regularly. The child may play with younger siblings and generously share toys with them. The adult feels pride and pleasure at seeing the child behave in these ways.

The third kind of behavior is neutral. **Neutral behavior** neither pleases nor displeases us. At these neutral behavior times we hardly even notice the child. The child may be reading a book in the school library, petting the cat, lying outside on the grass watching ants, or helping big sister build a model car. When the child walks through the kitchen as you are working at the sink, or walks into the classroom on the way back from the rest room, for example, he or she is engaging in a neutral behavior. There is nothing special about neutral behavior. At these times the child is neither a bother nor a help. The child is just there, alive and breathing, doing his or her own thing in the world. When adults do notice this kind of behavior, they do not feel much of anything about it. In fact, the child's neutral behavior is often taken for granted and generally ignored.

An important idea to keep in mind concerning these three types of behavior is that each of them, negative, positive, and neutral, is strengthened when we give emotional attention to them. In other words, when we socially reinforce any of these behaviors, whether negative, positive, or neutral, we encourage the child to continue in that type of behavior. Tricky, isn't it? As parents and teachers, we are responsible for teaching our children attitudes and behavior. We cannot ignore a child's negative behavior and still function as responsible parents and teachers; we must intervene at times to teach desired behaviors. Yet, the more emotional attention we give to a child's negative behaviors, the more we strengthen his or her negative behaviors. We will return to this in detail later.

As parents and teachers, we pay attention to children's behaviors with positive and negative behaviors of our own. (We are also often neutral with kids, but then of course we are not giving them any emotional attention.) Ordinarily, the kind of attention you give a child depends on how the child is behaving. If René ignores your call to come into dinner, your emotional response will be negative and so your own behavior towards him is probably going to be negative, too. "René, I said *get in here this minute.*" In this case, a negative behavior in the child has provoked a negative response in the parent. If, on the other hand, René immediately comes running to the dinner table and says, "Boy, am I hungry. This stuff looks really good," your emotional response will be positive and your own behavior towards him will probably be positive also. René might even get a hug from you, or at least a big smile. The difficulty with this perfectly normal reaction pattern is that the child becomes the initiator of the adult's responses. The child acts, the adult reacts. Or, another way of putting it, the child controls the responses of the adult.

If the child's behavior is positive, there is no problem. Most adults are quick to respond to a child's positive behaviors by giving back positive verbal and nonverbal cues. Positive interactions flow back and forth between parent and child until it becomes hard to know who started them. It does not matter who started this positive response cycle. No one really cares as long as everyone is happy. The problem arises when the child somehow slips into a negative behavior pattern. The natural reaction for the parent or teacher is to respond in equally negative ways. Since the adult is more powerful than the child, the adult is often able to get temporary control of the situation, but eventually the child initiates new negative behaviors. This, in turn, elicits more negative responses from the adult. Soon a full-blown power struggle is under way, a power struggle that neither the adult nor the child wants, but that both are unable to stop. In order for parents or teachers to help the child break out of this downward spiral, adults must first learn to deal with the child's negative behaviors without giving the emotional attention that unwittingly encourages the very behaviors they are trying to prevent.

We can usually recognize a positive and a negative behavior when we see it in a child, but we are not always so adept at realizing when we are the ones giving a negative or a positive attention to the child. The reason it is important to learn to recognize our own positive and negative attentions is because they are loaded with emotional energy, and emotional energy is what the child needs from us.

Our verbal attentions to the child are easy to recognize. When we say, "Cut that out, Jackie," there is no doubt that we have just given a negative verbal attention. When we say, "What a careful job you did, Jackie," it is clear that we have given a positive verbal attention.

On the other hand, when we give nonverbal kinds of messages, we are often unaware of the nonverbal attention our bodies are giving to our children. The first language your child learns to interpret is nonverbal. Even babies are extremely good at understanding this body language. Although we may seldom express feelings verbally, our bodies almost always give an indication of the feelings inside—the look on our face, the way we walk, the tone of our voice, the kind of eye contact we do or do not make—all reveal our inner state. When an adult who has been taught as a child that it is wrong to express anger says, "I'm not angry," but the clenched fist, flushed face, and tight voice, say, "I'm so angry I can barely control myself," children will know which of the two messages is true. Nonverbal messages from you, whether negative or positive, are highly charged with emotional attention for the child. If you can develop a basic awareness of your own body language, you will not be fooled into thinking that words are the major way you pay attention to children.

Nonverbal attentions are extremely powerful, even when we are unaware we are giving them. A touch, a smile, eye contact, your tone of voice, a scowl, a hug, a sigh can express myriad moods and emotional attitudes. When you smile at one of your students and make warm eye contact when he is listening to you attentively, you are communicating values and emotions you do not have to put into words. When you grab your child's hand in exasperation and pull her down the grocery aisle because she will not quit whining about wanting more expensive junk food, no words are necessary for the child to know how you are feeling about the behavior.

One family, who managed to raise five responsible and loving children, engaged in so little talk that a typical dinner-time discussion consisted of "Please pass the butter." These parents were very successful at teaching values and behaviors by using subtle nonverbal cues. Observers of certain so-called primitive societies have commented on the fact that, compared to our industrialized culture, much less talking about discipline goes on between children and adults. Hard as it may be to believe for those of us who love to talk, nonverbal communication is probably even more effective than verbal communication in teaching behaviors to children.

The Importance of Paying Attention at Neutral Times

Adults often ignore children's neutral behaviors altogether, giving neither verbal nor nonverbal attention. Maybe we ignore neutral behaviors because we are afraid that if we intervene, the child will stop being neutral and start being a bother, or maybe we think of it as rewarding an ordinary behavior that deserves no reward. After all, when children are doing what they are supposed to be doing, why make a big deal out of it? There is a very good reason for giving emotional attention at neutral times: *Paying attention to a child's neutral behavior is a powerful tool for bringing about positive behavior change.* Giving positive attention to a child at neutral times may not seem to make much sense at first, but it is a fact that children blossom when parents and teachers make a concerted effort to give them positive attention at neutral times.

Karin was a first-grader who refused to answer when adults spoke to her. She also passively resisted doing her schoolwork and chores. Yet, when she was with her peers, she was talkative and animated. If you have ever been around a child who will not talk to you, who even resists making eye contact with you, you will understand how frustrated her teachers and parents were. Her parents finally learned to develop a program of regular, positive, nonverbal contacts. The plan especially focused on touching because this little girl tended to be stiff as a board when any adult reached out to hug her. Her parents understandably felt rejected and discouraged by her refusal to hug and be hugged. Consequently they reached out to her less and less.

The parents' day was divided into three parts. During each time segment, one parent or the other, depending on which one was home during that time, was to touch Karin four times when the child was engaged in neutral behavior. The touching was to be light and undemanding. (Tickling was forbidden, since tickling is an extremely demanding kind of touching and is often experienced as aggressive.) They were to touch her hair, put an arm around her waist, or touch her hand when they gave her an object. If she pulled away from them, they were to let that happen without any kind of notice. They were to continue to be pleasant and try their best not to feel rejected by any withdrawal on her part. The parents were cautioned that it might take a month or more to begin to thaw Karin out. To everyone's amazement, within two weeks Karin's teachers were asking, "What happened to Karin? She is so cooperative and downright bubbly lately." The parents reported that their daughter was not only smiling and talking to them, she had even begun to lean against them and put her arms around them for hugs.

What was so powerful about giving this child attention during neutral times? To be sure, to be held and touched is a powerful human need. Yet they had tried touching her at positive times before but were usually rejected. The power of giving positive attention at neutral times comes from the fact that if children are attended to in a positive way only when they are successful or achieving, they begin to doubt that people value them for themselves. As children grow older, they may even begin to suspect that the adult is using their accomplishments as a kind of parental or teaching trophy.

A father told about the time his sixteen-year-old neighbor earned an Eagle Scout badge. The father was then twelve years old. One day at a neutral time, his mother talked to him about how wonderful it was that the neighbor boy had been awarded the Eagle Scout badge. She smiled at her son pleadingly and stroked his hair. "You can do it, too." He remembered the moment clearly. "But it takes years and years and hardly anyone gets to be an Eagle Scout," he said. "Do it for me," his mother said. Do it for *her.* He recognized that, at some nonverbal level, she was seeking to meet, not his needs, but her own. Within the year he quit the Boy Scouts.

When learning the concept of paying attention to kids at neutral times, one mother told about her favorite uncle. "Actually, I never knew him very well. When he came to the house to visit my folks, I would sit and listen to the grown-ups talk. Nobody paid much attention to me except him. Once in awhile he would look over at me and give me a grin and a big wink. I've always had this feeling that he loved me best, that I was his favorite. I think I just realized why."

Another example of paying attention at a neutral time: every morning, teachers at the Waldorf School in Portland, Oregon greet each child at a neutral time by standing at the door to the classroom, shaking each child's hand as they arrive, and saying something like, "Good morning, Jimmy, welcome to our class." At the end of the day, each child is again given a formal handshake and some form of goodbye, "Goodbye, Jimmy, see you tomorrow." Eye contact and a smile further transmit the teacher's message that this child is valued "just because." No praise or advice is given, just hello, goodbye, the friendly handshake, eye contact, and a smile. (Although the Waldorf School did not need a second supervising adult, for some classrooms an additional adult might be needed each morning so the teacher can give her full attention to each arriving child.)

Michele Miller, director of Garden's Noise Preschool in Portland, Oregon advises parents to pay attention only to their own child when they come to take their child home at the end of the day. No talking to the teachers, no multi-tasking taking or sending cell phone messages, just smiles, hugs, and warm eye contact with their child. The non-verbal message to the child is, "You are a valued person. I am so happy to see you again." There are to be no questions or comments as in, "Was he a good boy today?" or "I hope you were a good boy today;" just a smile, a hug, a high-five or some other touch, warm eye contact, then a goodbye to the teacher, who now steps in to add her own goodbye. If there is something parents would like to discuss with her, Michele asks them to contact her by phone or email, or schedule a private meeting. In this way, at the end of their often hectic day, the parents at Garden's Noise Preschool are given the gift of a stress-free neutral time to interact with their children and to convey the powerful non-verbal message that this child is unconditionally loved "just because."

We need to be noticed and loved just because we exist. By paying positive attention to children at neutral times, adults convey a sense of unconditional love. Nothing bolsters our sense of self-esteem so much as knowing we are loved not because of what we have achieved or will achieve, but because we are here and alive, because we are who we are. The knowledge that we are unconditionally loved is a prerequisite for healthy, positive behaviors. The knowledge that we are loved just because we are lovable makes it unnecessary for us to seek out attention in other, more negative ways. The withdrawn, resistant first-grader, for example, had learned how to get the attention she so badly needed in her busy family by retreating into herself and hiding behind a mask when she was with adults. It was another form of the hiding game children play when they want an adult to find them. When she began to get attention just for being alive, she had no need for her old negative withdrawal behaviors.

Child's Staircase of Needs

But, you may ask, why should children ever want to accomplish anything worthwhile in life if they get all this attention for doing nothing special? People cannot just sit and pet the cat or read all the rest of their lives. Indeed, what is it that motivates human beings to learn and to achieve, to become the best they are capable of becoming? The psychologist Abraham Maslow, in his study of emotionally healthy human beings, proposed an answer to the question of what prompts a human being to become one of those people at the "growing tip" of humanity.

Maslow believed that all human beings have certain needs that must be satisfied before they are able to grow towards self-esteem and what he called self-actualization. Just as plants need water, sunlight, and nutrients to attain the promise of their genetic codes, so people need certain basic requirements in order to grow toward the best they are capable of becoming.

First Step on the Staircase of Needs: Physical

The first thing humans need is to have their basic PHYSICAL needs provided for. We need air to breathe, water to drink, the right kind of food to eat, shelter from the elements, and sometimes we need healing medications. Until we get these things, we have no time, energy, or inclination for thinking about much else. The need for food, healing, shelter, water, and air are clear-cut needs. Other physical needs, like the need for touching, are not as obvious. Yet being held and touched, especially for the very young child, is one of the most crucial of the basic physical needs. Growth hormones are released when a child is held and touched. Children will not thrive and babies can actually die from not being cuddled.

Western culture has been slow to recognize that all primate babies need to be carried snug and secure next to the mother's body until they begin to walk. In *The Continuum Concept,* Jean Liedloff tells of her experiences living in the jungles of South America with the Tauripan Indians, where adults keep children close to their bodies until the children choose to go off and begin to explore the world around them. *The Continuum Concept* is worth reading for an understanding of how far our Western culture has strayed from a natural physical closeness with children.

Second Step on the Staircase of Needs: Security

As one need is met, another arises. Next comes the need for SECURITY. We not only need to feel physically secure, for example, to know that bombs are not going to drop on us, that the plague will not strike us down, and that we will not be beaten, we also need to feel safe emotionally. We need to know we will not be sexually harassed and intimidated. Children need to know that when they go to school their teacher will not humiliate them in the classroom and that bullies will not bother them on the playground or bus. Children need to know that dad or mother will not get drunk, or drugged in any other way, so that they neglect or abuse them.

A kindergarten teacher tells the story of Manuel, a five-year-old boy, who since the first day of class had been a joy to know. He was always cooperative with adults and kind to the other children. One Monday morning Manuel came to school withdrawn, almost sullen. As the week went on, his behavior got worse to the point of Manuel hitting another child. Finally, the puzzled teacher called Manuel's mother to ask if there was something wrong. "I thought we were doing a good job of hiding it from him, but I guess not. Manuel's dad lost his job last Friday and we have been worried sick about it." When parents are worried about finding enough money to keep the household going, children usually know it. As the safety/security step on his staircase of needs is weakened, even a boy like Manuel will respond with negative behaviors.

If a child believes that adults are no longer in control of the situation, the child will take the burden of worry and responsibility onto his own shoulders. I will never forget the seven-year-old boy who quite seriously told me, "It's my job to keep Mom and Dad from fighting. If I can keep Dad from getting mad, then Mom won't get hurt." This was a boy who always tried to please adults, who behaved like a little old man, so serious and unsmiling. His childhood, instead of being a time of exploration and joy, was burdened with responsibility and guilt for the out-of-control behaviors of his father. Children often believe they are responsible for the negative emotional climate in their families, even though in reality they are powerless to change things. And so, because of the integrity of their honest little souls, they burden themselves with a heavy load of guilt.

Children's security needs are also threatened if they constantly hear their parents arguing over how to discipline. Learning not to argue over the children is a major area of challenge for any parent, and not arguing about the children is especially hard for divorcing parents. Working out visitation and discipline arrangements that support each other's role as a parent is extremely difficult when there is a long history of hurtful incidents between the two adults. Divorcing parents who make the effort to get early mediation help in order to clarify visitation and discipline agreements, and who jointly work to convince their children that *divorce is never the children's fault*, will be rewarded with happier and better behaved children.

Physical touching and holding by the adult is also a part of Maslow's safety need. Toddlers can be brave about going off and exploring the world on their own as long as there is an adult nearby who will hold and protect them if things get too scary. At many stages of childhood, children need to be able to run back to the parent and be picked up or hugged whenever they need the comfort of being close to their mother or father. Only in this way will children grow up feeling a sense of rightness and trust about life, a feeling of, "Hey, this is a great and secure world."

Adults and older children, too, never outgrow the need for someone to be there to support them with a hug or two when the going gets rough. A friend tells the wrenching story of when her husband died after a long illness. Two days after his death, she woke to find that every one of her five children, even the fourteen year old, had climbed into bed with her during the night. The security and safety needs for this family had been yanked out from under them. What better place to begin to rebuild a feeling of security than in the warmth and closeness of their mother's bed.

Equally important for strengthening the security needs of children is the knowledge that adults around them are in control, that limits and rules are clearly defined. The need for clear guidelines for children of all ages can be compared to needing handrails on a high bridge. Even if we never have to reach out and grab the handrail, just knowing it's there gives us a sense of security. A Head Start teacher tells the story of her first days in the classroom. The procedure was to lay out a few games on the tables for the children to work with during the first part of the morning. The first morning, the children played with the games for a little while and then, when the parts were out of the boxes and scattered on the table, a boy pointed at a game above him on the shelf and said, "Can I have that one, teacher? Please, can I have that one?" Being an agreeable C-adult, she got it down for him. Other children began to ask, "Can I have that one, teacher?" She ended up getting down all the games from the shelves. The children became more and more unruly ("bedlam" was her word for it) and by clean-up time, no one wanted to help restore order. Game pieces were scattered all over the room. Like most of us, this teacher learned from experience that children will often push their limits to try to find out just where the handrails are. If there are no handrails, they begin to feel insecure, and behavior deteriorates.

The need for security is also a reason young children thrive on routine and predictable outcomes. Anyone with a toddler knows how upset a child becomes if the daily routine is disturbed. Often, all a child who has trouble going to sleep at night needs is a regular, predictable bedtime ritual. Substitute teachers know that the younger their students are, the harder it is for them to accept a new person and a new way of doing things. Many a substitute teacher at the kindergarten or first grade level dreads to hear this constant refrain, "But our teacher never does it that way." And how many of you have moved into a new apartment only to have your youngster wail at bedtime that first night, "But I want to go *home.*"

Third Step on the Staircase of Needs: Belonging

As our PHYSICAL and SECURITY needs begin to be met, at least in some minimum fashion, another need arises. We need to BELONG. At the most basic level, we need to belong to some human society, however small, even if only to one other person. We need to know that no matter what comes, this other person or persons will be there and will never leave us or push us away from them. Duncan Campbell of Portland, Oregon believes that a child can survive even the worst family situation if only he or she can find one good adult friend to belong to throughout childhood. His group, Friends of Children, hires caring adults whose job it is to be an adult friend. Each Friend has a caseload of only eight children. Friends are assigned to children in first grade and stay with that child until the child is eighteen years old. Friends of Children is proving that giving a child just one person to belong to, one person who will always there for you, can turn a child's life around. Duncan believes that he, himself, was saved from a life of crime and misery because he was befriended as a child by his fifth-grade teacher, his high-school football coach, and by his friends' fathers.

Even those of us who are lucky enough to belong to a solid family need to belong to larger groups. The need to belong is one of the reasons we participate in the social activities of our church, and why we join the Elks club, a hiking group, the Rotary, the Girl Scouts, the Cub Scouts, fraternities, sororities, the Lions, Eastern Star, and why we identify and cheer for favorite sports teams. The need to belong (as well as the need for security) is an important part of the reason so many teenagers join a gang.

Elementary teachers know how important it is to help a new child feel a sense of belonging to their classroom group. When children arrive on the first day of school, they find a sign with their name on it pasted to the desk and over the coat hanger. These signs say to the child, "I was expecting you to be here because this is your room, this is your class, this is where you belong." Children who enroll in a new school in midyear are lucky if their parents remember to notify the school ahead of time so their teacher can have another desk moved in, put a sign on it, and tell the other children about the new arrival. In this way, the new child will be greeted with the same message of, "I was expecting you to be here because this is your room, this is your class, this is where you belong."

As we mature, in order to fully strengthen our stairstep of belonging, we need to develop the faith that, in some way, we belong to the universe. We need to know that even though the reason for our existence will never be fully understood, we are an integral part of All That Is. In the movie "Roots" is a powerful scene in which a father lifts his newborn baby high overhead, under a night sky blazing with stars, to show him the great Universe to which he belongs. For many people, belonging to a formal religion is the key to experiencing this sense of belonging. Others only experience the sense of belonging when they are outdoors, sleeping under the stars, sailing on a great ocean, climbing a mountain, or fishing in a quiet stream. Many Vietnam War veterans moved into wilderness areas to live, like the Olympic Peninsula in Washington state. These natural outdoor places were the only environments in which these veterans could find a sense of spiritual peace, environments in which they could find the faith to believe they belong to the Universe. Other people find the sense of belonging to something greater than themselves when they are gardening, nursing a baby, or listening to beautiful music. The old saying is true: "There are many roads to the same mountain."

Fourth Step on the Staircase of Needs: Being-Love

A next step up the staircase of needs is the need to be unconditionally loved. Maslow called this unconditional love BEING-LOVE. Children need to feel loved and accepted by at least one adult just because they are alive, just because they are lovable. This kind of love loves us for no other reason than that we are who we are. We are loved even when we have not earned that love. Imagine how the six-year-old boy, Rafer, felt whose mother, whenever he was "bad," refused to wear the Cracker Jack ring he had given her. Rafer's father had already left the family. The mother's live-in boyfriend had recently dramatically packed his suitcase and threatened to leave because the boy consistently did not hang up his clothes. Rafer's mother was the only person he could count on, and it seemed to him that her love, too, was conditional. "I will only wear your token of love when you are good. I will only love you when you are good." It is not surprising that Rafer exhibited almost frantic behaviors and that at school he was, incorrectly, perceived as a child with a physically based attention deficit.

This, then, is the answer to the earlier question of why it is important to pay attention to a child at neutral times. Paying attention to a child "just because" satisfies the need to be loved for just being alive. Paying attention to a child at neutral times is an expression of that unconditional love Maslow called Being-Love. Not long ago, a teaching assistant who had been having problems during recesses with a second-grade boy began paying attention to him at neutral times. She smiled at him in the halls. She made a point to greet him each morning when he got off the bus. Two weeks later she was telling us that not only was he not misbehaving with her anymore, but he was actually hugging her around the waist when he saw her on recess duty.

The need for unconditional love exists for adults as well as for children. During one of our parenting classes, a young mother said, "This business of paying attention at neutral times works for adults, too!" She told us how the relationship between her and her husband had been worsening for the past few months. Her husband was always working or studying for his college classes. She was left to take care of the children plus do her own job. It seemed they were always tired, never had any fun anymore, and very few kind words had passed between them lately. So she decided to start giving her husband nonverbal positive attention at neutral times. Every night when he retreated to the bedroom to study at his desk, she made it a point to go in for a brief time, just long enough to stand by him for a moment, stroke his hair, and lean over to kiss him on the cheek. "At the end of the week, he brought me flowers.

He's never brought me flowers in all the years we've been married!"

In thinking of my own relationship with my husband, the times which most convince me that I am loved are not the times we make love, but those times when he touches my hair as he walks by or gives me the warmth of eye contact and a smile across a room crowded with people, unasked for, unearned, expecting nothing in return. If the need to be given positive attention during neutral times is this important for an adult, imagine how much more powerful it is for a child.

Fifth Step on the Staircase of Needs: Competency

Once a basic level of PHYSICAL, SECURITY, BELONGING, and BE-ING-LOVE needs are met, the human being is freed to step up to the next higher need, the need to be COMPETENT and to be RESPECTED for that competency. Every healthy human being has experienced the fun of learning some new thing. It may not be the thing others want him to learn. The boy who loves working on cars instead of his history and math lessons is a classic example. But for each person there exists the excitement and the deep satisfaction that comes from grasping some new concept, attaining some new level of mastery. Have you ever seen a first-grader who did not want to learn to read and count and write? There must be something in our genetic code, something in the makeup of our DNA that elicits an intrinsic joy in learning some new thing. Maybe it is because the use of our minds has meant our survival as a species. Whatever the reason, the need to learn skills, and to feel competent in the application of those skills, is enormously important. It is a wise adult who can find a way for each child to feel not only that he or she is unconditionally accepted as a valuable member of the class or family, but that he or she is respected as a competent person learning to be in charge of his or her own life.

Reaching the Top of the Developmental Staircase: Self-Esteem/Self-Actualization

Finally, if all the stair-steps on the developmental staircase of needs are strong, human beings are free to move towards and blossom into what Maslow called self-actualization. A self-actualized person has high self-esteem, integrity, honesty, and self-discipline and is a person who learns for the joy of learning, builds for the joy of creating, and trusts that the world, in spite of its sorrows, is basically a good place. Without even being aware of it, the self-actualized person becomes a force for civility, creativity, and compassion in the wider community.

Many of us never make it to the very top step of this developmental staircase. Sometimes our PHYSICAL needs and our needs for SECURITY and BELONGING and BEING-LOVE and COMPETENCY/RESPECT are satisfied so meagerly that our character development is stunted. In this way we never achieve our full potential. We are like plants that struggle to grow in light so dim they can never really thrive.

Each one of us has experienced a falling back down the stairway of personal growth at some time in our lives. When our staircase of emotional needs crumbles, we trip and tumble back down the stairs. And when we fall, our behavior deteriorates. Most of us have had times in our lives when we were hungry, maybe even homeless, times we felt abandoned, sick, unloved, incompetent, frightened, times when it seemed there was not even one other human being who cared about us. Any parent who has suffered through a divorce with a child, for example, knows the negative, age-inappropriate behaviors that are manifested in both the child and the parents at this time. Parents, as well as their children, feel their needs for security, belonging, being-love, and competency/respect threatened during a divorce. You can probably think of times in your own life when the lack of one of these needs triggered some "childish" behavior on your part that now amazes you.

I clearly remember my own behavior as a fifteen-year-old high school junior. Because of my family's constant moving, I had lived in a state the year before that did not require a second year math credit. Since the state we were now living in required two years of high school math, I was forced to make up my missing second year of math by sitting in the midst of people a whole year younger than me, all of whom (I was certain) thought I must be a stupid person who had flunked math the year before. Compounding the problem was my father's alcoholism, of which I was ashamed and trying hard to keep secret from my new classmates. I sulked, argued with the teacher, avoided doing schoolwork, and talked to my classmates when the teacher was talking; yet in all my other classes

I was a model student. The concerned and puzzled math teacher talked to me after class one day, "What's the matter, JoAnne?" I was unable to tell him. I was keenly aware of a whirling mass of painful emotions, but could not articulate the problem. From the vantage point of forty-one years later, I realized that my need for belonging to my new peer group was threatened, as was my need for competency and respect.

The fall back down the stairway is usually temporary; our character and emotional development is arrested only momentarily. Eventually, when some basic level of needs is met, we realize again that someone does care, that we do belong somewhere, that we are competent, respected, lovable human beings. When this happens, growth up the staircase towards self-motivation and self-actualization begins once more. Each human being, if he or she has been nourished by having some basic level of needs satisfied, continues up that staircase, pulled along by an inborn urge to learn and grow.

Exercise

Once we are aware how important it is to give positive attention to our kids at neutral or positive times, it is relatively easy to do. The main obstacle is that we often just forget to do it. In positive and neutral situations our children are a delight to us and we are emotionally able to let them know we love them. The dilemma that arises for most of us is what to do when our children are misbehaving. What kinds of attention do we give them when their behavior is negative? Parents and teachers certainly should not give positive attention to a child during periods of misbehavior, yet positive attention is what a child needs in order to have the needs for security, belonging, unconditional love, and competency/respect satisfied. It is hard to even like a child at negative times. What on earth is a parent or a teacher to do? Is it possible to be a strong disciplinarian and still not strip away a child's self-esteem and leave unfulfilled the needs for belonging, love, and respect? The answer to that question is an unqualified YES. The following exercise is the first step on the way to learning how to discipline while at the same time you help the child to strengthen his or her personal self-esteem staircase.

1. **Learn to recognize the differences between the child's negative, neutral, and positive behaviors.** The following "Child's Staircase of Needs" chart has three boxes. Each box represents one of the three basic categories of behaviors. Set aside twenty minutes a day for at least five days to mark down checks or circles in the appropriate boxes, depending on the type of behavior you are seeing. Make a check in the negative box when you see the child engaging in a negative behavior, and put a circle in the neutral or positive box when you see the child doing something neutral or positive. You can choose to observe only one child, preferably your "problem" child if you have one, or you can observe any child at random. Do not put the observed child's name on the chart. If the children ask what you are doing, tell them you are learning some new things about being a parent or a teacher. "I am learning some ways to make things go better in our family (or classroom)." Say nothing more about it. Find a handy place to post the chart, maybe on the side of the refrigerator or inside a cabinet door. Teachers will have to find some other special spot so the chart does not disappear into desk papers.

2. **Do not try to change the child's behavior this week.** Just observe and check off what you notice happening. When you notice a negative behavior, make a check in that box. When you notice a neutral or positive behavior, make a circle in the appropriate box. Neutral behavior seems to be the tough one for many people to learn to recognize. A good internal clue to help you distinguish between neutral and positive behaviors is to remember that positive behaviors usually make you feel proud and pleased. You will not experience much emotion about neutral behaviors. Neutral behaviors are just there. Often you will not even notice them. Examples of neutral behaviors are when a child walks through the room, when she is sitting gazing out the window, or just watching television.

3. **Behavior that is neutral for one child might be positive for another.** If Gracie never just sits and reads in the classroom, and then one day you look over and see her sitting and reading, that is positive behavior for Gracie. After all, you feel mighty proud and happy to see

her finally involved in a book. However, in Carlos's case, reading is a neutral behavior. When you look over and see Carlos just sitting and reading, you will not have much emotion about the behavior because Carlos often sits and reads.

4. **Do not insist that your spouse or partner keep a chart.** Your spouse will resent it if you attempt to force him or her into participating. If your partner does want to participate, it would be wonderful because change for children happens much faster if all adults are involved. But if the other adult does not want to take part, please respect his or her wishes. You can accomplish a great deal on your own. Keep in mind Rudolf Dreikurs's advice to stop trying to change your partner and instead just concentrate on what you yourself have the power to accomplish: "Do what you can do." You have no right to insist that your spouse or your fellow teacher or your friend do things your way (unless of course, they are actually abusing the children). By the same token, you do not have to do what they tell you to do. If your spouse, or another teacher, tells you how you should discipline the children and you can see that following their advice will make things worse instead of better, you can refuse to do what you are told. As long as you remember *not to argue about child-rearing methods in front of the kids,* which will inevitably cause them to feel insecure and worsen their behavior, you are free to "Do what you can do."

CHILD'S STAIRCASE OF NEEDS *

What Human Beings Need for Healthy Emotional Growth

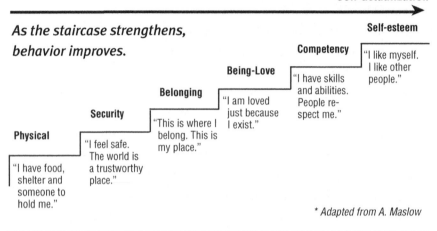

Self-actualization

As the staircase strengthens, behavior improves.

Self-esteem

Competency

"I like myself. I like other people."

Being-Love

"I have skills and abilities. People respect me."

Belonging

"I am loved just because I exist."

Security

"This is where I belong. This is my place."

Physical

"I feel safe. The world is a trustworthy place."

"I have food, shelter and someone to hold me."

* Adapted from A. Maslow

WORKSHEET
TOTAL OF CHILD'S BEHAVIOR

Behaviors You Give Emotional Attention Will Continue

Positive	Neutral	Negative
Pleases you—a joy for you	Child doing his or her own thing—not a problem for you	Angers or irritates you —a problem for you

from *Caring Discipline: Practical Tools for Nurturing Happy Families & Classrooms*

Chapter 2 Discussion: PAYING ATTENTION

1. Share the positive/neutral/negative behavior exercise that you charted throughout the week. Is everyone clear as to the difference between a neutral and a positive behavior? Did anything particularly interesting happen regarding the neutral behavior you observed?

2. Was there ever a special time of your life when any of the basic needs that Maslow outlined were not provided for you? Would anyone like to talk about that experience and what you remember about it?

3. Are you aware of any times in your child's life in which it was especially hard for you to see that his or her needs were met?

4. If your spouse has decided not to participate with you in your attempt to learn some new parenting methods, would you like to talk about any feelings or thoughts you have regarding that decision?

CHAPTER THREE

How Parents and Teachers Sabotage Their Discipline

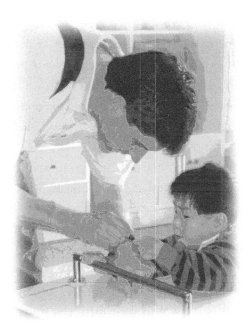

Many parents and teachers feel they are failures as disciplinarians. Some read every new article and book on the subject that comes along. They take people's advice and try getting tougher. They take other people's advice and try being more lenient. They even enroll in classes in child psychology, but nothing seems to help. Finally the day comes when they throw up their hands in bewilderment and say, in anguished tones, "I've tried everything. Nothing works with that kid." Usually the problem with these dedicated but ineffective parents and teachers is that they are sabotaging themselves. Without realizing it, they are subverting their own disciplinary efforts.

Procrastination

There are four basic ways to sabotage yourself. The first is Procrastination. Sometimes parents or teachers keep hoping that if they are patient enough or kind enough or reasonable enough, children will see the light and do what they are asked without so much fussing. These adults ask the child to do something once, a second time, then a third time, even a fourth time before they finally run out of patience and get upset enough to do something about it. An example of procrastination: a four-year-old boy who starts jumping on the couch when his mother is trying to visit with guests. Mother says, "Get off the couch, Aaron." Aaron ignores her and keeps on jumping, Mother says, "Aaron! You heard me." Aaron keeps on jumping, his eye on Mother. "Aaron. If you don't get off that couch, I'm going to get out the spoon and give you a spanking." Aaron keeps on jumping and at last responds, "Oh, Mom. Why can't I?" Mother, her voice rising to peak levels, shouts, "Okay, young man. You asked for it!" She lunges at him but he leaps off the couch and dashes outside. Mother shakes her head and complains to her friends, "I can't understand why Aaron is so naughty."

Unfortunately, Mother's procrastination is only teaching Aaron that it is okay to wait until the fourth time she tells him before doing what his mother says. After all, Mother never gets really serious about things until at least the fourth command. What Aaron is learning from this display of patience is that it is safe to ignore the first three or four commands. You could even make a case that Aaron has trained mother to tell him to do something four times before she acts. To avoid sabotaging yourself, you must *act the first time you see the misbehavior.* If you do not act at the first sign of misbehavior, and instead just keep on reminding, warning, and scolding, you will only make yourself miserable. It is even possible that the kids will learn to simply ignore you. One mother said she overheard her ten-year-old daughter telling her new stepbrother some of the unwritten rules of his new family, including this one: "You don't have to pay any attention to Mother when she hollers at you. She never does anything about it."

Acting on the very first sign of misbehavior is extremely difficult for some parents and teachers, especially C-adults, who often have the sneaking suspicion that they do not have the right to make demands on the child anyway. Difficult or not, it is essential for you to expect children to carry out reasonable requests, or else you will not be able to teach children the behaviors and values that you know are important for them to learn. If the problem is that you do not know *what* to do about the misbehavior, be patient a bit longer. Subsequent chapters will answer your questions about what to do in each situation.

Besides teaching that you mean what you say the first time you say it, a further benefit of "act-the-first-time" is that if you act immediately, you will not get so angry at the child. The longer children avoid doing what you want them to do, the more frustrated and angry you become. Everyone gets angry occasionally. If anger is constructively dealt with, it poses no problem to any relationship. The problem with unresolved anger that builds over a long period of time is that it will not only sabotage your discipline and damage your relationship with your children, it will also undermine the building of their developmental staircase.

If you are the kind of person who lashes out with your anger, you will find yourself yelling at the kids, or hitting them, far beyond what you yourself feel happy about. Continual screaming at children and blaming them can be as destructive, sometimes even more so, than hitting. A mother in one of the parenting groups once said, "I would rather have been beaten than told the things I was told. My mother used to put her face up against mine and scream at me that she wished I had never been born, that it was my fault she couldn't have a happy life."

On the other hand, if you are the kind of person who deals with your anger by withdrawing rather than attacking the child, you will probably want to retreat. You cannot withdraw physically, of course, since as a parent or a teacher you must be with the child. The danger is you will withdraw from the child emotionally. It is possible for a parent or teacher to be in the same room with a child and completely ignore the child's presence. Positive behavior is ignored, neutral behavior is ignored, even negative behavior is ignored as long as possible. When a child is constantly ignored, the nonverbal message sent by the adult is, "You are not a lovable person and I don't like being with you." We have already talked about how painful it is to be ignored by anyone, but it is especially painful to be ignored by someone as important as a parent or teacher. The only way the child has to gain the withdrawn adult's attention is to behave in more and more negative ways. Finally, the child's behavior becomes so outrageous that the adult explodes, directing pent-up rage at the child with abusive language or extreme physical punishments. Even the long-suffering C-parent and teacher can be provoked to this extreme. After the explosion, the adult again withdraws, refusing to acknowledge the child's presence until the child goads him into another explosion.

Pete was a quiet, reserved man who began his experience as a parent wanting to be a good father, but not knowing what to do whenever his young son misbehaved. Pete was determined not to repeat the mistakes his own father had made, but he had no role models for positive ways to interact with his own child. As the years went by, his son escalated his negative behaviors in order to get his reserved father to pay attention to him. As John Bradshaw once said, "If I am thirsty, I would rather have clear water, but if there is no clear water, I will drink it muddy." Pete grew increasingly puzzled and resentful of his son's negative behaviors. Since Pete's habit was to withdraw from people when he was angry with them, he not only ignored his son at negative behavior times, he began to ignore him all the time. With every misbehavior, Pete withdrew further from his son, ignoring the boy's existence until the boy would do something so outrageous, Pete would explode. By the time the boy was a teenager, Pete and his son seldom talked to each other except with scorn and blaming. Both felt hurt and abused by the other. The boy continued his pattern of negative and irresponsible behaviors well into his adult life and never developed a healthy sense of his own worth as a human being.

Repressed anger cannot be entirely hidden. If the adult is carrying around a heavy load of resentment and anger against the child, the child knows from the adult's nonverbal behaviors that somehow the parent or teacher does not approve of him or her. When the adult is forced to talk to the child or has to be with the child, there is no real affection expressed. The child is deeply hurt. He or she is at first bewildered, then hurt, resentful, and angry. Inevitably, because children are so dependent on adult attention, they will continue, and even escalate, their negative behavior, making the adult want to withdraw from them even further. In this way, the sad, downward cycle is continued in which the child's behavior worsens and the adult finds it harder than ever to look at the child without feelings of resentment and anger.

On the other hand, there are few of us who have not lost our cool and ended up whacking our children on the bottom at least once. Sometimes our patience cannot be stretched one millimeter further. I remember my own early parenting days when I sometimes yelled at my children and hit them on the bottom with my open hand. I still feel terrible inside when I remember those spankings. It is a common story whenever parents get together to share the difficulties of parenting, "I hit them and I yell and I feel so bad about it afterwards." Most of us feel bad about hitting and yelling at our kids because deep inside we know that hitting and yelling are demeaning both to the one who hits and the one who gets hit. Hitting and yelling tear down everyone's staircase of emotional needs.

If you find that you are doing a lot of yelling and spanking or are often threatening to spank, do not give up. There are much better ways to discipline your children. Frequent spanking and unkind words may help you to vent your own frustrations, but will eventually rob your children of the self-esteem and dignity they need to grow emotionally and will cause them to become increasingly sullen and angry. Their misbehavior will not only continue, it will intensify. Hurting a child may drive the misbehavior underground, but it will not bring about positive long-term behavior change.

Not all cultures approve of hitting children as a form of discipline. In Sweden, for example, spanking of any kind is against the law. The Tauripan Indians of South America don't need a law against spanking since hitting a child would never occur to them in the first place. It is worth remembering that both Stalin and Hitler experienced childhoods filled with extreme emotional and physical punishments inflicted by their parents. Dr. Alice Miller, in her book, *For Your Own Good,* makes a convincing argument that the rage rooted in the punishing childhoods of people like Hitler and Stalin comes back to haunt humanity with a vengeance.

Some people think it is all right to spank as long as the spanking is not done in anger, but I have noticed in my years of working with families and schools, that children who are regularly disciplined by spankings, whether in anger or not, often do not develop adequate inner controls for regulating their own behavior. These children continue to misbehave in settings where they know spankings are not allowed, and may even continue the pattern into adulthood of always needing powerful forces outside themselves to set limits on their behaviors.

In our culture we use the word "spank" instead of "hit." Spanking is acceptable whereas hitting is not. It is against the law to hit another adult, but spanking a child is somehow socially acceptable. We often "spank" children for "hitting" another person. It seems ludicrous, even irrational, when we think of it in this way. Why is it okay to hit a child but not to hit an adult? The answer is that disciplining children by hitting them and shaming them has been handed down to us for over a hundred years as a legacy from our Victorian ancestors. Since the Victorian approach to child rearing is the basic method our culture has absorbed, many of us simply do not know any other way to control our children's misbehaviors. Most of us would like to change the old punishing parenting approach, but we haven't yet figured out exactly what should replace it. Hence this book. Read on. You will find there are many more effective ways to stop misbehaviors and teach value systems.

In the meantime, if you are concerned that you are doing too much hitting and giving frequent verbal expressions of anger toward your children, there are some immediate and short-term ways to let your resentment and anger out without hurting your children. When the urge comes on you to hit the kids, try going into the bedroom and punching a pillow. Try whacking your bed with a tennis racket a few times. It makes a satisfying thump and does not hurt anything except for raising a little dust. A counselor friend keeps a huge pillow in her room at school for anyone, big or small, to come by and give it a few kicks when they have "had it."

A mother who had a violent temper and frequently hurt her children learned to punch a pillow instead of hitting her kids. She felt silly about it at first. She was embarrassed to have her preschoolers standing by, wide-eyed, while she beat her fists against the pillow. Eventually, she realized it was a far saner method of expressing anger than hurting her children. She was a verbal woman who also did a lot of screaming at the same time she was hitting the pillow. She would yell, "I'm so damn mad I'm going to hit this god damn pillow! I'm not going to hit you kids but I sure as hell am going to knock the god damn stuffings out of this god damn pillow!" The neighbors were probably horrified at the language she used in front of the children, but it worked. She had more to learn before she began to understand how her own hidden unmet needs were sabotaging her life and feeding her anger, but at least she was no longer directing her verbal or physical assaults at her children. Another plus was that her kids were learning there are other things you can do when you get angry besides hit and yell at people. This same mother later told about a time her five-year-old daughter got angry at her four-year-old brother. The girl ran into the bedroom, and started whacking her pillow, all the while shouting, "I'm so damn mad, but I'm not going to hit you! I'm going to hit this god damn pillow!" Working with anger at this level is only a beginning, but the important point is that this family was starting to learn some workable methods of coping with anger that did not focus on punishing each other. In the context of the former physical and verbal violence in this particular family, swearing was a minor problem. (We'll talk more about anger in Chapter Four.)

Anger is much less likely to arise if you can act immediately to carry out the correction the first time you see the misbehavior taking place. By having a plan and by acting immediately, you will take control of the situation, thereby avoiding the downward spiral of frustration, anger, and punishment. As a general rule, it is best not to get carried away with any intense feeling during disciplinary times. Intense feelings give too much attention and power to the misbehavior. As much as possible, and this will be difficult, save your emotional energy for the neutral and positive times. *Emotional energy is what children want and need from you. Try not to give it to them when they are misbehaving.* It will only fuel the power struggle and encourage the misbehavior.

Children are learning an incredible amount these first years of their lives. Behavior is just another thing they have to learn. Keep in mind what you want your children to learn and which methods you are going to use to help them learn it. Try not to become emotionally distraught when children make behavioral mistakes. We all make mistakes. It is an integral and necessary part of learning. That does not make us bad parents or teachers. This is how we all learn. The same is true for the child: *The fact that the child makes mistakes does not mean he or she is a bad child.*

Talking and Talking

The second major way we sabotage our own discipline is through Talking and Talking about it. A disciplinary action should be carried out, finished, and forgotten. You need to be firm about carrying out the correction the first time the misbehavior occurs and then *do not mention it again.* As Rudolf Dreikurs so beautifully phrased it, "Act, don't talk." Both A and C-adults have problems sabotaging themselves with this one.

Example A

Dad sends Shelley from the dinner table because she is messing with the food, making loud burping noises, and generally causing everyone else at the table to lose their appetite. Dad tells Shelley to go to her room without any more to eat. Shelley goes off to her room complaining all the way that Dad is mean. On the way down the hall she whines that she is hungry, and finally, just before she goes into her bedroom, she loudly promises not to do it anymore if she can come back to the table. Dad sticks to his decision and refuses to give in. So far, so good.

But now Dad proceeds to sabotage himself. When dinner is finished, Dad goes into the bedroom where Shelley is sobbing, her face buried in a pillow. Dad is a C-type parent, a loving father who does not like being the "bad guy." Dad tries to explain to his daughter why he did what he did. He sits down on the edge of the bed and pats her on the back. "Look, Shelley. This wasn't any fun for me either. Do you think I can enjoy my dinner when you can't have yours? Next time, think about that when you start acting like a goof ball at the table, Okay? Okay? Come on. Let's see a big smile. That's Daddy's girl." Dad picks Shelley up, puts her on his shoulders and carries her out of the bedroom. Dad believes he has handled the whole thing pretty well, but is exasperated and amazed when a week later at Grandma and Grandpa's, Shelley repeats the performance. Shelley has learned she can get lots of special, emotional attention from her father by misbehaving.

Example B

Or take the A-type parent, also a loving father, whose ten-year-old son left the bicycle out in the driveway right behind the car where Dad nearly backed over it. This A-type father does not think of himself as the "bad guy" because he has to discipline his child. He is quite comfortable in the parental leadership role, and doesn't feel the need to explain himself about why he did or didn't do certain things, but still he proceeds to sabotage himself.

First Dad takes the bike and hangs it up in the garage. Then later, when his son comes asking for help in getting the bike back down, Dad says, "No. You can't use the bike for two days because you left it out right behind the car and I nearly backed over it." So far, so good. But now comes the talking and talking sabotage.

"How many times have I told you to take better care of your bike? How long do you think it took me to earn the money to buy you that bike? We can't afford to be buying things for you that you don't even care enough about to take good care of. Maybe not using it for two days will teach you a lesson you'll remember about learning to be more responsible. And if you do it again, next time I'll hang the bike up for a week!"

That night at the dinner table, Dad tells Mother in front of his son and two daughters, "Chuck's bike is grounded for two days because he left it out right behind the car where I nearly ran over it. He has got to learn to be more responsible. You girls take a lesson from this. You all need to be more careful with your stuff."

When the two days grounding is over, Dad gives the bicycle back to his son and launches into a final lecture. "Okay, Chuck. Remember this the next time you park your bike in the driveway. What if I hadn't seen it? It would have been run over. Then you wouldn't have any bike at all to ride. I can't afford to buy you a new bike every time you wreck one. I wouldn't do that even if I could afford to because you've got to learn to be more responsible. I was all ready to leave for work and I had to get out of the car and waste my time because you were irresponsible. This isn't the first time either. Now I hope this helps you to remember." Dad is totally disgusted when a couple of weeks later, Chuck leaves his bike out behind Dad's car again.

Both of these fathers used sensible corrections with their children's misbehavior that should have been effective. Instead, both children continued to misbehave. The problem with both fathers' approach was that they sabotaged themselves with all their talking, which in these two instances took the form of cajoling, advising, pleading, warning, reminding, reassuring, and scolding. Like many adults, these two fathers believe the way to teach children positive behaviors is by talking at them.

As strange as it seems, *talking undermines effective discipline,* even if the talking takes the form of good, reasonable advice. First of all, talking gives a tremendous amount of emotional attention to the child for misbehaving. Misbehavior is encouraged when you give this kind of social reinforcement. The attention you give your child at the time of a correction should be as brief and nonverbal as possible. Pretend you have put a piece of duct tape over your own mouth. Bite your lip. Count to ten.

Advising, lecturing, moralizing, or verbally trying to teach in any way when either the adult or child is seething with negative emotions will turn off the child's ability to listen. *Let the correction be the teacher.* Children have an inner door they can lock tight against any adult if they choose. The child can simply refuse to accept what the adult is saying, even when both child and adult know full well that everything the adult says is true. Children are exactly like adults in this matter. Think of a time someone gave you advice you did not want to hear. What was your response?

The classic example is a man who comes home from work after a day of extreme tension and anxieties about his job. He comes storming in the door, slams it behind him, and starts complaining about his no-good, stupid, power-hungry boss. His wife herself has just come home from work. If she were to sabotage herself, she would say something like this, "Now Honey. You know your boss is having a hard time of his own right now, going through a divorce and everything. And remember, when you took the job, Carl warned you that your boss was difficult even in the best of times to get along with. You knew from the beginning he was an S.O.B. Why don't you just go take a nice bath. Things will seem better in the morning. How about a big smile, honey?" Or, if she is feeling discouraged about her own job, she might say, "Well, I've had a hard day, too. My job isn't all that easy you know." Imagine this husband's reaction. The fact is, we usually do not talk this way to other adults, but we often talk this way to children.

The normal human response when we are forced to listen to unwanted advice is resentment and anger. The advice may be good advice, it may be reasonable and well-intentioned, but if we do not want to hear it, we will not hear it. Not only will we refuse to heed the good advice, we will blame the person who expects us to listen to it.

Some children sit quietly with downcast eyes while their parent or teacher advises, reminds, or scolds. They have learned to keep their resentment hidden. Other children very early begin to find flaws in the adult's logic and learn to argue endlessly as to the fine points of the case. "No one told me I had to do it by today," or "Why can't Susan do it? Why do I always have to do everything?" or "I was going to do it right after dinner." Any adult who tries to respond reasonably to these arguments ends up in an endless debate in which the child always has the last word or gesture. The parent or teacher ends up frustrated and angry, while the child feels demeaned, his or her sense of integrity threatened by having to sit and listen to all this talking. The resentment that arises from being forced to listen to things children do not want to hear triggers a powerful negative response, "They can force me to listen, but they can't force me to do what they say." This is a crucial point: *In order to maintain a sense of integrity and self-respect, the child very often feels compelled to do exactly what the adult is warning against.* The self-sabotage of talking about the misbehavior has created a power struggle between adult and child. You are the latest in a million-year-old line of teachers and parents. Adults have an obligation to pass along cultural expectations to their children. You have the authority of all society and all nature behind you. Do not sabotage yourself and all those thousands of ancestors by turning this into a personal power struggle.

Power struggles are especially destructive to the adult's efforts to instill a sense of responsibility in the child. When the parent or teacher lectures, advises, warns, scolds, even by so subtle and nonverbal a method as arching an eyebrow or using a tone of voice that implies, "Now you've done it, after all the times I warned you," it becomes easy for the child, who is trying to protect his inner sense of integrity and self-worth, to blame the adult. The child begins to feel that he or she is the injured party, and it is the adult who is responsible for the problem. In the eyes of the child, the adult becomes the cause of the child's misbehavior. "It's not *my* fault. If they weren't always picking on me. I would do it if they'd get off my back. I'll show them they can't push me around." Children caught in these power struggles grow up making decisions based on whatever the adult does *not* want them to do. If Mom says do it, Natalie will *not* do it. If Mom says *do not do it*, Natalie will try to do it at least once. Children like this often grow into irresponsible adults and continually blame everyone else for their own poor decisions.

I am not suggesting that adults stop talking with their children about important values or their philosophy of life. The sabotage problem arises when adults try to verbally teach their values during negative, emotional, high-stress times. Talking and talking, when both you and the child are in a confrontation situation, only results in increased resistance and tension between you and the child. Of course you want to talk with children about your deeply held beliefs, about the importance of manners, about all variety of values and opinions. But the time to teach children these things is when you and they are in neutral or positive situations, for example, when you are planning the day's schoolwork together, working on the car, walking across the school yard, or raking leaves.

Forgetting to Pay Attention to Positive and Neutral Behaviors

The third way we sabotage our discipline is Forgetting to Pay Attention to Our Children For Positive and Neutral Behaviors. We sabotage ourselves when we focus only on the child's negative behaviors. I cannot overemphasize how important this is. *The ratio needed to bring about desired behavior and attitude changes is to give the child at least four positive attentions for every one negative attention.* This means that every time you give one negative attention to a child, you need to concentrate on giving four positive attentions to the child as soon as you see him or her in a neutral or positive behavior. The four-to-one ratio might seem impossible to you if you and the child are presently stuck in an extreme negative behavior pattern. How can any adult be positive with a kid who is constantly misbehaving? Do not get discouraged. Things will get better. Meanwhile, try to catch the child at neutral times with as much positive attention as you can muster. Use lots of nonverbal attention if you cannot think of anything positive to say. Give frequent friendly eye contact to the child during group conversation times if you cannot think of anything else to do. Most adults can carry this kind of attentive behavior off successfully even if they are not feeling particularly loving towards the child at the moment.

Marcella and her teenage son were locked in a power struggle which she was unable to break. One day she was taking him to a soccer game. They were driving along in the car, her son seated in the passenger seat beside her, sullen and withdrawn as usual. She thought about what she had learned in her parenting class, to try to pay nonverbal attention at neutral times. Even though she was afraid of being rejected, as she had been so many times before, she summoned up her courage and reached out to touch his hand. To her surprise, he squeezed her hand in return and looked over at her with a big, affectionate smile on his face. "Things aren't perfect, but they've been better ever since," she told the group. As Marcella discovered, nonverbal attention is often even more powerful than verbal attention. (Chapter Two gives many more ideas for paying attention at positive and neutral times.)

Negative Scripting

Finally, we come to the fourth sabotage, Negative Scripting. In the same way that actors in a play learn what to say and how to behave by reading the script of the play, children learn what part they are expected to play in their family or classroom by listening to the opinions of important adults. Children begin their lives believing that parents and teachers are all-knowing. Children therefore believe that what the adults who take care of them think about life and about them must be true. As children grow older and their brains function at a more abstract level, they will begin to question adults' value systems, but not until the adult belief systems have sunk deeply into the very core of their beings.

Imagine then, the impact on a child overhearing his mother talking about him on the telephone to her best friend, "William is just impossible to be with. He drives me crazy sometimes. Sometimes I think every parent should be able to throw away the oldest kid and start in all over again." Mother does not really mean this. She is just venting some frustrations and even trying to make a half-hearted joke. But consider how William must feel. Or take Lupé, who is in the third grade, whose teacher says to the principal in front of her, "Lupé just can't be trusted. She is a born liar." Consider what kind of decisions Lupé and William are beginning to make about the kind of roles they are expected to play in life.

Below is a list of negative scripts that are commonly used, either spoken directly to the child or within the child's hearing. As you read them, pretend that you are the child and that you believe the person saying these things is all-knowing and all-wise:

1. "She is so clumsy. She's been this way since she started to walk. Honestly, every family needs a klutz and I guess Mary Sue is ours!" (Spoken to a friend at a baby shower over the head of her four-year-old granddaughter who, in passing the nut dish, dropped half of them on the floor.)

2. "She complains from morning till night. She was *born* whining!" (Spoken to a friend within the child's hearing.)

3. "If you don't shape up, you're going to end up in jail just like Uncle Ed. The police will come and take you away just like they did him."

4. "Sure you can take her out of the class. Keep her forever as far as I'm concerned. She's driving us all nuts." (Said in a clearly audible whisper by the classroom teacher to the school counselor, who has come into the classroom to take Mia to her office for a visit.)

5. "What a bad boy you are. Bad, bad boy!"

6. "Prue has an awful hard time in school. She just doesn't catch on fast. But school is so easy for Sid. He never seems to have any problems. He got all A's and B's last term." (Spoken to Grandma within Prue's hearing.)

7. "Come here, Dummy!" (One parent told her group that as a very young child she thought her name was Stupid because that is what her parents always called her.)

8. "I give up on him. He never listens. Things just go in one ear and out the other." (Spoken to a friend within the child's hearing.)

9. "Shame ... Shame on you!"

10. "My God! Sometimes I wish I'd never had any kids. They're driving me crazy." (Spoken to a friend within the children's hearing.)

Using a harsh, scornful, or disparaging tone of voice is often part of negative scripting. Even if we speak to the child in a foreign language when we say these things, if we use a harsh, scornful, or even flippant tone of voice, the child will clearly hear the negative message. From your voice and your body language the message is, "You are not a competent and respected person." At its deepest and most extreme level, children can interpret the message of the negative script to mean they should never have been born, "*You have no right to exist.*"

These few examples give you some idea of how common and destructive negative scripting is. If we talked to, or about, our friends and acquaintances like this, we would soon be without friends. In fact, most of us would never talk this way in the presence of an adult with whom we feel irritated, yet we often, unthinkingly, say these things to a child. This is ironic, because it is the child who will actually believe what we say. Children have not yet acquired the conceptual ability and the world experience that allow them to be critical of your opinions. They believe that you know everything. They believe that what parents or teachers say about them must be true.

"They say I am bad. She wishes she could throw me away. The teacher and all the kids wish I were not in the class. I am an outsider. People don't like a person like me. I am going to end up in jail. I'm just naturally clumsy. I am a dummy. I'll never be as smart as my brother. I should never have been born. Everybody would be better off if I were dead. I'm a bad person. I am the reason Daddy's life is so unhappy."

Not only does the child make intellectual decisions about himself or herself based on the negative scripts given by beloved adults, the child is also being deprived of the emotional needs described in Maslow's staircase of needs. Remember the needs for security, belonging, being-love, and competency/respect? The staircase of needs is chipped away and undercut each time a negative script is repeated to the child by an important adult.

Fortunately, adults can also write positive scripts for the child. Every time you give positive verbal attention to the child, think of it as an opportunity for positive scripting. Imagine how children begin to think of their roles in life if they overhear statements like these:

1. "Rufus was a big help to me today. He set the table and got me diapers for the baby." (Mother says this to Dad in front of Rufus when Dad arrives home. She ignores the fact that Rufus whined a good deal about going down for his nap.)

2. "Kayla played quietly with her Legos when the baby was taking a nap today. It was a big help to me because I needed a rest too." (To a neighbor within Kayla's hearing.)

3. "Daniel must have been working hard on his math because his math grade went up this term. I knew you'd be proud of him." (To Grandma over the telephone when Mom knows Daniel can hear.)

4. "I was so proud of Serena today when she spoke out and defended her friend against some kids who were teasing." (Teacher to Serena's father who has come to take Serena to a dentist's appointment.)

5. "Ask Arturo to show you the art work he did. He worked all period on it." (Teacher to school counselor in a pleased tone of voice.)

6. "I noticed you helped Richard carry all those books. I bet he appreciated that." (Teacher to child.)

7. "Carla worked on her social studies map for a whole hour this afternoon. She sure stuck to it and didn't give up." (One teacher to another in Carla's hearing.)

8. "This morning when I woke up I thought to myself, 'I'm so happy the kids were born!' " (Father to Mother within the children's hearing.)

9. "I am so grateful to have kids who will pitch in and help with the housework like they did this morning." (To Grandpa within the children's hearing.)

10. "Davina spent a whole hour helping Lamar practice catching and hitting. I hope she enjoyed it as much as he seemed to." (Spoken to a friend over the phone within Davina's hearing.)

What a difference in children's perceptions of themselves to hear this kind of positive scripting. Just as before, the child believes the adult is all-knowing. But this time, the child uses the information to make the decision that he or she is a respected and competent person. The emotional needs for security, belonging, unconditional love, and competency are met. Children who are given these kinds of messages are free to grow and learn from their mistakes instead of being stuck in the negative role of the bad guy, or the stupid guy, or the clumsy guy, or the child who should never have been born.

Hidden Unmet Needs

Once you become aware of them, the four sabotages are fairly easy to deal with. They at least have the virtue of lying at the surface, where we can see them, talk about them, and try to change them. The deepest sabotage of all is so hidden that it cannot be classified with the other four. The vast underlying base of all the other sabotages is our own hidden unmet needs. We may be grown-ups who are parents and teachers, all-wise and all-powerful to the still developing minds of our children and students, but you and I know we are fallible human beings. Like our kids, we have needs of our own right now, and we had needs of our own when we were children that may not have been met for us. The mass of these unmet needs lies hidden under the surface, often hidden even from ourselves. Like the underwater bulk of an iceberg, they lie waiting to sink our best efforts at relationships with other people and especially with our own children. The base of the iceberg, our unfulfilled needs, is the source of much of the puzzling anger and resentment we so often hurl blindly at the very people we love the most.

So the father who was physically and emotionally abused as a child is likely to abuse his own children and spouse. Over the years he has tried to forget the pain he endured as a child. "Sure I used to get the belt, but it was good for me. I had it coming." He is not in touch with the humiliation and hurt he suffered as a child. He is not in touch with his own low self-esteem, which is the result of his long childhood experience of never having enough sense of security, being-love, belonging, and respect. As an adult, he tries to hide from his own inner pain. But now he is powerful enough to protect that small child within him against his tormentors, maybe even at last extract some revenge. Unfortunately, he now sees his tormentors as his wife and children. "Why do they irritate me like this? Why do I always have to tell them? Why do they get me so angry? It's their fault I have to hurt them." His bewilderment is real, since his unmet needs are hidden even from himself.

Or, consider the mother who was taught she should always take care of other people's needs before her own. She is the good little girl who, as an adult, feels guilty at the very thought of directly asking for what she wants. After all, as a child she was belittled and shamed whenever she asked anything for herself. "You should wait to be asked. You should take the smallest piece. You should go last through the door. You should speak only when spoke to." As an adult, she is closed off from the burial grounds of her own unmet needs. But the bones still lie there and, in some hidden place, she still remembers. So she finds quiet ways to protect the small child within her. She is continually disappointed in her children and her husband. "I always did what I was told. Why can't my children be more considerate. Why don't they come to see me more often? Why am I so unhappy?" She spreads the guilt around unceasingly. In her quiet way, she self-sabotages on as grand a scale as the punitive father. John Bradshaw calls these hidden unmet needs a "gaping hole" somewhere deep inside that yearns to be filled. But children cannot fill that gaping hole left over from our own childhoods. If we expect that they will, we will always be disappointed and angry at them.

I vividly remember talking about parenting to a group of young single mothers who were enrolled in a community college program designed to help them develop the skills and confidence they needed to get good jobs. When I got to the part about our hidden unmet needs, one of the women asked, "But can't our children fill those needs for us?" I had to tell her the truth, "No, children will sometimes show you they love you and make you feel wonderful for a little while, but as a usual thing, no. Children don't yet have the inner resources to help their parents fill the hole of unmet needs left from their own childhoods. It wouldn't be fair to ask it of them." To my amazement and consternation, half of the group began to cry.

If you, like those young mothers, are feeling totally drained from your parenting role, and wonder what you can do to fill your own unmet childhood needs, you might try doing what one marriage counselor suggests. When you get into a negative situation with your child, stop for a moment and try to imagine yourself as a child. Be as vivid as you can be in your remembering. Next, love and protect the child that you were, and still are. Now pretend that the child you once were is your son or daughter. Think about how you would have wanted to have been treated by your parents. What kind of discipline would have made your emotional needs staircase strong and still taught you limits and responsibility? In this way, by acting as your own protective and caring parent, you can begin to heal the wounds from your own childhood, as well as experiencing the here-and-now satisfaction of becoming a more competent and supportive parent for your children.

If you often feel angry or resentful at the children in your care, it would be helpful to spend some time trying to discover the source of that anger. As in the two incidents given above, the anger may be coming from long ago, unresolved emotions from your own early childhood experiences. As children, we are often taught that anger is a "bad" emotion and that we are "bad" if we express or feel anger. But anger is not "good" or "bad." It exists. It is a part of reality. There is nothing wrong with anger unless we use its energy to hurt ourselves or someone else. *Unfortunately, when the basic feelings that give rise to the anger are not dealt with openly, the anger builds and builds until it blindly takes control of all facets of our life.*

For example, one father told the members of his parenting class that he frequently erupts with rage at other people, including his children. As he talked about the experiences of his childhood, of being moved from foster home to foster home, of never belonging anywhere or to anyone, of being scolded for talking to the neighbors because "they don't want to be bothered by the likes of you," the other members of the group helped him identify his primary emotions of rejection, humiliation, loneliness, and shame. A constant and terrible rage arose out of those primary feelings. The anger was necessary, even helpful, to him during his childhood. Without the anger, he might have given up totally. The anger gave him the energy to survive the suffering of his bitter childhood.

Unfortunately, like this father, many of us use our anger to hurt ourselves or other people. It is how we use our anger energy that can be harmful, not the anger itself. We need to explore, share, and talk about those early primary feelings and the situations that gave rise to them before we can let go of the anger.

Another hidden unmet need that gives rise to anger is when we are not having any fun right here and now. When our life gets to be a drudgery, when we have no time to take care of ourselves, no time to play, no time to laugh and relax, we start feeling resentful. Eventually the resentment erupts in anger, which often ends up hurting those we love the most. Recently, Rita was so busy on her job and feeling so harassed that she asked her husband if he would do all of the housework jobs for a couple of months. Since his life was calm at that time and since he is a loving person, he agreed. A few weeks later, Rita told us she was looking through the cupboards for a plastic container to store some leftover chili and could not find the lid. The damn lid was not where it was supposed to be! She felt frustration and then rage at her husband for putting the lid in some stupid place instead of where it should be. Luckily, the feelings lasted only for an instant before Rita noticed what was happening. She said, "I think the anger erupted because I was feeling sorry for myself. I was working all my waking hours. I wasn't having any fun. I realized it was time to do something nice for me, even if it was only to take a long hot shower." Rita recognized that her husband had nothing to do with her anger. In the same way, our children often have nothing to do with the anger that sabotages our discipline and relationships with them.

If, after you work your way through this book and things still are not markedly better in your relationships with your kids, it may be time to look for clues in your own childhood for the roots of how you are sabotaging your relationship with your kids. Find a good therapist or support group for adult children of dysfunctional families to help you uncover the hidden pain of your own early unmet needs and of those feelings you were never able to express openly. The purpose of a counselor or a support group is to help you heal those old, festering wounds. It may be that this is the root cause of problems in the adult/child relationships within your family or classroom, and that only with this kind of healing will you be able to stop sabotaging your discipline and your relationship with your children.

Exercise

This week, concentrate on learning to identify the four sabotages when you see them. Use the following "The Self-Sabotages" worksheet to observe yourself or other adults interacting with children. Watch for any of the four kinds of sabotages: Procrastination, Talking and talking about the misbehavior, Forgetting to pay attention at positive and neutral times, and Negative scripting.

Also watch to see if your own hidden unmet needs are getting in the way of your interaction with the children. If you see any self-sabotage going on, write a brief description of the incident in the appropriate box so you can share it with your group at the next meeting. As you did last time, either give yourself a twenty-minute time segment each weekday to observe. Or if you prefer, you can watch less intensively throughout the entire day. Remember, do not chart your spouse or partner. It is very important that you do not observe and analyze your spouse.

WORKSHEET

THE SELF-SABOTAGES

PROCRASTINATION

TALKING AND TALKING ABOUT THE MISBEHAVIOR

NOT GIVING POSITIVE ATTENTION AT POSITIVE AND NEUTRAL TIMES

NEGATIVE SCRIPTING

HIDDEN SABOTAGE: The unmet needs of the adult

---

from *Caring Discipline: Practical Tools for Nurturing Happy Families & Classrooms*

REVIEW: How Parents and Teachers Sabotage Their Discipline

The Four Self-Sabotages

1. **Procrastination**

   Instead, act the first time you see the misbehavior.

2. **Talking and talking**

   Instead, carry out the correction with as few words as possible and do not mention it again.

3. **Forgetting to pay attention to positive and neutral behaviors**

   Instead, give the child at least four positive attentions for every negative attention given.

4. **Negative scripting**

   Instead, use positive descriptions and tone of voice in talking about your child.

The Underlying Base of the Four Self-Sabotages Is Our Own Hidden Unmet Needs

1. The unmet needs from our own childhood, or present day circumstances, give rise to feelings of anger and resentment, which we sometimes direct at other people. Because of this, our children often have nothing to do with the anger that sabotages our discipline and relationships with them.

2. If you suspect that your hidden unmet needs are now sabotaging your discipline with the children, it may be time to find a good therapist or counselor or support group to help you uncover the hidden pain of your own early unmet needs and to help you heal those old, festering wounds.

from *Caring Discipline: Practical Tools for Nurturing Happy Families & Classrooms*

Chapter 3 Discussion: SELF-SABOTAGE

1. Share this week's charting of the self-sabotages you observed.

2. Are you involved in a power struggle right now with any of your children? Talk about what happens.

3. When you were a child, did your parents sabotage their discipline in any way?

4. Do you sabotage yourself in any way in the process of disciplining your children?

5. Everyone write down five things they remember their parents saying to them when they were children. Do this very quickly. Do not take more than a couple of minutes. Take turns sharing your list with the other members of the group.

6. Are you aware of any scripts you are giving your children?

7. Make a two-column list. First column: Ways to express anger that will not hurt either you or the people around you. Second column: Ways to express anger that are hurtful to yourself and the people around you. Make a similar two-column list for ways in which children express anger. Are the two lists different in any way?

8. Ask if anyone in the group wants to talk about any of their own unmet needs, past or present, that are getting in the way of their relationships with their children. Go ahead and share if you want to, but do not pressure anyone to do this.

9. If anyone is interested in joining a support group for adults who were, or still are, members of a dysfunctional family, call your local mental health association or Al Anon chapter for information. Suggested readings are: *Codependent No More* by Melody Beattie and *Healing the Shame that Binds You* by John Bradshaw.

Chapter FOUR
Listening to Inner Reality

Young or old, we are all moved by powerful emotions. The very young child experiences the same feelings as the adult: joy, sorrow, loneliness, humiliation, fear, anger, embarrassment, contentment. Human beings come fully equipped with the whole wide range of human emotions. As educator Jean Lawrence observed, "Feelings have no birthday." Of course, each individual has unique personal experiences and so interprets each situation differently. For example, a child may feel fear at the noise of an oncoming steam locomotive because the child has never seen one, while you may feel a touch of sadness and nostalgia because you have many memories of steam locomotives. At some other time, you may be the one to experience fear while the child feels sadness. The capability of the adult and the child for feeling emotions is the same, even though the experiences and the attitudes that give rise to the emotions may be different.

Yet adults often find it hard to allow children to express the very same negative feelings that adults commonly experience. If an adult learned as a child that feelings of anger, sadness, jealousy, or resentment are somehow wrong or frightening, it is hard for that adult to witness a young child openly expressing those same forbidden emotions. Complicating the problem is the fact that adults have often been taught that it is polite to hide their own negative feelings, whereas the negative emotions of children are right out in the open for everyone to see and hear. The usual response of the adult who has somehow learned to repress his or her own negative feelings is not only to stop the child's open expression of negative emotions, but to convince the child he or she should not be feeling that way at all. In other words, with the best of intentions, we often try to convince the child that the child's negative feelings are "wrong."

There are three major reasons why it is so hard for adults to allow emotions like jealousy, anger, and sorrow to be felt and expressed by children. The first is that as loving adults, *we want so much to protect their young lives from emotional pain.* To see our children hurting recalls our own memories of emotional pain and we hurt right along with them. It seems part of our duty as parents and teachers to try to prevent our children from suffering the inner hurts that we ourselves have experienced. The second reason is that because of the raw intensity of some negative emotions, *we are afraid our children might get themselves into trouble or might hurt someone else* if they do not learn how to "control" their feelings. And third, *we sometimes interpret children's expressions of negative emotions as acts of defiance and personal rejection of us.*

These three reasons, each based in powerful emotional needs of our own, often compel us to try to convince children that they are wrong to be feeling what they are feeling. In so doing, we unintentionally weaken the competency/respect step on their staircase of needs by sending them the nonverbal message, "If you were a competent person, and as smart as I am, you would know that what you are feeling is the wrong way to feel." Inevitably, the child also begins to assume that if his or her feelings are wrong, he or she must also be a bad person for feeling that way. In this way, the being-love and competency steps on the staircase of needs are undermined, as the child asks, "How can I be a lovable and competent person when I have such wrong feelings inside?" Self-esteem is eroded and all the negative feelings are strengthened.

Children have an inner core of integrity that compels them to be true to themselves. They know that what they feel is true, even when they are not able to verbalize it by giving the feeling a name, and even when other people tell them the feeling is wrong. They know their feelings are real, even though the feelings become increasingly confusing to them when important adults try to convince them they *should not be feeling* that way, or *are not feeling* that way. In order to defend their inner selves and to keep in touch with feelings they know are firmly rooted in their own inner reality, children can slam shut an inner door to block any attempt to argue them out of their negative feelings. With the inner door shut, the words of the adult cannot penetrate. A child's ears may hear you, but his or her heart will be closed.

Lois's husband had recently left her and their five-year-old son. The husband had not called or written the boy for four months. Other than the letter he left behind, Lois had not heard from her husband. Their son, Phil, cried easily and often erupted in angry outbursts at his mother. Occasionally, Phil tried to verbalize his feelings, "I miss Daddy." Lois continually tried to take away some of his pain by telling him what she believed to be true, "Daddy misses you, too, Phil. He is just upset right now. He has so many things on his mind. I know he loves you very much. You are his own special boy." Phil invariably responded to Lois's attempts to comfort him by yelling, "Shut up! Shut up!" and running from the room. There were many wet eyes in our parenting group as Lois told this story. We realized how painful it must be for her to helplessly watch her child go through the pain of abandonment.

After learning about the importance of not arguing children out of their inner-reality feelings, Lois, in spite of many reservations, decided to try to stop all her well-intentioned reassurances about Daddy. The next time Phil said, "I miss Daddy," Lois was quiet. She went over to sit by her son and put her arm around his shoulder. "I miss him, too, honey." She gave him a hug. He hugged her back and cried a bit. They sat like that for a little while, neither of them saying anything more. Then Phil got up and started playing with his toy trucks in a perfectly calm manner. "I don't really understand it," Lois told us. "The angry feelings he usually had just melted away."

Here is a paradox: By allowing the child to feel the intensity of his or her inner pain, the child is able to finally let the painful feeling go, whereas, if someone tries to convince the child he or she should stop experiencing the intense inner pain, the child clutches it even more tightly.

Further, children experience a second emotion of anger when people around them try to cajole, or reassure, or argue them out of their first feelings. In Phil's case, for example, his first feelings may have been rejection, feeling unloved, and loneliness. When Phil yelled, "Shut up! Shut up!" and ran from the room, it was the secondary emotion of anger that fueled his behavior. Yelling "Shut up!" at his mother was not a rejection of her as a person. His expression of anger was a defense, which helped give him strength to protect himself against the confusion of being told he was mistaken to feel what he felt, when, deep in his inner-reality core, he knew that even if Mother said his feelings were wrong, what he felt was real.

Here is another painful inner-reality situation related by a grandmother. Five-year-old Laura is sitting on the living room floor building a complicated block structure. Her two-and-a-half-year-old brother, Roald, is playing with his cars nearby, occasionally helping by handing his sister some blocks. The grandparents are seated in chairs on either side of the children, talking and watching the kids play. Unexpectedly and without meaning to, Roald bumps into Laura's block structure and the whole edifice comes tumbling down. Laura starts to wail, "Oh, it's wrecked! It was almost done! I was going to use it for the little dolls to live in." Laura begins to sob. The adults recognize these are not crocodile tears. Laura is deeply pained over the loss of her creation.

Both grandparents try to comfort and reassure her by giving what they perceive to be helpful outer-reality information. "Don't cry, Laura. We'll help you rebuild it," and "Never mind, honey. We'll help you make it as good as new." Laura cries even harder at this and begins to stomp her feet and shout, "Why do things I make always get wrecked? Why do I have to have a little brother?" At this point, Mother comes into the room, immediately realizes and accepts the state of Laura's inner-reality feelings and says, "Oh, you must feel so sad that your block house got wrecked." Laura nods, sniffles, and stops yelling. She gets back down on the floor and says calmly, "Well, I can fix it again." Roald, who has been watching the whole affair with round eyes, now says, "I'm sorry," and goes over to hug his sister and tries to help her rebuild the block house. To her grandparents' amazement, Laura even accepts her little brother's apology and inexpert assistance.

The grandmother told us she knew how important it is to let children experience their own painful feelings, but she wanted so much to protect her granddaughter from the pain of losing her block house that she went right ahead and tried to convince her not to feel sad anyway.

Here is the dilemma for all loving adults: How can we convince ourselves that children are strong enough to endure their own inner pain? How can we convince ourselves that children will not necessarily hurt themselves or others when they experience strong negative feelings? And how can we learn not to take it personally when a child expresses negative emotions like resentment or anger?

Here is a situation in which a second-grader named Scott comes home from school, slams his books on the table and yells, "I'm not going to that dumb school ever again!" We adults instantly assume that Scott is having a problem at school that we must solve. We are upset that he is upset. We try to make him feel happy again. We generally try to convince the child that he should be reasonable and rational. We are reasonable and rational in our advice to him. We ignore his inner-reality feelings and instead try to convince him of the outer-reality situation that we clearly perceive, even if he does not. Here are some typical outer-reality responses adults are likely to give Scott.

"But look, you have to go to school. It's the law. I know things are tough some days, but it's tough for everyone some days. Going to school is your job. I can't quit my job just because I have a hard day. You're making too much of this. It's better to try to forget all about it. Let's have a cookie. Tomorrow will be a better day." The adult may even go over to the child, rumple his hair, try to tickle him into giving a laugh. Or the adult may try to get to the root of the problem by questioning and attempting to place blame: "What happened? Are you sure you didn't do something to cause it?"

From the adult point of view, explaining to the child the facts of the situation is a rational and helpful way to approach the problem. This is why it is so puzzling and frustrating to a concerned adult when Scott responds to all the good advice and reassurances by becoming even more upset. At this point, Scott may even run angrily from the room, slamming the door behind him. Some children will stay in the room but will withdraw inwardly. They will answer the adult's questions with a sullen expression and downcast eyes and respond, "I don't know … I don't know." Like all healthy children, Scott has an inner door he can slam tight against anyone in the outside world who threatens his inner-reality feelings and his honest, inner core of integrity. Bang. He closes the door. When he does, he stops listening to you. He will no longer share his feelings. You can force Scott to sit there, but you cannot force him to really hear what you are saying.

Adults, too, have this same inner-reality core, but it is often buried so deep we sometimes forget it is there. Unlike the young child who is still very much in touch with his or her inner reality, we adults sometimes confuse what we *should* feel with what we *do* feel. It is not unusual to find adults who cannot figure out what they want because they are so accustomed to wanting what other people have wanted them to want.

At any rate, communication is now closed. If you are the adult in the situation given above, you may be talking but Scott is refusing to hear you. He is fending off your words like Wonder Woman fends off bullets with her magic bracelets. Since his feelings are not acceptable to you, he has stopped trying to share them. He may leave or sit in sullen silence or he may flip into a kind of self-indulgent behavior by arguing. You can be as rational and reasonable as you like, but Scott can match you point for point. If you are going to act like a judge or a detective, he will be the lawyer for the defense. "Why do you always tell me things I already know?" or, "You can change jobs, why can't I change schools?"

What does Scott expect you to say? What does any child want from you when he or she shares a troubling feeling or inner conflict? Like every adult in the same situation, Scott wants someone to confirm that it is a common human experience to feel what he is feeling. Negative emotions and inner conflicts are scary for kids. "If Mom and Dad and Teacher are not blown away by what I'm feeling, I must be okay. If they are not repulsed by me because of these feelings, I must be normal. If they think I can handle it, I must be a strong and capable person."

In a moment of deep negative emotion, Scott has opened his inner door to share his inner reality with you. In order for that inner door to stay open, you must give up any sense of being superior to Scott in the matter of emotions. You must give up the role of being the all-wise protector, advisor, problem-solver, and judge. You must let Scott take the lead. You must trust that he is strong enough to deal with the power of his own feelings. You must allow him to feel what he is feeling.

What can you, as a caring adult, do when Scott comes home deeply unhappy about school and says, "I'm never going to that dumb school again." Whether you keep on doing whatever you are doing, or whether you go sit at the table on which Scott has just thrown his books, you can look and feel sympathetic. You can say something like, "Wow, what a day you must have had" or just, "Gosh." You do not have to say much. Remember how powerful nonverbal attention can be? Quiet listening, intent nonverbal attention, combined with short sympathetic verbal responses is the inner-reality response he craves. The fact you are taking his feelings seriously lets Scott know you respect his right to feel what he feels. You do not have to memorize anything special to say. You do not have to agree with his words and opinions. You do not have to agree with him if he says the teacher is stupid or that someone should punch out the principal. Try to accept the feelings that gave rise to those statements. The main thing is to believe *the child has a right to feel what he is feeling.* And believe that *the child is strong enough to endure the pain of what he is feeling,* just as you believe that another adult is strong enough.

Kids sometimes need to blow off steam, the same as adults. You may remember the example of adult steam-blowing given in the chapter on self-sabotage, but it is worth repeating here. This time it is the wife who comes home humiliated and discouraged by something that has happened at work that day. She throws down her coat and storms, "I swear to God I'm handing in my resignation tomorrow. We'll eat beans. I'll go on unemployment. I've had it with that S.O.B.!" Imagine this woman's reaction if her spouse gives her a rational, reasonable outer-reality response: "Now honey, you knew when you took that job there would be some bad days. You can't just up and quit. You'd never get a good recommendation for the next job with such short notice, and you know we have to keep up those payments on the new car." The fact is, her husband knows she needs to blow off steam and regain some inner balance by venting her feelings at the events of the day. He knows his wife understands all the outer-reality facts. She does not need to be reminded about the car payments and the fact that there are always tough days on every job. She would feel demeaned and patronized if he gave her rational advice or reasonable criticism. Instead he will probably give her the inner-reality response of a hug and a sympathetic comment, "Oh, honey, I'm sorry you've had such a rotten day." Children coming home from school feeling discouraged and demeaned also know they cannot quit school. They are looking for the same kind of inner-reality response we give so easily to other adults, but find so hard to give to children.

As in the earlier situations with the boy whose father had abandoned him and the girl whose block creation had been destroyed, parents and teachers report again and again that when they manage to keep to the inner-reality response, and resist the temptation to start rescuing and giving outer-reality advice, they can see a visible, physical sense of relief as the tension from the negative feelings melts away. By listening in a quiet and compassionate way, you let children know they are respected, that their feelings are normal and human. When they reveal their inner selves to you, by your quiet example you can let them know there is nothing "wrong" about them or their feelings. Consequently, there is no need for them to slam their inner door tight against your words or to close their ears to your voice. Instead of adding to his or her problems by unintentionally weakening their competency/respect stairstep, you are helping the child to grow confident and strong.

Many of us find it frightening to accept and listen when a child expresses extreme anger over a perceived or real problem: "I'd like to kill him!" or "I hate her!" Teachers often tell how they are able to listen to a student's feelings, but have a difficult time listening to the negative feelings of their own children. It is especially hard for parents to allow their children to experience negative feelings because we are so protective of our own kids. Sometimes we want so much to protect our children from the pain we ourselves experienced as children, we can't bear to hear them express similar painful feelings. We often think we are failures as parents when our children are feeling friendless or discouraged or jealous; at these times we cannot even admit to ourselves that our children feel this way, much less allow them to feel it. Sometimes the old tapes play from our own childhoods: "Nice children do not say these things, good children do not feel these feelings. Shame on you. What a bad boy you are to feel like that." Such a simple thing, to allow a child to feel his or her own feelings, yet so hard for a loving parent to do.

If Gloria says she would like to kill somebody, it is tempting to leap in with a lecture on outer reality and tell her why we cannot even think of killing people and what the Bible says about killing and on and on. But of course Gloria already knows that. She is not really planning to kill anyone. The truth is that children who are allowed to express all their emotions, including anger, will not need to act out their anger in aggressive ways. Children who are not allowed to talk honestly about their inner-reality feelings are the ones most likely to hurt themselves or others. People who bury their feelings are the ones who will ultimately take out their pent-up anger on others. But when feelings are listened to and accepted, they lose their power to create the anger that prompts us to lash out and hurt ourselves or the people around us.

ANGER AS A SECONDARY EMOTION

It may help you to accept a child's anger if you understand that anger is a secondary emotion that gives us the strength to survive the pain of some deeper first emotion. Was the child humiliated? Is the child afraid of failure? Does the child feel unloved? Rejected? Stupid? Helpless? As has been mentioned earlier, emotions that are experienced first are what fuel the secondary emotion of anger.

Here is an example from my own experience of how anger arises from primary, underlying emotions. Several years ago, my husband and I were both working long hours. We were both exhausted. At one point it seemed to me we were just eating and sleeping together, living together in a house as mere acquaintances. One evening I came home and found him sitting in the living room reading the paper. I felt such a longing to be playful and carefree and intimate again; I went over and tickled him. He jerked my hand away and said angrily, "Can't you leave me alone when I'm reading?"

Imagine my feelings. I went into the kitchen and stood by the sink. I experienced powerful feelings of anger. I was about ready to go storming back into the living room and tell him what I thought of his insensitivity when I suddenly thought, "Wait a minute. What did I feel *before* I felt the anger?" You can probably guess most of my primary feelings: rejection, loneliness, and fear. The fear was that our relationship was disintegrating. In verbalizing to myself the primary feelings, my anger faded somewhat, although the pain of the first feelings hit even harder.

I went back into the living room and sat down beside him, "I've got to talk to you. I'm scared and I'm lonely." Immediately the paper came down and my husband's concerned eyes looked out at me. "What is it?" The paper was forgotten. He listened to me tell of my fear that our relationship was crumbling. I listened to him explain how he was resentful of having so many people to deal with at work, and how he had looked forward to coming home to peace and solitude only to find that even I had not respected his need to be alone for awhile. (Tickling is an extremely demanding kind of touching, by the way.) At this point, I was finally able to imagine *his* feelings. We talked about how the stresses of time and energy were creating a barrier between us. We sat for a long time saying nothing, holding each other. Intimacy was restored. Not only did the anger evaporate, the fear and the loneliness also melted away. If I had gone back into the living room and confronted him with the secondary emotion of my anger (even if I had put it in a polite form of "I feel so angry at you" instead of "How can you be so uncaring, you louse?"), we might have had a major problem build between us for days or even weeks. Most likely we both would have taken our unresolved anger back to hurt not only ourselves, but also the children and adults we worked with.

Children are usually not going to be able to verbalize their primary emotions for you. Many adults are also not able to verbalize the primary emotions that cause their own anger to flare. As a young adult, I certainly did not know how to share my primary feelings. Unfortunately, many adults and children have this in common: The emotion they can share most easily with others is the secondary emotion of anger.

Most people think of anger as a negative or a "bad" emotion, but anger also has a positive face. Anger is an expression of a human being's strength and energy. Anger gave me the energy to walk back into the living room and confront my husband with my pain. Without the anger, I might not have been able to do anything about my pain. Without anger, children too might give up, lose their inner integrity, wither emotionally, maybe even physically die, as has happened to so many children in orphanages. Anger gives each human being the energy to go forward, to change things, to get what he or she needs.

The reason so many of us are afraid of anger is because we have so often witnessed the power of anger to hurt ourselves or other people. Alice Miller's book, *For Your Own Good*, is well worth reading if you would like to understand just how devastating and far reaching are the consequences for all humanity when the primary emotions of children are not heard and accepted. Her account of Hitler's repressed childhood is a chilling example of the childhood rage that can fuel a violent adulthood, leaving a trail of sorrow in its wake. In a more recent book on the same theme (*Real Boys: Rescuing Our Sons from the Myths of Boyhood*), psychologist William Pollack describes the unspoken "boy code" that teaches American boys to cover up their emotions. The unfortunate result of valuing silence and toughness in our sons is fragile self-esteem, academic and emotional difficulties, school violence, and even suicide.

When children express deeply felt and negative emotions, they just want to be listened to. Usually, they do not expect anything else from you. The very act of airing their emotions lessens the need for taking any other action. On the other hand, sometimes you can sense a child needs help in problem-solving the situation. Resist the temptation to leap in and take control by giving outer-reality advice. Listen and let the child take the lead. If you sense the child needs help in finding a specific solution, first always ask his or her permission. Here are some ways to offer your help, while still allowing the child to stay in charge of his or her own feelings:

1. "Is there something I can do to help?" Only agree to do what you feel good about doing. You do not have to agree to anything that would whittle away at your own inner core of integrity.

2. "Do you have any ideas for making things go better?"

3. "Do you want me to think of some ideas for you to try?"

At first it will be hard not to slip back into the outer-reality response. After two minutes of successful inner-reality listening, you may find yourself falling back into giving the same old unasked for, outer-reality advice. Habits die hard. Do not be discouraged if this happens to you. Keep at it and you will gradually feel more comfortable at not leaping in to solve the child's problems. If you cannot think of anything to say, just keep quiet. Look sympathetic and pay close attention. You can even try telling the truth, "Gosh, I just don't know what to say."

Use the inner-reality response only when children express a deep and troubling emotion that is tied to a real problem in their lives. *Do not use the inner-reality response when you are carrying out a correction for a self-indulgent misbehavior.* It is up to you as a sensitive adult to decide whether the child is really having a difficult time coping with his or her emotions, or whether the child is engaging in a self-indulgent, attention-getting misbehavior. If you are not sure, first try an inner-reality response. You will be able to see from the child's reaction whether this is a real problem for the child or whether it is just a habitual self-indulgent misbehavior. Many well-intentioned and caring C-adults have sabotaged themselves by giving lots of listening attention to a child who used feelings as a smoke-screen for self-indulgent behavior. (More about self-indulgent behavior in Chapter Eight.)

Eight-year-old Beth could always deflect her parents' demands for responsible behavior by using feeling language she had learned would trigger their reflective listening skills. One noteworthy example was for her to furrow her brow and say sorrowfully, "I feel very sad when you make me do the dishes all alone in the kitchen." This would divert her parents attention from the task of getting her to do the dishes while they had a long discussion with her about her feelings and their feelings. The parents came away from these encounters with Beth feeling frustrated and angry, but not exactly sure why. No wonder they were upset. Their own inner sense of integrity was threatened. They felt outwitted and manipulated by their eight-year-old daughter. In fact, Beth had no deep troubling feelings in this matter other than she definitely did not like to do the dishes. She had learned to use the language of feelings to manipulate her parents into discussing emotions instead of her chores. When these parents learned to ignore the self-indulgent behavior of feigned sadness and concentrate on some logical consequences for dishwashing, everyone was happier.

Finally, there is no formula you need to memorize, no correct word pattern you need to remember. The key to really being able to listen to human beings express deep and hurting feelings, whether child or adult, is to believe they have a right to feel what they are feeling, and to believe that they are strong enough to bear the pain.

Exercise

Study the charts on the following two pages. Using the two "Inner and Outer Reality" charts as a guides, use the worksheet to write down any inner- or outer-reality responses you give to your children during the coming week.

INNER AND OUTER REALITY

Helping the Child Cope With Painful Emotions

Child's Opening Remark	Outer-Reality Response	Inner-Reality Response
"Jane gets to go everywhere! I never get to do anything good!" (Stamps her foot.)	"Jane didn't get to do all these things either when she was your age. When you are her age you will get to do all the things she does. Anyhow, I think you get to do more than Jane got to do at your age!"	"I bet you wish you were the oldest one in this family … " (spoken with understanding, not as a put-down) or just a sympathetic look, and "Hmmm," or "Gosh!"
"1 don't want to go to school anymore! I hate this dumb school!" (Throwing school books on the floor.)	"But everyone has to go to school. Its the law! You just have to learn that everything in life isn't fun. I have to go to work, even when I don't want to!"	"Gosh, what a tough day you must have had!" or just a sympathetic look, and "Hmmm," or "Gosh!"
"I can't do it … " (Slumped shoulders and downcast eyes.)	"Of course you can! You are just as smart as anyone in this class. I'm sure you can get it. Just keep trying. Maybe you just need to work harder."	"You're feeling pretty discouraged today … " or just a sympathetic look, and "Hmmm," or "Gosh … "
"I'm never going to play with that stinky Ginny again!" (Frowning, with hands on hips.)	"Well, you might be angry right now, but you'll get over it. Remember the argument you had with John last week? And now you are friends again."	"Something happened between you two that was really upsetting," or just a sympathetic look, and "Hmmm," or "Gosh … "
"There's nothing to do around here." (Drooping head and whining voice.)	"Have you thought about making something with the Legos? Or maybe you could see if Jimmy wants to come over. Or … how about helping clean up that garage?"	"One of those boring days … " or just a sympathetic look, and "Hmmm," or "Gosh … "

from *Caring Discipline: Practical Tools for Nurturing Happy Families & Classrooms*

OUTER-REALITY RESPONSE Characteristics	INNER-REALITY RESPONSE Characteristics
1. Closes the door to two-way communication.	1. Opens the door to two-way communication.
2. The adult does lots of talking (advising, analyzing, moralizing, criticizing, consoling, judging, ordering, questioning).	2. The adult does lots of quiet listening along with short verbal responses that clarify the child's feelings.
3. Insists on logic, reason, rationalization.	3. Accepts the fact that feelings often seem irrational or illogical.
4. Argues the child out of his or her feelings and makes judgments about those feelings.	4. Accepts the child's feelings— does not judge them.
5. Assumes the adult must take away the child's pain. The nonverbal message to the child is, "You aren't very strong. You aren't very capable."	5. Trusts the child to deal with his or her own pain. Nonverbal message to the child is, "You are a strong and capable person."

WORKSHEET

PRACTICING INNER-REALITY RESPONSES

Child's Opening Remark	Outer-Reality Response	Inner-Reality Response

from *Caring Discipline: Practical Tools for Nurturing Happy Families & Classrooms*

Chapter 4 Discussion: LISTENING TO INNER REALITY

1. Using the "Practicing Inner-Reality Responses" worksheet, share the stories about your inner- and outer-reality responses this week.

2. Do you remember a time you were angry as a child? Do you remember a time your parents were angry? What happened? Can you identify the primary feelings that came before the anger erupted?

3. Think about a recent time, as an adult, when you were angry. Can you identify the primary emotions that gave rise to your anger?

4. Divide into groups of three. Have each person take a turn playing the part of a child, an adult, and an observer. Have each "child" choose either a situation from the chart or a situation from real life. Remember, *do not use a situation where the adult is carrying out a correction for a misbehavior.* It must be a situation in which the "child" has a real-life problem and is sincerely trying to cope with painful emotions.

5. First, have the person playing the adult role give the outer-reality response. Then start the situation over again and the second time have the "adult" give the inner-reality response. The observer can then lead the discussion with the "child" and the "adult" to explore what happened between the two people during the outer- and inner-reality interactions.

   Do this three different times so each adult has the opportunity to experience being the child, the adult, and the observer.

6. Check back to the discussion guidelines at the end of the first chapter. Is your group still following the guidelines? Is everyone getting a chance to talk? Does each member of the group feel his or her own inner reality is being listened to?

from *Caring Discipline: Practical Tools for Nurturing Happy Families & Classrooms*

CHAPTER FIVE
Describing
Outer
Reality

Human beings are verbal beings. Our rich use of the spoken language sets us apart from all other species. Talking and listening is a major way we learn from one another and is one of the ways we bond emotionally with other human beings. For most of us, conversation is a large part of the joy of living. We have already talked about the fact that talking and listening are most productive and fun during times of positive and neutral behaviors. During these times, grown-ups and kids can usually just go with the flow and enjoy each other's company. Occasionally though, when we attempt to verbally praise a child at a positive or neutral time, the child suddenly withdraws and may even become belligerent.

Sometimes the child responds to verbal praise with negative behavior, leaving the adult bewildered and wondering, "Well, what brought that on?" Have you ever had the experience of giving praise to a child when the child suddenly drew inward or ran away? Here is a common example of this kind of situation. A child has drawn a picture. The adult looks at it and says, "Oh, what a beautiful picture." The adult really thinks the picture is beautiful. The adult is honestly telling the child what he or she thinks. But the child grabs the picture from the adult's hand, scrunches it up, and throws it into the wastebasket. The child yells, "No, it isn't!" and runs from the room, slamming the door behind her. This is so common a situation, in fact, that many parents and teachers never comment at all on a child's picture but instead make it a rule to ask, "Do you want to tell me about it?" In this way, the adult avoids misinterpreting and possibly offending the child.

Asking children's opinions about their artistic creations is certainly a much better way to react than to belittle the child by asking "Is it a horse?" while turning to another adult in the room and giving a laugh. Or, in an attempt to be helpful, some adults will take the drawing and begin improving on it, "That's a very nice house, but look, if you add just a few more lines, it will look three-dimensional." One little boy gave up drawing by the time he was five years old because his father, who was a loving, concerned parent, kept improving on his son's drawings in an attempt to teach him how to do it even better. The message to the child in both of these situations is, "You are not a competent person." The same applies in every facet of life. We have all known daughters of good cooks who were afraid to cook for fear they would make a mistake and carpenter's sons who refuse to even own a hammer. Without meaning to, each parent convinced his or her child that the child was incompetent in the very area the parent most wanted the child to succeed.

But back to our first example, in which the adult sincerely said, "What a beautiful picture." Now how on earth can sincere praise cause a child to become upset? The answer has to do with that same inner core of integrity talked about in the last chapter. The child needs to be true to his or her inner self. If the inner self believes that the picture is not beautiful, then the child cannot accept the adult's praise. From the child's point of view the picture was not beautiful. The child crumpled the picture and threw it away because inner honesty demanded that the child not accept praise for something he or she did not deserve.

Martin, a new sixth-grade student to our school, is a memorable example of the strength of a child's inner integrity. Martin was in continual trouble with his teacher, the playground personnel, and the principal because he was frequently involved in fights with other children. After getting to know Martin better, his teacher tried to work out as many ways as he could to begin to supply Martin with some of the emotional needs Martin yearned for: security, belonging, being-love, and competency/respect. Without the help of Martin's troubled parents, the teacher could not supply much, but even the little he could do seemed to help because the incidents of fighting went way down. One day at the end of lunch period, the teacher brought Martin to my counseling office to visit. "I want to tell you how good Martin has been this week," the teacher said. "He has been just wonderful." Martin was sitting on my desk chair (all the kids liked sitting on my desk chair, which had rollers on the legs). He began to move nervously back and forth. The more the teacher praised him, the more frantic Martin's movements became until finally he and the rolling chair were practically bouncing off the walls of the room. The bell mercifully rang and they walked off down the hall. After school this exasperated teacher told me, "Do you know what Martin did after we left your office? He walked into the room just ahead of me and the very first kid he met, he doubled up his fist and punched him in the face. The other kid never even looked cross-eyed at him."

Martin was a boy who had come to believe in his inner self that he was not good, that he was a bad person. We could not have known all of Martin's behaviors that week. Only Martin knew all of his behaviors. Maybe that very morning at the bus stop, Martin had taunted one of his classmates about being fat and made her cry. How could Martin remain true to himself and accept the verdict that he was good when he was convinced he was bad? Martin chose to hit the first child he saw to show the teacher the truth, to prove to the teacher that he, Martin, was not really a good kid. "See, this is how I really am! This is the real me!"

Here is that inner core of integrity again, driving human beings to make their own honest and independent judgments. Maybe this inner integrity of ours is a survival instinct. How could human beings have survived for over a million years without the ability to make reality-based and independent decisions? Individuals or nations who consistently deceive themselves about their real-life situations will not survive. Wherever the urge toward inner integrity comes from, it is especially strong in children because they have not yet learned to repress it.

Using Describing Language to Give Praise

Martin obviously needed some kind of praise, some kind of recognition for his new positive behaviors. What could the teacher have said that Martin could have accepted? Martin could have accepted a *description* of what he had done, a *describing praise.* Martin's inner integrity can accept a simple statement that describes the specifics of what happened because *a statement of fact cannot be argued with.* If it is a pure describing statement, even Martin will have to admit that what the teacher said is true. The teacher could have used far fewer words and just stated the facts of the matter by saying, "Martin hasn't been sent to the office one time this week for fighting. Not even during lunch period. Mrs. Jones told me she has not had to get after him once on the playground all week." The pleased tone of the teacher's voice, his arm on Martin's shoulder, make the process of giving describing praise warm and caring. Even though the words are starkly factual, there is nothing clinical or cold about describing praise.

Well-intentioned adults can evaluate children every day by telling them they are good artists, or that they are beautiful or good or lovable. Yet children will refuse to accept this kind of evaluating praise unless they already believe in their honest inner selves that the statement is true. Children will not believe an evaluating statement is true, or feel good about it, until they themselves make a long series of independent judgments based on factual information from the world around them. The pure, describing bits of factual information that you give to the child are individual bricks the child uses to build and strengthen his or her staircase of needs. Children must build their own staircase, brick by brick, one small piece of information at a time. They need to make their own judgments about being capable and smart before they can accept your opinion that they are capable and smart. Whether child or adult, one brick at a time is how each of us builds our own stairway to self-esteem and competency. Only when Martin believes he is smart, can he accept it when you tell him he is smart. Only when Martin believes he is good, can he accept it when you say he is good.

If you evaluate a child in any way, even if you use positive evaluations like "good," "wonderful," "beautiful," or "smart," you have put yourself, and not the child, in control. You do not want the child to be always dependent on your opinions about him or her. Our goal should be to help children learn to make their own positive decisions about themselves. Children who are not overly dependent on other people's opinions will grow up with the inner confidence to be able to think for themselves. When evaluating praise is the only kind of praise they hear, children are likely to value the opinions of other people more than they value their own. Even as adults, they will need constant reassurance from others in order to believe they are okay. The security and competency stairsteps on their staircase of needs will have been weakened because they are always looking to other people to define what is right and what is wrong.

Even when children agree with you that they are smart or good or beautiful, evaluating has another serious pitfall. Evaluating causes rivalry between children and sometimes even a belief that they must be perfect in whatever they do. The following incident is an example not only of the power of describing praise, but is also an example of how evaluating praise can cause children to limit themselves because of the fear they might not be perfect at everything they do.

Jacob was a four-year-old boy who willingly took his turn painting at the preschool easel. He seemed to enjoy painting and created pictures for which the staff continually praised him with comments like, "What a beautiful painting!" "Great job, Jacob!" But every day Jacob took his painting, wadded it up into a ball, and stuffed it as far down as possible into his take-home tub. Jacob's mother always retrieved Jacob's cast-off paintings, smoothed them out, exclaimed at how beautiful they were, and said, "Let's take this home and hang it up." But the mother's praise and entreaties were of no avail. Jacob stubbornly continued to stuff his finished paintings into the basket and refused to take them home. To all of us adults who worked at the preschool, Jacob's paintings were beautiful, radiant with varied forms and colors. Jacob, however, obviously believed they did not measure up. His mother evaluated his paintings by pronouncing them beautiful, but he, being in touch with his inner integrity, could not in all honesty agree with her evaluation. He had a seven-year-old sister who had been given evaluating praise for her beautiful paintings for many years prior to his artistic attempts. Jacob was convinced his sister's paintings were beautiful and that his art work could never measure up to hers.

The preschool director finally suggested that everyone, teachers and parents alike, stop evaluating Jacob's or any other child's paintings by saying they were "nice" or "beautiful" or "super" and instead stick strictly to describing what we saw. No interpreting and no evaluating. Describing praise is harder than evaluating praise because you have to really pay attention to whatever is being described. Describing simply cannot be done in an off-hand manner. It requires total attention. Some examples: "You're using reds and blues today." "A big, big circle over there and lots of lines below." "Three boxes in the corner." "Lots of red dots." "You mixed that blue and that yellow to make green." Describing Jacob's paintings gave him outer-reality information that could not be argued with. Everything the adults described was acceptable to Jacob's honest inner self.

Finally, the day came when Jacob proudly held up a finished painting for his mother to see, "Look, Mama!" It took two months, but Jacob finally made his own independent decision that his paintings were worth admiring. Brick by brick, he had come to some independent conclusions. Jacob now believed his paintings were interesting, that the process of painting was a fascinating one, and that he was a capable person who was able to control and play with the process of making patterns on paper. The idea of whether or not his paintings were beautiful or not beautiful as compared to his sister's paintings no longer mattered to Jacob. By describing what he was doing, we had helped him focus on the *process* of painting instead of the final product. Earlier, we had unwittingly compared his completed paintings with his sister's completed paintings (and with all the other children's completed paintings) by evaluating them as "beautiful" or "good." Without meaning to, we had pushed Jacob into the scary situation of thinking he always had to produce a perfect and praiseworthy product.

Once a child believes that he or she has to be perfect, that child will no longer reach out and explore new areas of her life unless she knows she will succeed. You can probably remember something in your own life you never tried because you were afraid you might fail. Juan's brother, who was five years older than Juan, was a model student. Juan decided very early that he could never be as successful in school as his big brother. Feeling the need to be competent at something, Juan gave up on schoolwork and learned to be the best baseball player in the neighborhood. Competing with his older brother academically was too scary. Many a perfectionist child refuses to try anything he or she thinks will not have a praiseworthy outcome, whether it be going out for a sport (one of the most intensely evaluated activities in our schools) or signing up for a class they might not get an "A" in. The child assumes, "If I am not good at that subject, then people will think *I* am not good." In this way, many doors are closed at an early age because of the fear of being evaluated.

Describing focuses on process. Nobody fails at process. You do one thing and then you do another thing. This thing works and this other thing does not work. Learning how things work is interesting. Sometimes the process is frustrating. Sometimes the process is exciting. Sometimes the process gets boring. Sometimes the process is fun. Process is just the way things work.

Evaluation, on the other hand, is intimidating. Evaluation means there is a right way to do things. *Evaluating means there is an end product and a standard to which we must measure up.* Things must turn out good, or beautiful, or right, or even perfect. If it doesn't turn out perfect, then it wasn't worth doing. Evaluating means some people are better than others, smarter, more capable. Evaluating means if he is the best, then I am not as good as he is. If she is beautiful, than I am not as beautiful. If he is the smartest, then I am dumber.

You may remember some examples of positive scripting given in Chapter Three on self-sabotage. If you will look back and reread those examples, you will see that each of the positive scripts described one specific incident. Each is a description, not an evaluation (pages 48-49). Because each positive message is a description of a fact, the child has to accept the statement as true. Even the example of the father who says, "This morning when I woke up I thought to myself, 'I'm so happy they were born,' " is a description of fact. That was how he felt when he woke up that morning. Each of these describing statements is one more solid brick that the child will use to build his or her staircase of needs.

Even though some evaluating labels can at first sound very positive, children may still feel trapped by them, powerless to be any different than what the adult has given them permission to be. An example of how restrictive even a positive evaluation can sometimes be was told by fifty-two-year-old Amanda. Amanda's parents had decided almost from the moment of her birth that she was the lucky child. Her older sister had been severely crippled from polio two years before she was born. Amanda often heard the script, "Amanda is so lucky." Amanda agreed she was lucky not to be crippled by polio, but unfortunately all through her childhood, she never dared ask for help nor does she remember ever expressing any negative feelings to her parents. She tried to live up to her lucky script by smiling on the outside and keeping any pain she may have felt totally to herself. "I never thought I had the right to ask for anything or to feel badly about anything. It was very lonely sometimes," she told us. Or, consider Maria, whose family and friends gave her the evaluating script of "She is such a beauty." As Maria grew into old age, she desperately tried everything to hold on to her youthful beauty. Without it, she felt she had nothing left. Her old age was robbed of the contentment she might otherwise have experienced, partly because of her frantic attempts to hang on to the childhood script that defined who she was: "Maria is a beautiful woman." Without her external beauty, Maria believed she was worthless.

Using Describing Language to Reduce Stress

Describing language can also be used to lower stress in negative situations between people. For example, take a situation where a teacher steps in to stop a fight and help two children problem-solve a disagreement. If the teacher starts out by evaluating or judging the situation and asks, "Okay, which one of you started it this time?" both kids will slam shut their inner doors. From that point on, they will try to close out whatever the teacher says. But if the teacher begins by describing the situation, without blaming or evaluating, by saying, "I see two boys who want a turn on the swing," the children will be able to listen to her. By describing the situation, the teacher can give accurate outer-reality information that both children can accept as true and inarguable. Both children will be more able to listen to their teacher as she leads them through the problem-solving process.

Here is an example of a negative situation in which the mother knew her rebellious eighteen-year-old daughter, Sara, would never obey if she gave her a direct command. On the night of Sara's high school graduation, Sara came home from a party at 11:30 p.m. to change into her jeans. She ran into the living room where her mother was still waiting up for her to come home, and said, rather defiantly, "I'm going to the beach with some of the other kids so don't wait up for us. We'll probably have breakfast down there."

The beach was a two-hour drive over mountain roads. Some of her friends had probably been drinking. The mother wanted to scream, "It's not safe. You are not going and that's that!" but she knew she could not tell her eighteen-year-old daughter what to do. The mother was silent for a moment while she focused on her own inner reality. Then she said, "I would be so worried about you, I don't think I could sleep all night." For a moment, Mother and daughter looked into each other's eyes, then Sara turned and went back down the walk to the waiting car, talked with her friends awhile, then came slowly back into the house. "I don't really need to go. Some of the guys have been drinking anyway."

The mother had given her daughter an important piece of describing information and trusted her to make her own evaluation of the situation. The mother took a risk. The daughter might have said, "Oh, don't be such a worry-wart," and driven away with her friends. But she did not. The same inner integrity that would have compelled Sara's inner door to clang shut, had her mother evaluated the situation and made the decision that Sara could not go, now compelled Sara to make her own honest evaluation and her own responsible decision.

As a general rule, whenever you get into difficulty trying to communicate outer reality to a child, use describing language. Here's an example of a mother who came home from work and found her school-age children had strewn books, toys, and coats all around the living room and dining room. The mother was exhausted and she needed to fix dinner. She experienced feelings of being discouraged and unappreciated. Her anger flared and she thought, "What do they think I am? A slave?" But she kept herself from evaluating the situation and refrained from the sabotage of too much talking. Instead she tried to describe the situation in as few words as possible. She let her tone of voice sound as exasperated as she felt and said, "I see coats and hats all over the living room and toys all over the dining room floor. And books, books, books everywhere!" Then she went to the kitchen to start dinner. She had given them basic outer-reality information and tried to trust that their inner integrity would help them make an honest independent decision of what to do. In this case, the kids did pick up their mess before they came out into the kitchen to visit and share the events of the day. Mom remembered not to sabotage herself. She did not mention the messy house again except to say, "I really appreciate that you straightened things up."

You can also use describing statements whenever you need to share your own inner-reality feelings with someone you love. Do you remember the situation in the chapter on inner reality when I described my primary feelings of loneliness and fear to my husband? "I feel lonely and I'm scared." At that moment, my inner reality was part of my husband's outer-reality world. He needed information about the condition of my inner self in order for his own inner integrity core to make a decision. He would not have listened to me if I had started the conversation by evaluating him, "You are constantly ignoring me. I don't think you even care about my feelings anymore." From my husband's point of view, these evaluating statements would not have been true. He did care about me and he did not perceive himself as constantly ignoring me. His inner integrity would not have allowed him to listen to this judgmental, evaluating message. When I used describing language, he did not withdraw from me but instead put down his paper and listened to what I had to say.

Because describing is such a pure language form, it is a powerful and effective method of communicating with another human being, no matter what age the other human being happens to be. Whenever you are in doubt and wonder what on earth you can say to get through to the other person, try using describing language. Other people may not make the decision you want them to make, but they will be able to listen and consider what you are saying. And very often, if other people are at all in touch with their own inner selves, their inner core of integrity will impel them to a fair decision.

Exercise

Study the charts on the following pages. With the two "Describing Praise" charts as guides, use the practice worksheet to write down any evaluating or describing responses you observe or participate in during the coming week.

DESCRIBING PRAISE

Situation	Evaluating Praise Examples	Describing Praise Examples
Mother to her five-year-old who has just wiped up his spilled milk:	"What a good boy!"	"You wiped up all the milk!"
First-grade teacher to one of her students who is showing her his picture:	"What a beautiful picture!"	"Look at that! You used greens, blues, and reds. And lines that curve and squiggle!"
Music teacher to her girls' choir:	"That's the best job any class in this school has ever done on that song!"	"I especially like how your voices blended while you sang. I couldn't hear one single voice louder than the others."
Mother to Dad, who has just come home from work and is holding three-year-old Johnny in his arms:	"Johnny was super good today!"	"Johnny helped me feed the baby and change her pants, and he put the lunch dishes in the sink, too!"

from *Caring Discipline: Practical Tools for Nurturing Happy Families & Classrooms*

EVALUATING PRAISE Characteristics	DESCRIBING PRAISE Characteristics
1. Implies that one child has performed better than another. Tends to encourage rivalry and jealousy between children.	1. Accepts each child where he is and encourages cooperation among children.
2. Emphasizes the end product of learning.	2. Emphasizes the process of learning.
3. Temporary: Even if adults give a positive evaluation today, they can take it away tomorrow with a negative evaluation.	3. Permanent: No one can take away from the child the fact of what he or she has done.
4. Encourages dependence on the opinion of other people for a sense of self-worth.	4. Gives children the basic building bricks to build their own competency and self-esteem stairsteps.
5. Is open to honest argument. If children think your judgment is in error or is an attempt to manipulate them, their inner integrity will not allow them to believe your evaluation.	5. Is not arguable because it is a statement of fact.
6. Behavior may worsen if children feel compelled to prove to you that they are not as good as your evaluation of them.	6. Behavior is likely to improve. Children do not have to defend their inner integrity by proving to you that you are wrong.

from *Caring Discipline: Practical Tools for Nurturing Happy Families & Classrooms*

WORKSHEET

PRACTICING DESCRIBING PRAISE

Situation You Observed or Participated In	Example of Evaluating Praise	Example of Describing Praise

from *Caring Discipline: Practical Tools for Nurturing Happy Families & Classrooms*

Chapter 5 Discussion: DESCRIBING OUTER REALITY

1. Share examples of the evaluating and describing praise exercise that you did this week. Is the difference between evaluating and describing clear to you?

2. Has one of your students or children ever refused to accept evaluating praise from you? What happened?

3. Do you remember a time as a child when your inner integrity was threatened, causing you to close your inner door on an adult? Will you share that with the group?

4. Has anyone had a chance this week to help a child by listening to his or her inner reality? Were you able to continue to listen and be quiet, or did you revert to the old habit of jumping in with outer-reality information? If you could not continue to listen, be patient with yourself. It takes time to change old habits.

5. Does anyone want to talk about a misbehavior and a correction they are having problems with?

6. How are the self-sabotages coming? Would anyone like to talk about a self-sabotage that is particularly causing a problem?

CHAPTER SIX

Negative Behaviors
How To Tell the Difference

So far, we have lumped all negative behaviors into one category called "negative behaviors." We are now going to separate these negative behaviors into specific types. It is important for you to learn to identify specific types of negative behaviors because each of these negative behaviors requires a different response from you. We will examine how to interpret the patterns of the negative behaviors you see happening so that you can make an intelligent decision about how to prevent them in the first place, and how to respond to them at crisis times when you cannot prevent them from happening.

Finding patterns in human behavior is not so different from finding patterns in any other sphere of human activity. One example of a pattern is the way people have learned to measure the earth with a grid system of parallel and meridian lines. The meridian lines stretch from pole to pole.

The parallel lines measure the distances in ever-decreasing circles parallel to the equator. We find our way around the surface of the earth by locating ourselves relative to the intersections of these parallel and meridian lines. It sounds simplistic, but it works. The earth goes on as before, complex and mysterious, but we are able to navigate our way around it. Even on a small sailboat over great oceans, we can find our way without getting lost because of the patterns we have learned.

In the same way, you can learn to recognize the pattern of your children's negative behaviors and how to respond appropriately. Learning the patterns of children's negative behaviors and the appropriate responses for those behaviors will enable you to begin to find your way around in the complex web of discipline interactions between you and your children.

An important part of the specific response patterns you will be learning in Chapters Seven through Ten involve four misbehaviors and four basic corrections. Corrections are not punishments. Punishments humiliate and degrade the other person. Punishments erode the staircase of human needs. The needs of security, belonging, being-love, competency, and respect are worn away by punishment. Corrections, on the other hand, are a teaching method that, if carried out without self-sabotage, will keep the child's staircase of needs intact and strong at the same time you are teaching desired behaviors.

Equally important is for you to learn when a negative behavior is not really a misbehavior at all, but instead is an effort by the child to solve a real problem in his or her life.

The Four Misbehaviors

As a first step in this process, you need to become skillful at recognizing and categorizing the four misbehaviors as you notice them occurring in your children. Once you learn to recognize which of the four kinds of misbehaviors is occurring, you will be able to apply the appropriate correction for that misbehavior. As you read through the explanation of each type of misbehavior, can you pick out the category most typical of your child?

1. NOT-MINDING

Children who are misbehaving by not minding do not follow reasonable directions the first time they are asked. Not-minding behaviors are often associated with the very young child who is in the process of learning what is expected. Not-minding often involves situations in which children would not have known they were supposed to do something until an adult asks them to do it, for example, "It's time to go home now," or, "Now it's time to put your game away." They may argue and complain while they avoid doing what they have been asked to do, they may be very agreeable and tell you they will do it pretty soon (which they never get around to doing), or they may give every indication that they did not even hear you as they proceed to go quietly about their business. They have to be told again and again. Eventually they may do it, but only after great effort on your part.

2. SELF-INDULGENT

Children who are being self-indulgent behave in aggravating ways that bring them lots of attention. They may whine, argue, intimidate with accusations such as, "You like her better than me," or "Why do I always have to do all the work?" or "I hate you!" They may refuse to speak when they should be talking, or they go on and on about what a bad, mean person you are, or they constantly ask questions to which they already know the answers, or hide from you, or are bossy with adults as well as children, or make a fuss when they do not get their way. Bickering and fighting are often self-indulgent behaviors.

3. ROUTINE NOT-MINDING

Routine not-minding behavior happens when children do not carry out tasks that they know in advance must be done on a regular basis. This misbehavior is similar to not-minding but is more often associated with the older child and routine tasks that you should not have to keep reminding the child to do. Examples are: cleaning a room on Saturday, brushing teeth before bedtime, going to bed at 8:00 p.m., getting off to school by

7:30 a.m., doing schoolwork on time, not touching off-limit items in the school or home, not going to off-limit places, and observing school rules. If there is a problem with routine not-minding, it becomes increasingly apparent as children head into the teenage years. Older children know what is expected of them. Adults feel they should not have to be constantly telling the child what to do. As in not-minding behavior, the child may eventually do what needs to be done, but seldom takes the initiative to go ahead and do it without continual reminding and prodding by an adult. Parents and teachers usually feel they are working harder at these routine tasks than the child.

4. AGGRESSIVE

Aggressive behaviors are those actions that deliberately hurt people, either physically or emotionally, in an attempt to get even. In aggressive behavior, children behave in ways that use situations to their own advantage in a deliberate attempt to hurt others. Occasionally, the child loses all self-control and starts to destroy property and physically hurt people (sometimes including himself) in a kind of blind rage. These extreme forms of aggression can usually be prevented. After using the *Caring Discipline* approach, you will see violent incidents markedly decrease, whether in the school or at home.

If children turn their aggression inward and hurt themselves—for example, if they bite themselves on the arm hard enough to actually draw blood, bang their head against a wall, pull out their own hair, abuse drugs, or threaten suicide—you will need more help than this book can give you. These inward-turning aggressive behaviors require that you contact someone who can give you personal counseling assistance.

It is sometimes difficult to distinguish between self-indulgent and aggressive behaviors. Fighting between children, as was mentioned earlier, is often a self-indulgent behavior designed to get the attention of adults, but if a child is really intent on getting revenge and seriously hurting another child, it is an aggressive behavior. (If your children only fight with each other when you are there to see it, their fighting is probably a self-indulgent behavior.)

Three Major Problem-Solvers

Not all negative behaviors are misbehaviors. Before you begin to observe and chart the four misbehaviors, you need to be able to identify those times when negative behavior is *not* a misbehavior. Negative behavior can often be an attempt by the child to solve a real life problem. In other words, sometimes the child is earnestly trying to get out of a difficult situation and doesn't know how to improve things without acting in negative ways.

It is important, therefore, that as you begin to learn to recognize the differences between the four basic types of misbehaviors, you also need to stop and ask yourself whether the child is actually misbehaving or, instead, whether the child's negative behavior indicates he or she needs some help from you in solving a problem.

There are three major problem-solving areas in which the adult can help the child.

A. ADJUSTING THE ENVIRONMENT

Sometimes the child is not developmentally or physically capable of performing up to the adult's expectations. When adults have unrealistically high expectations of a child, which the child cannot fulfill even if he tries, adults usually assume the child is misbehaving by not doing what he or she is "supposed to." An obvious example of unrealistic expectations is the parents of a fifteen-month-old baby who expect their baby to be potty trained by fifteen months. While it is possible that a rare fifteen month old can learn to control his or her muscles of elimination, the vast majority, especially boys, cannot, and so efforts to push the child to achieve bowel and sphincter control are doomed to failure. The parents can help the child by adjusting the environment so that the problem disappears. By providing diapers as long as needed and being calm and matter-of-fact about matters of wetting and messing, the adult can turn an apparent misbehavior into a normal, age-appropriate, neutral behavior.

A basic rule to remember is that *babies and toddlers never misbehave.* When babies and toddlers behave in ways that seem negative to you, it means they need their environment changed. Negative behaviors on the part of babies and toddlers mean they are hungry, tired, curious, lonely, have a tummy-ache, ear-ache or are teething. They need to be held, fed, comforted, have dry diapers, be removed from certain situations, and, sometimes, have their diet changed. As Fitzhugh Dobson said, don't worry about spoiling babies and toddlers. "Babies don't spoil. Only fruit spoils."

Parents of two-and-a-half-year-old twins complained that their twins were constantly out of their car seats and bugging their eight-year-old sister whenever the family went for a ride. Rather than treat this as a misbehavior, other parents in the parenting class began to think of ways to adjust the environment. How about putting one of the twins in the front seat with one of the adults sitting in the back seat between the other two children? What kind of a car seat was it? Someone suggested bringing the car seats to class next time so we could figure out a way to buckle them up so they could not undo the buckles. Another example of adjusting the environment to meet developmental needs: Preschool teachers know that if preschoolers are given juice in Styrofoam glasses, they will constantly spill their juice, not because they are misbehaving, but because at this age they do not have the coordination to use a light-weight glass without tipping it over. Another type of glass needs to be used instead, ones with a weighted bottom perhaps.

Every age has its own developmental rate beyond which children should not be pushed. Children need to be allowed to grow up at their own inner pace. Many young parents talk with their friends about each other's children. They compare notes: "Clyde started walking at ten months." "Lilly was speaking in whole sentences at twenty-two months." "Jason could kick the soccer ball more than thirty yards when he was only six." "Buelah was reading before she started first grade." In this way, parents sometimes get very competitive about developmental rates and, without even being aware of it, push their children along faster than is good for any child. If this is happening to you, try to stop and take comfort in knowing that once your kids are all grown, you will laugh to think you ever cared how young they were when they started walking or talking or playing soccer or learning to read. The important thing is for your child to know that you accept them as they are right now. What matters in the long run is for your child to know that you are taking joy in their day-today progress. In this way, you will strengthen their developmental needs staircase so they can grow into a confident and competent adulthood.

One of the values of working through this material with a group of people is that you can compare your expectations for your child with theirs. Ask yourself the questions: Am I expecting too much of my children? Could I change the environment for now and just wait awhile for them to get a little older?

The unnecessary environmental burden of pushing kindergartners to read and write

While some children can learn to read and write at age five, it is a herculean task for many five-year-olds and interferes with the far more important requirements of that age group's brain development. From four to seven years old, a child's brain develops best from creative play and positive social interactions. By seven years of age, most children's brains are finally wired to the pre-frontal lobes in a way that allows for more abstract thinking and an introduction to academic learning. No wonder the Finnish educational system, which doesn't start children learning to read until their brains are ready at the age of seven, and allows tremendous amounts of free time for explorative play throughout a child's school career, has one of very best academic outcomes in the world.

It is unfortunate that so many adults regard learning to read and write at an early age to be more important than for the child to develop a sense of competency and trust in the world around them. When I was an elementary school counselor, all first graders came to school the first day in the fall bright-eyed and eager to learn, but after a few months there were always some children, with brains not yet developed enough for academic work, beginning to show signs of believing they were failures. I often noticed them walking dejectedly down the school hallway, or saw them beginning to act out in negative ways.

While it is true that occasional failures throughout our life-time can make us stronger, constant daily failure at a time of life that should be an exuberant, trusting, and joyful exploration of the world, is counter-productive. For young children whose brains have not matured enough to succeed at academic lessons, failure at learning to read and write can create a downward spiral of negativity towards themselves and others, all because of a false assumption by so many well-intentioned adults that early reading skills are crucial to success in life.

Numerous studies show that learning to read at an early age, and having high grades and high test scores, does not correlate with success in life. Success in adult life is directly linked to the development of what Abraham Maslow called Self-Actualization, which you will remember is the goal at the top of each child's staircase of developmental needs, which is also a goal of the extremely successful Finnish educational model.

A stressful environment can affect your child's brain development *

Many researchers are convinced the influence of a stress-filled culture is another reason we are seeing more American children exhibiting short attention spans and impulsive behavior. One researcher, Bruce Perry, author of the *Childhood Trauma Academy*, said, "Simply stated, children reflect the world in which they are raised. If that world is characterized by threat, chaos, unpredictability, fear and trauma, the brain will reflect that by *altering the development of the neural systems* involved in the stress and fear response."

A baby is born with billions of brain cells that support trillions of interconnections. Nature has given the developing fetus extra brain cells so that any cell or connection not needed for survival can be pruned away. The pruning process begins three months before the child's birth and continues until sexual maturity at around twenty years. By the time a child is three years old, the brain still has over one thousand trillion interconnections, but by the time the child is an adult at twenty the process of discarding neurons will have reduced the number of brain connections by half. By the age of twenty, the number of 86-100 billion brain cells will stay fairly stable, barring ill health or drug abuse, for the rest of the person's life.

One of the messengers for telling the brain which cells are impor-

---

* I am indebted to the insights and research of Thom Hartmann, author of *The Edison Gene*, for much of this information on brain development.

tant to keep and which are okay to discard is cortisol. The more stress and subsequent cortisol production a child experiences, the more the old brain, the source of the "flight or fight" response necessary for protection in a dangerous environment, is strengthened. The less stress, the more the newer/pre-frontal lobes of the brain, source of rational thinking and planning, will be strengthened. Because cortisol stays in the bloodstream from eight to twenty-four hours, many small fear responses can add up to as much as one large fear response in convincing the body that the old brain needs to be strengthened. When the world is experienced as a hostile place, the old brain needs to be strong in order to make the split-second survival decision to either run away or stay and fight.

Brain researchers have consistently found that if the child is adequately nourished and not taking drugs, *one of the most significant factors in brain development is the child's exposure to stress.* It is obvious that a child living in a war zone or other area of conflict such as an unsafe neighborhood, or experiencing continual negative feedback in the school classroom or playground, will have high cortisol levels. But another not so obvious source of powerful stress for children, one widely present everywhere in our modern culture, is television and the internet.

Thom Hartmann, in his book *The Edison Gene: ADHD and the Gift of the Hunter Child* says, "Television producers and, particularly, advertisers, know that in order to capture the attention of a casual viewer and hold the attention of a serious viewer, they must produce a steady flow of startle flickers. Quick changes of camera angle, rapid changes in sound, punctuations in color and movement—all of these produce very small startle responses in the (old) brain, preparing the body to react and riveting attention to the television just as surely as it would be riveted to a cobra or tiger. The effect of this is a continuous stream of low-level cortisol entering the bloodstream." The outcome of all these fear and startle responses is a continuous strengthening of the ancient fight-or-flight brain at the expense of the newer pre-frontal lobes, and for many kids, an eventual diagnosis of ADHD.

No wonder the American Academy of Pediatrics recommends no screens of any kind in a child's bedroom. The AAP warns that children under the age of two should not watch any media and for children under the age of three, TV watching is associated with disrupted sleep schedules. AAP research also indicates that the more television children watch, the more at risk they are for delayed language development. Person to person interactions, including cooperative play experiences, are what promote language skills, not watching someone else talking or playing on the television, even when the program is educational.

Another basic environmental need for all children is sleep

The sleep-deprived child exhibits many of the symptoms similar to those of ADHD: difficulty following directions, short attention span, impatience, impulsivity, restlessness, and risk-taking. One likely reason for a huge increase in sleep-deprived kids is the wide-spread over-use of electronic screens. Thirty and forty years ago, we didn't have internet-enabled devices that made it easy for kids to play online with other kids at 2:00 in the morning.

How many hours of sleep does your child need? The common agreement among professionals is: 11 hours for children aged 2-5; 10 hours for children aged 6-12; and at least 9 hours for children aged 13-18. If your child has misbehavior problems, you could begin by logging how many hours of sleep he or she spends in bed each night, except that you won't have any way of knowing how many hours of sleep is happening if your child is taking an electronic device with him to bed. In 2013, the American Academy of Pediatrics released recommendations for use of media by children and teenagers. They advised there should no screens of any kind in the bedroom: no TVs, no mobile phones, no computers or tablets. A child's bed should be for sleeping.

Banning all electronic gadgets from your child's bedroom will not be an easy task to accomplish, especially if your child has already become accustomed to taking any of these items to bed at night; it certainly will make things easier if the rules are in place *before* your child receives an electronic device. If the devices have already been acquired, limiting the use of electronics can seem a daunting task, but don't give up, keep in mind that children do not have the maturity to make this kind of a decision. Remember that you have the authority of a million years of parents standing in a long line behind you. (Chapter Eleven will teach you how family meetings can be used to reduce the power struggle that may arise from your decision to limit electronic use.)

One admittedly extreme example of limiting television viewing happened many years ago when television was the only electronic screen available in most homes. A young father of two girls appeared one day at his mother's front door carrying his family's only television set and asked, "Will you keep this for four years until the next Winter Olympic games? The kids can watch TV in other people's houses but not in ours." His astonished mother agreed even though she was certain her son's plan was doomed to failure. But sure enough, four years later he came back to retrieve the television so his family could watch the Winter Olympics. After the games were over, to the amazement of the grandmother, he brought back the television to store in her basement for four more years. "I never thought they'd give up television for another four years without staging some kind of a major protest, but it worked!" By this time the two girls were in high school, happily involved in a well-rounded social and academic life, a situation that their parents attributed in part to the lack of television in their early years.

A more recent attempt to reduce the use of electronic devices was started by some Seattle based Microsoft employees who put a moratorium, for themselves as well as for their kids, on the use of all electronic screens in their homes one day a week. One day a week with no electronic screens provided a framework for an environment that encouraged meaningful interaction between family members: time for playing catch, building bird houses, coloring together in a coloring book, sharing the tasks of making dinner, going on a hike or a picnic. The one day off a week became a vacation from the sometimes invasive outer world and gave opportunities to convey unconditional love for their kids during the many neutral times that occurred during the day. Neutral times can also be used to pass on important family values, plus giving parents the opportunity to listen to their child's views about the world as he or she is experiencing it. The outcome of strengthening family bonds is well worth the initial shock of turning off the electronic screens.

Not all parents will agree with your attempts to limit electronic use. Here's an example of a non-supportive parent who tried to sabotage the rules my friend Cindy had established with her family: Cindy's eleven year old son had invited a friend for a sleep-over. At bed time, the friend insisted he shouldn't have to follow Cindy's rule to leave his smart phone in the kitchen table charging basket overnight. He felt he had the right to take the phone to bed with him just like he did at home. Cindy stood firm and said, "No, the rule in our house is to leave all our electronic gadgets on the kitchen table at night." The friend abided by the rule but was definitely not happy about it. On the following day, the boy's mother called Cindy to say that the next time her son stayed overnight it would be fine to let him take his smart phone to bed. Cindy said, "I'm sorry, but I can't do that. We don't let our kids take any of their electronic gadgets to bed, and it wouldn't be fair to them if I bent the rules for their guests. Besides, the kids need their sleep." Cindy was stunned when the boy's mother said, "Well, then I guess he can't sleep over at your house anymore."

Even the President of the United States has rules about the use of mobile phones. A few years ago, when I was fortunate enough to be given a tour of the West Wing, I noticed a small table with an empty basket on it outside the door to the Cabinet Room. When I asked my guide what that was for he said, "Whenever the President has a cabinet meeting, everybody leaves their cell phones in the basket."

Sometimes a busy parent tries to multi-task by using their smart phone at the same time they're talking with their kids, making a meaningful conversation with the child impossible. Unfortunately, the non-verbal message the kids pick up on is that Mom or Dad is more interested in the internet than in them. As one child recently asked his mother about his internet game-addicted father, "How can I get Dad to pay attention to me?"

For parents trying to establish boundaries on the use of electronics in their home, *Face to Face: Cultivating Kids Social Lives in Today's Digital World*, by Dr. Kathy Masarie, Kathy Keller Jones and others, is an important reference book for ideas on how to strengthen family bonds and foster positive peer relationships, as well as how to help your child deal with modern-day issues such as cyber-bullying and pornography. At the end of this chapter you will also find a guide for developing your own family rules for the use of electronic screens, adapted from "Tips for Maintaining Digital Sanity and Protecting Your Family," in *Face to Face*, by Kathy Keller Jones.

Influence of Diet on Behavior

Increasingly, a major area in which adults need to intervene to adjust the environment is in the area of health and diet. If your baby or toddler has one or more of the following symptoms: colic, cries and fusses a lot, frequent bouts of diarrhea, severe diaper rash, frequent ear infections, or doesn't sleep through the night, the problem may be an allergic reaction to common foods such as cow's milk, eggs, or wheat. Such allergies are very common and parents need to adjust the child's environment to eliminate the allergens. A mother with twins told about how her twins cried often during the day and never slept through the night for fifteen entire months. Finally a family member suggested giving the twins a soy-based formula instead of cow milk formula. (Be sure to check with your pediatrician before changing formulas.) When the mother told her pediatrician that since switching from cow's milk, the whole family was now able to sleep through the night and the twins had become happy, contented babies, the doctor said, "Oh, my gosh, they did have all the symptoms of allergy to cow's milk, didn't they?" Older children are also susceptible to allergic reactions from common foods. Bed-wetting, for example, can be caused by an allergic reaction to dairy proteins found in milk, which causes bladder tissues to become swollen and insensitive to the feeling of fullness. Ear infections, asthma, headaches, runny nose, even hyperactivity are all common reactions to food allergies.

A good first place to start researching possible allergies is the book, *Is This Your Child? Discovering and Treating Unrecognized Allergies in Children and Adults*, by Doris Rapp, M.D. Another helpful resource is *The Yeast Connection Handbook*, by William G. Crook, M.D. In chapter eight: "Children's Health Problems," Dr. Crook makes a convincing case for the interrelationship between refined carbohydrate/sugar diets, antibiotic use, and Candida albicans (a type of yeast) overgrowth in the intestines, resulting in problems ranging from continual ear infections to behavior problems such as attention deficit disorder and autism. He also has an extensive bibliography as well as names, addresses, and phone numbers of support groups and authorities in each area.

You can find additional information about allergy related behavioral problems on the internet. A widely used website for researching food choices is www.mercola.com. Internet searches are not always valid, but if you look at enough different sites, you will begin to see common elements emerge that may give you some clues. A basic reference book for learning about the roots of allergies and ways to keep your family healthy is *Natural Health, Natural Medicine* by Andrew T. Weil, M.D.

While it's commonly accepted that many children are calmer and better able to focus when they follow a low sugar diet, it's not so well known that exercise is also important. When a school in Taiwan required every child to participate in a ten-minute exercise period between classes with the goal of improving their mental functioning, the program had the unexpected result of reducing problem behaviors throughout the school. Another example of the benefits of exercise was the ADD college student who ran for an hour just before every written exam because exercise helped him sit and focus for a couple of hours afterwards.

B. HELPING SOLVE CONFLICTS

Fighting often happens not for revenge or to get attention, but because children have a real life issue that needs to be solved. Fighting to solve a problem between children is not a misbehavior because in these situations children are trying to solve a problem by attempting to get what they think they have a right to have. They do not want revenge (aggression). They do not want the attention of adults (self-indulgent). Their primary goal is to protect their own interests and get what they want. Infringing on another person's rights by hurting that person is secondary. Hence this kind of fighting cannot really be classified as a misbehavior. In these situations, children do not need to have a correction applied by an adult. They need help from an adult to learn other ways of solving the problem.

Children, especially very young ones, usually do not know how to go about solving problems without hitting and yelling. This is not surprising since human beings have an instinctive reflex to lash out and protect themselves whenever they feel threatened. In this culture, children also see hitting and yelling glorified on television. Further, hitting and yelling are widely used by adults to punish young people. The double standard is obvious. Adults are allowed to hit children but not other adults. Children are not supposed to hit either adults or other children. In this way, children learn that hitting and yelling are quasi-acceptable problem-solving techniques.

Occasionally, adults find themselves tacitly recognizing that fighting is sometimes the only viable solution they can find by advising a child to fight back against a bully. Maybe you have had this experience yourself. Here's an example told by a high school teacher.

Jerry was a huge, quiet, good-natured, high school junior. Tim was a small boy, the same age as Jerry, who had trouble making friends or gaining any positive recognition for himself. In an effort to win the admiration of his peers, and secure in the knowledge that Jerry was a non-aggressive person, Tim began to ridicule Jerry, making fun of him, accusing him of being dumb, an ape, and a coward. Since Jerry was aware of his own superior strength, he patiently tried to ignore Tim's taunts. Jerry continued trying to ignore Tim for several weeks, but the more he ignored him, the more satisfaction Tim seemed to take in the whole affair, escalating the teasing until he began to actually push and punch Jerry. Unfortunately, Tim gained tremendous amounts of negative attention from the other students who kept telling him to leave Jerry alone. Tim was starved for attention. Negative attention from the other kids was better than none at all. This went on for weeks with Tim making Jerry's life more miserable every day. Finally, a teacher advised Jerry, "First try warning Tim. Tell him, 'Leave me alone or I'll punch you out.' If that doesn't work, then hit him a good one." You can guess the result. One day, a much subdued Tim appeared with a swollen lip. There was no more harassment from Tim. And gentle Jerry went back to being gentle Jerry. In Jerry's case, this kind of fighting was not self-indulgent, nor was it aggressive in the sense that he was using another person in an uncaring way with the intent to hurt. This was clearly a case of trying to solve a problem.

In spite of how much we may sympathize with the occasional seemingly justified solution of "punching someone out," it is a desperation measure that we would like to avoid. Children often initiate fights with another child because they simply do not know how to handle the situation any other way. Yet there are other ways to resolve disputes that children can be taught from a very early age. Whenever you see a fight between children, first consider whether or not it is a problem-solving situation. Do not try to categorize it as self-indulgent or aggressive until you have first helped the kids learn some negotiating skills. Here is an example of a fight between two children that began as an attempt to solve a problem:

Six-year-old Sophia wants to take a turn on the swing during school recess time but six-year-old Imani will not get off the swing when she asks for a turn. Finally, Sophia grabs at the swing and stops it. Imani yells and kicks at Sophia who, in turn, yells and hits at Imani.

Imani and Sophia have a real life problem: how to share the swing. They are not fighting for attention from the teacher (self-indulgence), and neither child is so angry that they are trying to get revenge by causing real pain to the other child (aggressive). They have a problem in how to share the swing, and because they do not know how else to solve it, they are fighting to get what they think they have a right to have. They need an adult to intercede and help them learn some beginning rudiments of negotiation and problem solving.

PROBLEM-SOLVING STEPS

Here are five steps the adult can use to help children learn how to problem-solve.

1. Do not place blame or innocence on either child

Innocence or blame has nothing to do with problem solving. Both children have rights that must be protected. Keep yourself focused instead on how to help them solve the problem. *Describe the situation* by saying, "I see two people who want a turn on the swing," or "Gosh. Here are two upset people." Stay away from blaming statements like, "Okay. Who started this anyhow?" or "Can't you two ever get along?" Common blaming words are, "bad … wrong … always … never … stupid." Stay away from any word or phrase that implies the child intended to misbehave or that one of them probably started it.

2. Reduce the stress level in both children so they will be able to listen to you

Go over to the children and put one arm around Imani and the other around Sophia. First briefly comfort the child who appears to have gotten the worst of it, and then comfort the other one.

"I am sorry you are hurt, Imani." Then turn to the other child, "And you seem awfully upset, Sophia." Be calm and friendly with both children.

3. Prompt each child to use words to state the problem

To Imani say, "Tell Sophia what you didn't like." If Imani does not do this, pretend to be Imani, look directly at Sophia and say firmly, "Say, 'I don't like it when you stop my swing. And I don't like it when you hit me.' " Or, if Imani is able to say anything even approximating this, paraphrase it, nod your head in approval, and say, "Good for you for using words to tell Sophia what you didn't like."

To Sophia say, "Tell Imani what you didn't like." If Sophia does not do this, pretend to be Sophia and looking directly at Imani, say firmly, "Say, 'I don't like it when you won't let me take a turn. And I don't like it when you hit me.' " If Sophia is able to say anything even close to this, paraphrase it, nod your head in approval and say, "Good for you for using words to tell Imani what you didn't like."

Now repeat the above sequence, this time using the word pattern, "Tell Sophia what you want," and "Tell Imani what you want." Again, you may have to speak for a child if he or she cannot verbalize his or her own needs. For example, "Tell her, 'I want a turn on the swing, too.' " Stand beside the child you are speaking for as though you are that child. If you do this for one child, be sure to do it at some point for the second child, too, so the second child does not get the impression you are favoring one over the other.

4. Help them figure out some kind of solution to try

After you are satisfied both children had a chance to voice what it is they didn't like and what it is they want, say to them both: "Do you have any ideas for making it go better next time?" If they can't think of anything, make some suggestions, "I could look at my watch and tell you when three minutes are up. Then you could both have a three-minute turn. What do you think of that idea?"

They may like this idea, or Imani may very well say, "Well, she can have a turn and I'll go play on the merry-go-round." Remember it is not up to you to find a solution for their problem. Then give each one of them a friendly look or hug and leave the scene.

5. They do not have to find a solution

Strange as it may sound, the children do not have to come up with a solution. If they cannot agree, you can shake your head and say, "Well, maybe later on you will get an idea. Will you come let me know if you think of something? I'll think about it too." If there is an object, like a favorite toy they are fighting about, and they can't agree on a solution, as a last resort you can put the toy away until they figure out a plan. Do not do this in a punishing way. Just be matter-of-fact, "I'll just put this away until you get a plan that everybody likes."

The advantages to this approach to problem-solving fights is obvious. Both children feel heard and respected. They are consequently able to hear what you and the other child have to say. There is no placing of blame or innocence. There will be little, if any, residue of resentment left over to stain any future relationships with either you or the other child. The need for revenge will not develop. You have left the responsibility for choosing a solution up to them. In this way, they are gradually learning the art of assertiveness and compromise. You are empowering them to effectively take charge of their own lives. The example given involved very young children, but the basic ideas behind these five steps can apply to any age group.

The pattern given above is helpful to use with small groups of children during a crisis time. Later, in Chapter Eleven, we will discuss how the family and classroom meeting can be used to help children solve problems during crisis times and on an regular basis.

Notice that you do not ask the children to say they were sorry. If they are sorry they will probably say so. If they are not sorry, do not chip away at their inner integrity by pressuring them to lie about something as important as their own feelings, and to burden them with resentment because they do not feel sorry. Also, do not ask the children to share their feelings of humiliation or sadness or anger about what just happened. Turning the discussion into an exploration of feelings would detract from the task at hand. The task at hand is to teach problem-solving skills in a way that reaffirms both children.

C. DEALING WITH FEELINGS

At other times it is extremely important to listen to a child's feelings. Sometimes when a child complains, the child is not seeking attention (self-indulgent behavior) but is deeply bothered about something. For example, the eight-year-old boy who comes home from school and throws a spelling test down on the table yelling, "I'm stupid. I never get things right," is feeling inadequate and incompetent about not doing well in his schoolwork. And imagine the pain of the twelve-year-old girl who one day confides, "I don't have any friends. Nobody likes me." These are not examples of self-indulgent behavior, but are problems that you can help with by listening to the child's painful inner-reality feelings as described in Chapter Four.

The negative behaviors parents and teachers would like to eliminate are contained somewhere in either the four misbehavior categories (Not-minding, Self-indulgent, Routine not-minding, and Aggressive) or the three problem-solving areas (Adjusting the environment, Helping solve conflicts, or Dealing with feelings). You can no doubt add many specific examples of your own to each of the categories. After reading through the four misbehavior descriptions, can you choose the category that is most typical of your child or of the child in your classroom who gives you the most concern? For the moment, do not worry about what to do about these misbehaviors, just focus on trying to figure out which kind of misbehavior is occurring at the time it occurs. And try to notice which negative behaviors are not misbehaviors at all but instead attempts by the child to solve a problem.

Learning to distinguish between the four basic types of misbehaviors and the three problem-solving areas takes practice. Human behavior cannot be squeezed into a mold, but you can recognize and work with the patterns it forms. If you are not certain in which category a specific negative behavior belongs, just make your best guess. *You do not have to be right one-hundred percent of the time.* At the end of a week's charting, you should have a pretty good working knowledge of which kind of negative behavior is happening.

Exercise

Try to identify the negative behaviors you see this week. On page 112, you will find the "Negative Behaviors" worksheet that is designed to help you learn to recognize each of the four different misbehaviors (Not-minding, Self-indulgent, Routine not-minding, and Aggressive) as you observe them. You can focus your observations intensely for a twenty-minute period each weekday or be a casual observer all day long. Notice the top section is for recording the four misbehaviors, with a separate section at the bottom of the page for you to write about possible problem-solving situations. (Does the child's negative behavior indicate a need to adjust the environment, help solve conflicts, or deal with feelings?)

Keep in mind that many negative behaviors can be placed in several categories, depending on the context of the situation. We have already discussed how fighting can be classified as self-indulgent, aggressive, or problem-solving, depending on the situation. There are many other negative behaviors that can also be placed in several misbehavior categories. It all depends on the specific situation. Furthermore, maybe the negative behavior is not a misbehavior at all. Maybe it is a problem-solving behavior. Whenever you see a negative behavior this week, have a little fun with trying to decide which, or how many, of the misbehavior or problem-solving categories it could fit into. The Special Case at the end of this chapter is an example of how the misbehavior of lying can fit into three different categories.

You can choose just one of your children to observe, or you can observe an entire class or family. Do not write a specific child's name on the chart. You are not trying to change anyone's behavior right now. You are only an observer. Keeping a record of the negative behaviors for a week will not only sharpen your ability to distinguish between the four different misbehaviors and the three problem-solving situations, it will also help you zero in on which negative behaviors you want to work on changing first. If the children ask about the new chart just tell them, "I am learning some new things about being a parent (or a teacher)." You do not need to explain more than that.

WORKSHEET

NEGATIVE BEHAVIORS
The Four Misbehaviors and Three Problem-Solving Situations

NOT-MINDING (Not Doing What Is Asked)

SELF-INDULGENT (Attention-Getting)

ROUTINE NOT-MINDING (Will Not Do Routine Tasks)

AGGRESSIVE (Deliberately Hurting)

NEGATIVE BEHAVIORS Requiring Problem-Solving That Does Not Fit Above:

1. Adjust Environment   2. Solve Conflicts   3. Listen to Feelings

from *Caring Discipline: Practical Tools for Nurturing Happy Families & Classrooms*

REVIEW: Helping Children Solve Disagreements

1. **Do not place blame or innocence on either child.** Focus on the fact that there is a problem both children need to solve. Be calm and friendly with both children.

2. **Reduce the stress level in both children so that they will be able to listen.** First, comfort the one who appears to have gotten the worst of it, then comfort the other one. Example: "I am sorry you are hurt, Annie." Then turn to the other child: "And you seem awfully upset, Roger." Put your arm around each child, if that seems appropriate for their age.

3. **Briefly describe the situation.** "I see two upset people," "Here are two people who want a turn."

4. **Prompt each child to use words to state the problem.** To Annie say: "Tell Roger what you didn't like." If Annie does not do this, model her part and say firmly, "I don't like it when you stop my swing. And I don't like it when you hit me!"

   Then turn to Roger and repeat the process: "Tell Annie what you didn't like." Again, model for him if he cannot find the words.

5. **Prompt each child to use words to say what they want.** To Annie say, "Tell Roger what you want," and to Roger, "Tell Annie what you want."

6. **Help them figure out some kind of solution to try.** Say to them both: "Do you have any ideas for making it go better next time?" If they cannot think of anything, you can make a suggestion, but remember, they are the ones who must solve the problem.

7. **It is okay if a solution cannot be found.**

from *Caring Discipline: Practical Tools for Nurturing Happy Families & Classrooms*

Chapter 6 Discussion: IDENTIFYING THE FOUR MISBEHAVIORS

1. Share this week's "Negative Behaviors" worksheet. Do you see how the same negative behavior can often be placed in several different categories depending on the specific situation?

2. Which one of the four misbehaviors bothers you the most when you see it in your children?

3. Are you aware of any negative behaviors in your children that might fit into one of the problem-solving areas? *Remember that babies and toddlers never misbehave. Their behavior always fits into one of the problem-solving areas.*

4. Share with each other some examples of times when as a concerned adult, you had to go behind the scenes and adjust a child's environment without the child even being aware of it.

5. Work as a group. Make a list of the negative behaviors you would like to eliminate in your children. Using the observation charts you have worked with during the week, try putting each of the negative behaviors into the appropriate misbehavior or problem-solving categories. Be creative and have some fun with this. Spend some time discussing the differences in each specific situation. You will see that fighting and lying are two examples of misbehaviors that can be placed in different categories. How many others can you find?

6. If your group feels ready, try role-playing a situation in which two children are having a fight in an attempt to solve a problem. You can choose the situation given in this chapter of the two children who both want the swing, or choose any other situation you are familiar with. Be sure it is a true problem-solving situation before you begin. When you play the part of a child, choose to be a child you know well. Try to get into the feeling of how you think that child would behave and feel in a similar situation.

You will need two "children" and one "adult." Let other people in the group be observers who can offer their ideas after the role-play is over. The person playing the adult will try to help the "children" solve the problem as suggested in this chapter. Use the review sheet as a guide. After each role-play is finished, have the "adult" ask the children how they felt during the adult's efforts to help them solve their problem.

When you play the part of the "adult," remember, role-playing is a wonderful opportunity to experiment. Try not to be perfect. Making mistakes and getting feedback from your pretend "children" is how you will learn to help your real kids. Relax and have fun with the role-play.

Special Case: LYING
A Misbehavior That Can Fit Into Three Categories

One of the most upsetting misbehaviors to deal with is lying. Seeing a child hit another child is distressing, but hitting another child at least has the virtue of being out in the open. Parents and teachers feel they can understand hitting. Lying, on the other hand, seems deliberately premeditated and underhanded. There is an undertone of "sneakiness" about such behaviors that repulses most adults.

Lying is one of those misbehaviors like fighting that can fall into one of three different categories: Problem-solving, self-indulgent, or aggressive.

The Problem-Solving Lie

If lying is done for self-protection, it is a problem-solving behavior, and any correction is of secondary importance. Most important is not to back the child into a corner in the first place. If the child feels cornered, he or she is likely to try to get out of the problem by telling a lie.

Take the incident of Jonathan, whose father came home and found that his steel tape measure was broken. (Jonathan and a friend had been sword fighting with it.) Jonathan hadn't meant to break it, but he knew he would be punished both physically and emotionally if his father found out he did it. The father was furious. He promised, "It will go easier for you if you tell the truth." (By this the father means he will not physically hurt Jonathan if he tells the truth.) "If I find out you are lying, you are really going to get it." This is a catch-22 situation. No matter what Jonathan does, he knows he will be punished, if not physically, then emotionally by being shamed. He decides to lie in the hope his father will believe him and not punish him at all.

Children also learn to tell lies to solve the problem of getting what they want when they see important adults doing it. For example, a child overheard his mother telling his father's employer that her husband could not come to work that day because he was sick. The child knew perfectly well that his father was feeling fine but wanted the day off to go fishing.

In this way, the child learned that telling a lie is a quasi-acceptable way to get what you want. If mom or dad tell lies to solve problems, it must be an okay thing to do.

Sometimes children use a problem-solving lie for deeper reasons. The following incident happened to a grandmother who had taken her grandchildren camping at a state campground. On the next to last day of their outing, her nine-year-old granddaughter, Claire, came to her when Claire's older brother was out of hearing and said, "Mother said you should take us out for breakfast on our last day." (Claire loved eating out and she knew there was a restaurant in the private resort area nearby.)

The grandmother knew the child's mother would never have said such a thing. In fact, Claire's mother felt it was important to teach her children it was rude and selfish to ever ask for things. After her first flash of irritation, the grandmother realized that from her granddaughter's point of view, a child has no right to ask directly. She realized that Claire was trying to problem-solve the situation by using the authority of her mother to let grandmother know what she wanted.

Grandmother tried helping her granddaughter solve the problem in a different way. "Claire, if you want to go out to breakfast, I wish you would just ask me. Say, 'Grandma, can we go out to breakfast?' I would rather you would just ask me what you want rather than tell me things your mother said. If I had enough money, and if your brother wanted to go, we could go." Claire looked at her grandmother with round, serious eyes. She knew she had been found out. Grandma smiled at her granddaughter before she gave her one more piece of information, "After all, what is the worst that can happen? The worst thing that could happen is I might say no." And grandmother shrugged as if to say, this is no big deal.

Later in the day when they were alone, Claire directly asked if they could go out to breakfast. The grandmother replied, "Well, let's see if I have enough money left. If we do, we could ask your brother what he thinks." Of course, the brother thought it was a good idea. The next morning, on their way home, they all went out to breakfast. If grandmother had not had enough money, she could have said, "Gosh, Claire. It would be fun to go but I just don't have enough money this time." Claire's self-esteem will not be hurt from being told no, neither will she be more likely to lie again.

Claire was afraid to be honest about what she wanted. She was not afraid of being told "No." She was afraid of being emotionally punished by shaming: "How many times have I told you not to always be asking for things? We certainly will not go until you learn not to always be asking for things." It might be confusing at first for Claire to be told by Grandma that it *is* okay to ask for what she wants, when Mother has always told her it is *not* okay. But Claire is smart enough to learn that the relationship between her and her grandmother can operate under different rules: "With Grandma it is okay to ask directly for what you want, but I better not do that with Mother."

Claire lied to get what she wanted and to escape being shamed. Like everyone else, she wanted something. By lying, she tried to escape the emotional punishment of being told in a scornful tone of voice that she had no right to ask for what she wanted. Claire lied because she could not bear to hear the nonverbal message that she is not an important enough person to ask directly for what she wants.

The Self-indulgent Lie

Here is a typical example of the self-indulgent lie. Joe's friend Betsy has just returned from a Disneyland vacation with her family. She immediately runs over to Joe's house to tell Joe and his dad all about the wonderful things she saw and did in Disneyland. After listening to her for some time, Joe suddenly says, "I am going to Disneyland next month." This lie is a self-indulgent behavior. Joe has resorted to lying in order to get some of the attention now being focused exclusively on Betsy. Joe is not being aggressive in the sense that he is trying to get even and hurt Betsy in some way. He just wants everyone to know that he is as important as Betsy and deserves to have some attention, too.

This self-indulgent kind of lying can be best dealt with in the following way: Dad looks at Joe and firmly states the truth. "You *wish* you could go to Disneyland next month." Dad then proceeds to ignore any more references from Joe about the nonexistent trip to Disneyland. It is important that Dad make the statement about wishing. By stating what is actually the case, Dad does not ignore Joe's "lie" altogether. By quietly telling the truth, Dad is giving Joe a valuable reality check. "You wish it was true but it isn't." As soon as Joe shows any sign of neutral or positive behaviors, Dad can immediately give Joe the attention he is obviously craving, with warm eye contact or an arm around his shoulder.

Remember that young children have a rich fantasy life. It is okay for them to play pretend games, to pretend to have invisible friends, to be a fireman putting out fires, or welcoming a party of Martians who have just landed in the back yard. These fantasy stories are not lies, but part of the normal games of early childhood.

The Aggressive Lie

The following incident is an example of an aggressive lie because the child tries to manipulate the situation to deliberately hurt another person. Grandma and Grandpa have come to dinner. Walter and Janice have just brought home their report cards. Walter's report card is much improved over last quarter's report. All the adults are making a happy fuss over him. Janice's report card is also very good but hers is always good and everyone takes it somewhat for granted. A little later, Janice says to Grandma and Grandpa, "Remember that fire engine you gave Walter for his birthday? He said he didn't like it. He said it's too kiddish. He said you never get him good presents." (Janice has just exaggerated a remark Walter made last week about the fact that he is getting too old to play with trucks anymore.) Even if Walter did say what Janice has repeated, Janice should still be given a time-out, the correction for aggressive behavior, because repeating such a statement is deliberately hurtful both to Walter and to her grandparents.

One of the parents should carry out the basic five-minute time-out procedure, go back to the dinner table, and cheerfully continue the conversation with Walter, Grandma, Grandpa, and the other parent. If Grandma and Grandpa want to talk about Janice's accusation in front of the children, say quietly, "Let's not talk about it right now." Explain the strategy of not sabotaging to Grandma and Grandpa, as well as what

Walter actually did say, at a later time when the children are out of hearing. When Janice comes back to the table after her time-out has ended, carry on with your normal conversation and do not mention it again. As soon as possible after the time-out, at a neutral or positive time, be sure to tell Janice so Grandma and Grandpa can hear, too, how happy you are for her consistently good grades. It is her hurt feelings that nobody at the dinner table seemed to care about *her* grades that elicited her aggressive behavior in the first place.

Special Case: Understanding the ADHD Diagnosed Child

The diagnoses of ADHD has exploded during the past couple of decades with approximately 15% of all boys and 7% of all girls, a total average of 11% of our school population, now wearing that label. Today, 110 kids out of every 1000 in the United States are being diagnosed with ADHD, as opposed to only 12 kids out of every 1000 in 1979. It has been estimated that two/thirds of these children are prescribed either Ritalin or Adderall (an amphetamine), with some children as young as three years old even being given more powerful anti-psychotic drugs like Prozac with no long term studies having been done on how these drugs effect brain development. A recent survey showed that in the United States, 69 out of every 1000 children between the ages of 6 and 12 are on medications for ADHD; in the United Kingdom, only 9.2 children out of every 1000 in that age range are medicated.

A child is labeled as having Attention Deficit Hyperactive Disorder, or ADHD for short, when he or she exhibits some or all of the following behaviors: difficulty following directions; a short, although sometimes intense, attention span; is easily distracted; is impulsive, impatient, and makes snap decisions; daydreams, is disorganized and restless; is easily bored and prone to risk-taking. On top of this, the ADHD child is often highly creative and intelligent that causes adults in the child's life to think the reason this kid isn't doing well in school is because he/she is just plain lazy or ornery. These ADHD traits make it hard for this child to function well in social situations, especially in our present school system, but it does not mean there is anything basically wrong with this child's brain. The ADHD child's brain may be different from the norm, but it is not "disordered" or "diseased."

The American Psychiatric Association has ignored evidence to the contrary and has put the label of mental illness on ADHD symptoms in spite of the fact this diagnosis is hotly contested by many professional psychiatrists and doctors. One example of a doctor who disagrees with the mental illness label is the pediatric neurologist, Fred Baughman, who says, "All five to six million of children on these drugs are normal ... the American Psychiatric Association ... is representing ADHD as a disease when there is no scientific evidence to confirm any mental illness."

Because the child with ADHD behaviors does not fit into the learning environment of most American schools, the school becomes the most likely referral source to a doctor, and once a child is identified by a medical doctor as having ADHD or a "psychiatric disorder" the danger arises that instead of asking the open-ended and appropriate parenting question, "What can I do to help improve my child's behavior and opportunities for happiness?" the question a parent begins to focus on is, "Should my child be taking medication?" With this shift of questions comes a shift in responsibility from the parent to the medical profession, sometimes to the extent that some parents with children labeled ADHD have contacted me to ask whether they should even expect their child to follow regular societal rules of behavior. (The answer, by the way, is a resounding YES.)

Another significant problem resulting from a focus on drugs as the major tool for helping the child with ADHD is that the use of drugs tends to ignore other possible physical reasons for the behavior, such as a nutritional deficiency. Not enough research has been done in this area, but there is enough evidence of a link between nutritional deficiencies and behavior problems to justify asking your doctor for an extensive evaluation for possible nutritional deficiencies before you agree to medication for your child. For example: research at Purdue University indicates that a deficiency of omega-3 fatty acids may be tied to behavior and learning problems, and a double-blind study published by the *British Journal of*

Psychiatry in 2002 revealed a huge improvement in behavior after giving vitamin, fatty-acid, and mineral supplements to 231 violent young adult prisoners in Aylesbury Prison.

Dr. Leonard Sax, family physician and psychologist, warns that medication for ADHD behaviors is dangerously over-prescribed in this country, * "These medications are being used as a means of behavior modifications to an extent almost unimaginable outside North America … The most popular medications for ADHD are prescription stimulants such as Adderall, Ritalin, Concerta, Metadate, Focalin, Daytrana, and Vyvanse … The most popular medications now used to control temper tantrums and other acting-out misbehaviors in American kids are the atypical antipsychotics, especially Risperdal, Seroquel, and Zyprexa … the same medications that psychiatrists use to treat schizophrenia …" The result of long-term use of these medications "… may be a girl or boy who is more likely to be disengaged, and less motivated to achieve in the real world. We don't know for sure. Not yet … As a parent, you have to make a decision in the face of uncertainty … if you must use a medication, I recommend … using safer non-stimulant medications … such as Strattera, Intuniv, or Wellbutrin." Thom Hartmann, with many years of working with ADHD kids, recommends trying yerba mate tea as a safe stimulant and substitute for Ritalin.

Is there a genetic reason for some ADHD behaviors? Hunters, Farmers and the Edison Gene

Children with ADHD behaviors are often born into the same family, generation after generation, prompting many parents to suspect that ADHD might be an inherited condition, and sure enough, recent research has located a specific group of genes linked to ADHD behavior traits. Some researchers have called this genetic link the "Edison Gene" because many productive people, Thomas Edison being a prime example, have exhibited

---

* I am indebted to the insights and research of Dr. Leonard Sax, family physician, psychologist, and author of *The Collapse of Parenting*, for the information given in this section regarding the use of medication for kids diagnosed with ADHD.

many of the ADHD traits such as impulsiveness, creativity, and risk/novelty seeking behaviors. Unfortunately, instead of regarding the Edison Gene as a gift that can lead to great individual achievement and perhaps even contribute to the benefit of the entire world, as happened with Thomas Edison, Albert Einstein, Benjamin Franklin, Theodore Roosevelt and Winston Churchill, we often regard these kids as having some kind of a mental problem.

Why are more and more children being diagnosed with ADHD? Earlier we talked about how environmental influences, such as over-use of electronic devices, diet, nutritional deficiencies, and the stress produced by constant negative feedback from school or home environments, can influence brain development. Dr. John Ratey, M.D., assistant professor of psychiatry at Harvard Medical School believes that complex interactions between genes and the environment physically shape a child's brain, "I'm seeing a lot more ADHD now than twenty years ago … and I think it's because there actually is more ADHD now than there was twenty years ago. I don't think it's just that there are more diagnoses … there is a huge impact of culture on how the brain finally gets shaped … if you have the DRD4 7R allele (the Edison Gene) and you also grow up in our changing environment … rapid stimulation, rapid reward, Game Boys and the Internet, you're not going to learn to guide your attention very well …"

It has been estimated that 15 percent of Americans carry the 7R variation of the DRD4 dopamine gene, the major gene associated with ADHD. Seen in this light, the creativity, impulsiveness and distractibility typical of the ADHD child are not symptoms of a brain disorder, but rather an inherited learning pattern that appears to increase or decrease depending on environmental circumstances. Most of the research on the DRD4 7R gene shows that it occurs in about half of the children diagnosed with ADHD. The other half may have been diagnosed as ADHD not because of novelty-seeking behaviors (indicative of true, genetic ADHD) but because of a wide variety of cultural, nutritional, psychological, environmental, and educational factors that affect brain development ranging from growing up in a stressed-out environment to mineral deficiencies. *

* Thom Hartmann, *The Edison Gene*

Thom Hartmann, who was himself expelled from school for ADHD behaviors, got seriously interested in the controversy about the best ways to help children with ADHD when his own son, at the age of twelve, was classified as ADHD. During his early career of working with thousands of children with ADHD and adults with ADD (adults are diagnosed as having ADD Attention Deficit Disorder) he became convinced that there are two basic inherited brain types that he called the Hunter and the Farmer brain. In this scenario, the Hunter brain is associated with ADHD traits and was responsible for helping the human race to survive during times of constant change when humans were frequently on the move looking for food, as in the hunting and gathering cultures of our ancestors.

The Hunter brain is perfectly adapted for success in the nomadic hunting and gathering cultures where human beings lived and developed long before agriculture changed the way most people found food for their families. Hunters have to be flexible, able to change their strategy at a moment's notice; they are definitely not into long-term planning. They have incredible bursts of energy, useful for chasing game, but don't have a lot of staying power for the long haul. Hunters often describe their actions in terms of pictures, rather than words or feelings, and are not much interested in conversations dealing with abstractions. As one wife said about her ADD husband, "Everything he thinks goes right to his hands." They love the hunt but are easily bored by mundane tasks such as having to clean and dry the fish, or fill out the paperwork. Hunters take risks and will face dangers that "normal" individuals avoid; they love the feeling of competency and aliveness they experience when on the edge, like parachuting out of airplanes, and rescuing people during fires and floods; they're hard on themselves and those around them because when your hunting life depends on making split-second decisions, your impatience threshold necessarily tends to be low. This risk-taking trait is no doubt why Hunters represent a huge percentage of entrepreneurs in our society, Steve Jobs of Apple Computer fame comes to mind.

It's instructive to read the biographies of famous people suspected of having ADHD traits. Benjamin Franklin, for example, got easily bored and changed occupations constantly. He started on his thirty-seventh career when he was 80, and then went on to become a driving force in the American Revolution. Even a brief introduction to the life of President Theodore Roosevelt makes a convincing case that he is surely one of history's most outstanding examples of a person with ADHD and Hunter traits. Another one of our presidents, John F. Kennedy, in a biography endorsed by his wife, is described as exhibiting all the familiar Hunter traits including extreme disorganization.

On the other hand, the Farmer brain, with traits like those exhibited by President Kennedy's brother Robert (which made the two of them a perfect team) is perfectly adapted for living in the settled communities that were created 10,000 years ago when agriculture was invented. In an agricultural world, distractibility is a devastating trait. Crops have to be planted and harvested at precise times; you can't run off to chase deer, explore beyond the next hill, or investigate a noise in the forest. You must focus on, and stay close to, your crops. Farmers are good at attending to details, they are not easily bored, and unlike Hunters, once Farmers begin a project, they are likely to complete it. Farmers take the long term view and are able to sustain a slow-and-steady effort; even during high energy times of harvest, the farmer has to ration his energy to last for days, weeks, even months at a time. Farmers think ahead, and make better planners than fighters.

Most of us are a mixture of Hunter and Farmer traits. Our culture puts the ADHD or ADD label on the person who possesses mostly Hunter traits, and considers "normal" the person who has mostly Farmer traits. Since schools are an expression of our cultural values, schools have been organized to educate people with Farmer learning style traits, unfortunately creating a difficult, sometimes hostile, learning environment for the Hunter child.

If you get a chance to watch *Moana*, the 1928 documentary about life in a hunting/gathering society in Polynesia, notice the scene where a boy has learned the skill of hunting a lizard, and compare his actions with the behavior that would be expected of him to succeed in a modern school. Like this boy, many twenty-first century children also have a physical need to move around while they are learning. It is a lucky student whose teacher allows boys and girls to draw doodle pictures at their desks at the same time they are listening to a story or a hearing a lesson; after all, isn't this what many adults do while attending business meetings? Even luckier are students who are given the option of working at a stand-up desk, allowing them to turn their wiggles and squirms into natural movements and shifts of balance. When I visited President Thomas Jefferson's Monticello home a few years ago, I noticed he had designed a stand-up desk for himself, which made me wonder if perhaps President Jefferson is yet one more famous person who experienced the restlessness and inability to sit still for long periods of time exhibited by so many people with Hunter traits.

After Thom Hartmann figured out his Hunter/Farmer hypothesis, he explained the idea to his son and then gave him a couple of options, "You have two choices. One, you can learn to fake it during the school hours and behave like a Farmer: we can talk about how you can learn the skill-set to do that. Or, two, you can take these Farmer pills (Ritalin) that will make your brain work just like a Farmer's brain for about four hours. Or you can do both until you have the Farmer behaviors down pat." Thom and his son used the Ritalin for only a short time before dropping it. This discussion and subsequent efforts to help Thom's son learn new coping skills resulted in the boy's increased sense of competency and self-esteem, and eventually gave him the confidence to successfully follow his chosen career path that required a college degree.

If your child has been identified as ADHD, try to focus on the positive aspects of the Hunter/Edison gene brain traits, and begin to explore any appropriate environmental changes you can provide for your child. If the environmental change of medication is ultimately needed, follow Thom Hartmann's example, be extremely cautious and let medication be just one component of the solution.

If you'd like to learn more about the Hunter-Farmer hypothesis, and the skill-set needed to cope with having ADHD or ADD traits without the use of medication, as well as how to choose a career that fits with the Hunter/Edison Gene brain, I recommend that you study Thom Hartmann's book, *The Complete Guide to ADHD: Help For Your Family at Home, School and Work*, and his more recent book, *The Edison Gene:*

ADHD and the Gift of the Hunter Child.

I am greatly indebted to him for discovering and sharing this positive way of looking at ADHD/ADD; his books are a treasure trove of ideas for anyone interested in understanding and living with ADHD/ADD.

Special Case: Guidelines for Electronic Use

Adapted from an article by Kathy Keller Jones in *Face to Face: Cultivating Kids' Social Lives in Today's Digital World* *

Make sure your family has digital free time together

- Don't let smart phone rings and beeps interrupt face-to-face engagement, especially with your children. Your time with them is precious.
- Turn off adult's and children's cell phones and other hand-held devices during meals and when out with friends and family.
- Don't let TV and computer screens be focal points in your home; some families have a separate room for TV and computer use. Also, be sure to turn all screens off during dinner and when they are not being used.
- Consider having a designated "office" area for computer and phone use.
- Commit to a "digital Sabbath" one evening or day of the week. This is when a family turns off or stores all electronic devices to relax and have fun together.

Limit time spent with electronics

- Avoid the use of technology as an electronic babysitter.
- Limit the amount of time children can use screens for fun to an

---

* Used with permission from Kathy Keller Jones and Family Empowerment Network at www.family-empower.com.

hour or less total on school days; for example, tweens could earn a half hour a day to use the family Ipad after they have read, exercised, and finished homework or chores.

- If you allow video games, recognize the addictive nature of gaming and make sure the games being played in your home fit with your family values. Your children might experience violent games at someone else's house, but they will not associate them with their own home and self in the same way.

- Practice "appointment" TV. Use the latest technology, if you have it, to record worth-while shows and watch them at appointed times. Teach the skill of muting commercials and turning the TV off when the show or game is finished.

Protect good sleep habits

- Keep all screens out of kids' and teens' bedrooms.

- Collect all devices and put them in the "dog house" or charging basket at least a half hour before bedtime.

- Create a buffer zone between the time technology is shut down and bedtime. Allow time to get ready for bed, to talk and decompress. Safeguard this important transition time.

- Help your teens to figure out how to get their work done without staying up late on a regular basis. Getting up early is often a better alternative.

Delay the introduction of phones, texting, and social networking for as long as possible

- Ask well-meaning relatives to gift electronic devices such as Ipads to the family instead of to the individual child.

- Delay the introduction of phones and especially texting for tweens and teens. Phones rarely make your child feel safer, but they do expose them to overwhelming distractions and interfere with family connection.

• If possible, have a graduated introduction to cell phones. Start with a basic phone without texting, then add texting a year or two later based on good academic performance and maturity. Only introduce smartphones when your teen can use the internet and video games wisely.

• Purchase parental controls from your cell phone company (usually around $5 a month.)

• Delay the use of Facebook and other social networking as long as possible. If you need backup, read *Talking Back to Facebook* by John Steyer, 2012.

Use the Family Meeting process (Chapter Eleven) to develop a contract around the use of electronic devices

The Family Meeting process described in Chapter Eleven of this book will help you to lessen any power struggle that may arise from limiting your children's use of electronic devices.

CHAPTER SEVEN

The Correction for Not-Minding
Physical Assist and Broken Record

The next four chapters outline how to carry out the appropriate correction for each of the four misbehaviors. Corrections are not punishments. They are part of a step-by-step process of teaching the child to see the sense of behaving in certain ways. You are probably already using these corrections in one form or another. The key point about using the corrections is to learn when to use them, plus remembering not to sabotage yourself.

Some of the corrections will be emotionally difficult for the A-parent and teacher to carry out. The A-adult often has difficulty in allowing the child to make independent decisions. The A-parent and teacher can also find it hard to accept the concept that corrections should not be punitive.

Other corrections will be hard emotionally for the C-parent and teacher. The C-adult often finds it hard to carry out a correction because of the fear that if the adult is too controlling the child will not grow up to be an inner-directed adult, able to make independent decisions. The C-adult tends to worry that the child will not love the person who demands certain standards of behavior. The C-adult also finds it hard to stop rescuing the child from the consequences of his or her own behavior.

Both A and C-adults have strengths in different areas: We can learn from one another. A-adults can reassure C-adults that kids are strong enough to experience the consequences of their behavior, and that children will love the adult even when the adult insists on certain rules. C-adults can help A-adults see that corrections need not be punitive, and that children can be trusted to make independent decisions in many areas of their lives.

HOW TO GIVE A COMMAND

Not-minding behavior happens when the adult gives a reasonable command that the child refuses to carry out. If you can learn to give commands in a way the child interprets as fair and reasonable, you will find yourself having to use the correction for not minding much less often. Here are some basic guidelines for giving a command.

1. Give a choice if at all possible

No matter what our age, each of us wants to be in control of our own life. Healthy human beings will resist if they feel you are trying to control their lives. By saying to the child, "You can choose to do either this or that," you empower the child and give him or her a sense of control. In this way, making choices strengthens the competency step on the child's staircase of needs. However, the choices you offer must be choices you can live with. For example, a grandmother told about the time her three-year-old granddaughter, Tanisha, was visiting. When the girl's mother told her it was bedtime, the child started whining and complaining. The girl's father said, "Tanisha, you can go to bed right now or Grandma can read you a story and then you can go to bed." Tanisha immediately chose to hear the story, stopped fussing and went happily off to bed with Grandma (who had intended to read her a story anyhow).

Other examples of choice-commands are: "We can leave right now or we can go in ten more minutes." "You can finish your schoolwork at the work table or at the back desk." "You can finish playing your guitars in the garage or in the basement." "You can play with the kick ball on the playing court or on the back field." "You can play without pushing or you can sit out part of the game."

You can see that the choices are limited only to those choices the adult can live with. *Never give a choice when there is no choice.* Do not ask children if they *want* to do it. For example, "Do you want to go to bed now?" or "Let's go to bed now. Okay? Okay?" By asking children if they *want* to, or if it is *okay,* you have given them the choice of *not* going to bed. It is not fair to expect a child to mind when you have not given a clear choice or command. Rather than offer a choice you did not really intend to give, it is better not to give a choice at all and simply say, "Now it's time to go to bed."

An important point: If children refuse to act on either choice, *you must make the choice for them.* If the choice you gave was, "You can finish your schoolwork at the work table or at the back desk," and the child refuses to move, then you must choose for him. If the child still will not move, you can then step in to use the physical assist or the broken record, corrections that we will discuss later in this chapter.

2. If you cannot give a choice, describe the facts of the situation

Examples are: "It is time to go home," or "The table is not for sitting on." Another example: A two-year-old boy was grabbing all the cards from his three-year-old brother while their mother unsuccessfully tried to persuade the two-year-old to share. Finally, the grandmother simply said, "Those cards belong to your brother." Immediately, the younger child dropped his brother's cards and went off to do something else.

Another example of describing the situation happened on my first day as an intern at the Children's Psychiatric Day Treatment Center at the University of Oregon. I was sitting observing a small group of children when one of the children, who was about seven years old, came up to me, stood looking at me for a minute, and then reached out before I could stop him, and threw my glasses across the room. I looked at him very seriously, and in an equally serious tone of voice, said, "I don't like it when you throw my glasses." That child never touched my glasses again.

A similar incident involved a two-year-old girl who was sticking her tongue out at her mother's guests. At first everyone tried to ignore her, but unsuccessfully. The girl continued to put her face up close to each guest and then, smiling happily, stick out her tongue. Finally, one guest said very seriously, "I don't like it when you stick out your tongue at me." The little girl blinked her eyes in surprise and was visibly upset. She immediately stopped sticking out her tongue at the stranger. The adults continued to talk pleasantly among themselves and gave the little girl lots of positive attention. She never resumed the behavior during the rest of the visit. (It happened that one of the girl's uncles had been playing a stick-out-your-tongue game with her and she, no doubt, thought everyone would think the game was fun to play. At this point, all she needed was to hear the information that these adults did not like to play the game.) Human beings, even very young ones, are more apt to cooperate if they are given clear, describing information about the situation.

3. Use a positive tone of voice

No matter what kind of a command you give, concentrate on using a positive tone of voice. A positive tone of voice lets children know you respect them. Even describing information, if delivered in a harsh tone of voice, can invite a power struggle.

4. The fewer words the better

Be as brief as possible. Give only one, or at most two, commands at a time. Giving many commands at once is confusing. "Gary, go upstairs and bring me a diaper for the baby, and on your way, turn off those bathroom lights, and when you're done with that, you can choose to either take the letters on the hallway table out to the mailbox before we watch Sesame Street or before lunch." A command like that is too complex. It is too hard to remember, even if your child is a good auditory learner. The shorter the better. A one-word command is sometimes the best of all.

A Head Start teacher was trying to teach a five-year-old boy to hang up his coat when he entered the room. The boy was in the habit of just dropping his coat on the floor. The teacher went to stand by the coat and described the situation, "The coat belongs on the hook." The boy looked at him but continued to get out the blocks to play with. The teacher looked down at the coat. "Coat," he said. The boy came over to stand by the teacher and now they both stood looking down at the coat. "Coat," the teacher said, this time pointing at the coat. The boy picked up the coat and went to hang it up. Since the teacher remembered not to sabotage, the coat problem was soon solved.

5. Give lead time, if possible

Give some advance notice that you are going to want something to happen soon, for example, "In five minutes it will be time to start picking up the blocks," or, "In ten minutes we need to be ready to leave for Grandma's." Giving lead time is a way of showing respect for the child's activities and is much more likely to result in cooperation when you actually give the command that "It's time to go."

6. Be reasonable in the type and number of choices or commands you give

You will have to be the judge of how many commands a day are reasonable, but remember, the fewer commands you give, the more likely the child will take notice when you do give a command. As the child grows towards puberty, you should need to give fewer and fewer commands. The older the child, the more areas of life should be in his or her own area of control. We do not own children. Any command that orders children around just because the adult wants to wield power over them is not reasonable.

Any command that tries to force a bodily function on the child is unreasonable. "Eat that food," or "Stop wetting your bed," or "You have a bowel movement before you leave that bathroom," or "You better be asleep before I come in here again," or "You stop that crying right now" are all unreasonable commands in that they attempt to control another human being's interior bodily functioning. Even "I don't want to hear one word out of you while we are in the store" is unreasonable.

If you have exhausted all possible areas of changing the child's environment, and the child is over three years old, body-related problems like bed wetting, pants messing and eating can sometimes be dealt with as routine not-minding behaviors. We will discuss some possible solutions for these issues in the chapter on routine not-minding misbehaviors. But never give commands and then try to physically assist or use the broken record regarding a child's bodily functions. All body functions belong solely to the person who lives in the body, of whatever age.

7. Be sure you can follow through with the correction, otherwise do not give the choice or command

If you cannot carry out the correction, or follow through on the choices, do not give the command. If you are in a public place, like the grocery store, or at the school play, and you know you will be too embarrassed to carry out the correction, do not give the command. You must be consistent in carrying out the correction the first time the child does not mind. It is better not to give the command than to sabotage yourself by procrastinating.

8. Do not respond to self-indulgent behavior

Concentrate on dealing with the not-minding behavior. Do not let the child's accusations, complaints, whining, name calling, or scolding deflect you from carrying out the correction for not-minding. You will sabotage yourself if you get hooked into responding in any way to the self-indulgent behavior. (See next chapter.)

The Physical Assist and the Broken Record

The Physical Assist and the Broken Record is the two-part correction for Not-Minding. The physical assist and broken record are ways to help children learn to follow reasonable commands. Young children especially, because they are learning so many new behaviors in their brand-new world, need this type of guidance more often than older children. The physical assist is most effective with younger children; the broken record can be used with all children over three years old.

As children grow, the more they understand beforehand what is expected of them. When the new behavior has been learned so that children can integrate it into their belief systems, it becomes routine, something children "know in their bones" they are expected to do. Many not-minding misbehaviors of older children fall into the routine not-minding category, and call for a different correction that you will learn in Chapter Seven.

You are the latest in a million-year-old line of teachers and parents. Adults have an obligation to pass along cultural expectations to their children. You have the authority of all society and all nature behind you. Do not sabotage yourself and all those thousands of ancestors by turning this into a personal power struggle.

HOW TO CARRY OUT THE PHYSICAL ASSIST

> Teachers, agency personnel, foster parents and child care providers need special permission and training before using the following physical assist correction. (Exceptions would be the strategy of picking up a toddler and/or moving closer to the child.)

When the child does not mind the first time you give a choice or command, you physically lead him or her through the task. Leading the child through a task is called the Physical Assist. The physical assist is done in this manner: When the child has disobeyed, say "No." Then restate the command as you *physically lead the child through the task*. There are a wide variety of ways to physically assist a child: from walking over to stand very close to the child, to touching the child lightly on the shoulder, to actually picking up the child and removing him or her. The main idea is to use your own body in a nonverbal way to help the child do what you have asked the child to do. *Use as little physical force as you possibly can.* Very often, just the knowledge that the adult is right there, only a few feet away and ready to step in, is enough of a physical assist to convince the child it is time to carry out the command.

Do not restate the command more than once. Say nothing else throughout the physical assist procedure. Think of yourself as a force of nature, like a river or a steady breeze. You are carrying out the necessary teachings of human society that all adults have an obligation to pass on to their children. Try not to get too emotionally involved. Remember, this is not a punishment. This is a teaching method.

Example A

Mother and her two-year-old daughter, Reanna, are at Grandma's house. Reanna starts playing with Grandma's precious objects on the coffee table. Mother would prefer to adjust the environment by removing the objects to higher ground, but she knows Grandma does not approve of that, even for two-year-olds. So Mother both describes the situation and gives a choice, "Reanna, the things on the coffee table are not for playing. You can play with this." Mother gives Reanna a two-year-old kind of choice by offering her a toy to play with. Reanna continues with what she is doing. There is no sign that Reanna even heard what Mother said.

Mother, again with a pleasant but firm tone of voice, "No. Those things are not for playing." As Mother restates her command, she walks over to Reanna, picks her up and removes her to a different part of the house where she gives her the toy to play with.

The younger the child, the more easily she can be distracted with something else. For a two-year-old, being distracted by a toy is a form of giving her a choice. In cases where young children like Reanna cannot be distracted by another choice, you need to continue to use the physical assist to carry them away from the place they are not supposed to be.

Example B

Third-grader Kelly is pushing and shoving to break into the front of the line that is forming outside the school door as the children prepare to come in from recess. The teacher is too busy to stop and help problem-solve. Her mind goes blank. She cannot think how to give a choice, so she simply says in a firm but calm voice, "Kelly, you need to go to the back of the line." Kelly stands in his new spot at the front of the line, avoiding the teacher's eyes, with a pout on his face, and refuses to budge.

In the same pleasant but firm voice, teacher says, "Back of the line," as she puts her hand on Kelly's shoulder and walks him to the end of the line.

You may have noticed that when the command is restated in the two examples above, the adult did not use the child's name. This is because a person's name is one of the sweetest sounds in the world to that person. Using a name at negative times is giving too much social reinforcement. Your goal is to not give any more attention than absolutely necessary during the physical assist.

Example C

Sometimes the physical assist can be used without even touching the child. A diminutive resource room teacher told this story. She had a fifth-grade student who towered over her. Walking down the hall together they looked like Mutt and Jeff. The boy had been having a hard week. He had refused to finish his class work. "Cliff," she finally told him, "you will have to stay after school and finish your work before you can go home today." The teacher cleared this plan ahead of time with Cliff's mother who promised to come pick him up later in the day when his work was done. Immediately after school, Cliff tried to escape by taking his regular bus ride home. The teacher called Cliff's mother and asked her to bring her son back to school, but the mother said she had already tried and could not make him get in the car. The determined teacher marched out the school door, drove her car over to Cliff's house, knocked on the door, and commanded, "Get in the car." The astonished boy got in the car without protest. She did not have to touch him; her determined body language, and the waiting car, told him all he needed to know.

Never use more force than absolutely necessary. You can be firm without hurting the child either physically or emotionally. There should be no nonverbal message to the child of, "I'll teach you to disobey me, you little S.O.B." The nonverbal message to the child should rather be an inexorable, Mother Nature, matter-of-fact statement that, "This must be done. This is the way things are." The physical assist is not a punishment.

It is part of a teaching method that will temporarily stop the misbehavior and put you in charge of the situation.

When the physical assist is finished, go back to whatever you were doing. *Do not mention anything about what just happened.* Talking about the misbehavior is one of the surest ways to sabotage yourself. Talking about the misbehavior is perceived by children as demeaning, a way of "rubbing their face in it." *Talking about the misbehavior in any way will set up a power struggle in which children will attempt to protect their inner integrity by disobeying you again.* When the incident is over, let it be over. As soon as children exhibit the slightest neutral or positive behavior, immediately reinforce the new behavior with friendly eye contact or touch or word.

Your new behavior may be confusing to the child at first, especially if he or she has been accustomed to receiving negative feedback from adults for extended periods of time after misbehavior occurs. The confusion will soon clear, and your nonverbal, matter-of-fact type of physical assist correction will quickly convince them that it was their behavior you did not like, not them as individuals. The minute their behavior changes, why shouldn't you be friendly? After all, they are dear people and you care about them. Their misbehavior was just a natural part of their learning and growing.

HOW TO CARRY OUT THE BROKEN RECORD

The Broken Record is an assertiveness technique in which you state what you need to have happen, again and again, in the same even, calm tone of voice. *Notice that this is just the opposite of the physical assist, in which you give a command only once. So be clear in your mind, before you start, which part of the correction you plan to emphasize.*

Consider the example of Carlos, a student of mine when I was a high school teacher. Carlos was a withdrawn, sullen young man with many personal problems. He never gave me any trouble, but also never allowed me to get to know him. One day he came to class angry and upset. He started interrupting me and making insulting remarks. I tried to ignore him but finally decided I had to give him a choice, "You can stop what you are doing, or you can leave the room." Carlos was quiet for a while, but soon continued interrupting and insulting. I said, "I guess you choose to leave." Carlos started arguing. I closed my eyes, shook my head slowly back and forth and said, "No. Leave." More arguing from Carlos. I looked not at Carlos but at the door. "You will have to leave." I waited. The other students were absolutely silent. I tried to keep my voice low and even and said again, "No, leave." Finally, after repeating myself seven or eight times, Carlos slouched out of the room. The rest of us went back to what we were doing without comment. When Carlos showed up the next day, I greeted him with a smile and did not mention the incident. He did not exactly smile back but did give a grudging low, "Hello." Carlos never did anything like that in my class again. And I never found out what painful thing had happened in his life to trigger that event.

1. Avoid turning this into a personal power struggle

Avoid commands like, "I said you get down to the basement this minute," or "You better get out of this living room right now if you know what's good for you." Instead, put the whole inexorable force of nature and society behind your initial command, "It is time … You need to … ." Do not respond to self-indulgent arguments or accusations. Do not respond to anger. Be as firm and calm as you can. Concentrate on keeping your voice even. Let your nonverbal body language convey the message that you too have rights and that you are in this for the long haul. Plant your body in one spot and stay there. Remember you have a million-year-long line of teachers and parents behind you. Try to be a force of nature that must be obeyed, like a wide river, the ocean, a huge boulder, or a steady wind.

Limit eye contact during the broken record correction. Eye contact gives powerful emotional attention to the child during the misbehavior. It will fuel a power struggle. *Rather than look at the child, look in the direction you want the child to go, or toward the objects you want removed.* In the example just given, I concentrated on looking at the door and not at Carlos. Sometimes it helps to close your eyes and slowly shake your head from side to side as you quietly restate the command.

As with all the other corrections, remember not to sabotage by talking about it when children finally do what they have been told. Simply say, "Thank you," and go back to what you were doing before the incident started. Do not sabotage yourself by indicating in any way that you think you are the winner and they are losers. Next time you see them, pay attention to their neutral and positive behaviors. Try not to sabotage yourself by holding on to your resentment that they did not obey you the first time. Let the incident go.

2. Tell the child what you want to have happen

Give the command as many times as necessary in a calm, firm voice. Be a Broken Record. Tell the child what you want to have happen. If the child does not respond, be quiet for a moment, then repeat it again. If the child does not respond after another silence, repeat it again. Alternate repeating the command with a silence for as many times as necessary. For example, here is a situation where the choice-command was, "I'm afraid it's too loud for me when you play your guitars in the living room. You and Carol can play in the garage or in the basement." If, after waiting and giving the two children a chance to finish the piece they are playing, and still nothing happens, or if they start to argue with you, you must make the choice for them. Describe what you want to have happen. "You will have to leave." After the initial command, use only one or two words. The fewer words the better. You may have to repeat yourself many times. Remember to wait quietly for a moment after each time you repeat the command, "No. Leave."

Example A

Here is an example involving a five-year-old child. Dad is getting ready to set the table for dinner. His daughter Melissa is playing a game on the table. In a friendly way Dad says, "Melissa, it's time to pick up the game and clear the table." (Hopefully, Dad has remembered earlier to give Melissa some lead time so that she could plan ahead.) Melissa starts to wail, "I'm not done yet!"

Dad says, "No. I said it is time to pick up the game." Dad walks into the dining room, plants himself firmly beside his daughter and waits.

(Notice the physical assist.) Again he says, "The game." Melissa screams, "But I'm not done. You're mean!" Dad ignores this self-indulgent behavior. "The game," he says again. Finally, Melissa, grumbling under her breath, clears the table. Dad ignores the grumbling, says, "Thank you," walks back into the kitchen, and says nothing more.

Example B

One teacher tried the broken record technique while substituting in an inner-city middle school. Two ninth-grade boys started a fight on the ramp leading to the school door where she was standing at recess time. "Get off the ramp," she said. The boys looked over at her but kept on pushing and swearing at each other. She moved a step closer to them. (Notice the physical assist.) "Get off the ramp." They stopped and looked at her, each shouting that the other one had done or said something to start the fight. She moved another step closer and in the same, even tone of voice she repeated, "The ramp." They turned away and left the ramp. To her amazement, they also stopped fighting. This teacher's eyes sparkled as she held her hand high above her head, "And they were this much taller than I am."

Example C

Karen was growing increasingly concerned about the belligerent behavior of her fifteen-year-old son. He consistently defied her and refused even her most reasonable requests. He had even begun leaving knives around the house in prominent places, which she took as a deliberate attempt on his part to intimidate her. One behavior in particular that made her life miserable was his habit of playing hard rock music, which he knew she detested, at maximum decibel levels. Besides feeling assaulted by the noise, Karen felt she had lost ownership of her own home.

In spite of her growing fear of her own son, Karen decided to try the broken record. That night, as soon as the stereo was turned up full blast, she walked into her son's room and said, "The stereo is too loud. Will you please turn it down?" Her son barely glanced at her. "Get lost," he said. She moved a step closer and tried to visually imagine herself as a huge, immovable boulder. (Notice the physical assist.) "Turn it down, please." Her son reached over and turned it up as far as it would go. Karen closed her eyes and shook her head slowly back and forth. She waited. Her son ignored her. Karen looked at the stereo. "Turn it down," she repeated. The noise was so deafening, she knew he couldn't hear her but at least he could see her lips move. She kept looking at the stereo and continued to imagine herself as a huge, immovable rock. Every so often she said, in as calm a tone of voice as she could manage, "Turn it down." She was amazed and relieved when finally, her son reached over and turned the stereo to a bearable level. "Thank you," she said and left the room. No more was said by either of them about the incident but Karen felt that somehow their relationship had moved to an improved position of increased mutual respect.

Example D

A mother who was having endless troubles getting her three children (ages five, eight, and ten) to stay in bed at night had just started reading an early draft version of this book and had come upon the concept of the broken record. She decided to try it. She went through the regular bedtime routine, read them stories, gave them drinks of water, and kissed them all good-night. Then she came out to the living room, sat down with the book in her lap to await the onslaught. Soon they started calling for her. "I have to go to the bathroom. Whitney is bugging me. Can I have a drink of water?" She ignored all that. Finally, as usual, they came trooping down the hall continuing their complaints and requests for water. She kept looking at the manuscript in her lap. "Bed," she said in what she hoped was a firm, calm voice. They kept on complaining and whining. "Bed," she said. After she said, "Bed," about five times, the kids retreated down the hall. Mother could hear them in one of the bedrooms talking it over. "What's Mom doing anyhow?" Then they came out and tried complaining again. "Bed," she said, concentrating on keeping her voice even, still looking at the book. More complaints. "Bed," she said. That did it. They went back down the hall in silence and climbed in bed. The next night the kids tried it again, but with less intensity, and after the third night, Mother went through the usual bedtime routine of stories, kisses, and tucking them in with real pleasure, because after that they actually stayed in bed.

When children, of any age, do mind you, do not take it for granted. Let them know you appreciate them. Give them lots of immediate positive attention. In the bedtime situation above, "immediate" means the following morning. The next morning, Mother should not sabotage herself by mentioning how happy she was that they finally stayed in bed last night. It would be sabotage to *talk* about last night, but she can give lots of hugs and good morning smiles and even offer a super good breakfast. The rule of giving the child four positive attentions for every one negative attention still applies, and is absolutely necessary for changing the child's behavior over the long-term. The Physical Assist and the Broken Record correction primarily stops the misbehavior and puts you in control. Positive attention, given at neutral and positive times, is what will help to bring about long-term behavior change.

Exercise

Keep identifying the negative behaviors as you see them this week. Do not rush in to try the new corrections until you feel pretty confident you know where to begin. Before you start to administer any of the corrections, you need to become proficient at identifying which of the four misbehaviors is occurring, and whether or not the negative behavior is actually a misbehavior or rather an attempt to solve a problem. Using the corrections before you have some idea of *when* to use them will result in confusion for both you and the child.

Continue to write down your observations and experiences of the four misbehaviors and the three problem-solving behaviors during the coming week. Use the "Negative Behaviors" worksheet on the following page.

WORKSHEET
NEGATIVE BEHAVIORS
The Four Misbehaviors and Three Problem-Solving Situations

NOT-MINDING (Not Doing What Is Asked)

SELF-INDULGENT (Attention-Getting)

ROUTINE NOT-MINDING (Will Not Do Routine Tasks)

AGGRESSIVE (Deliberately Hurting)

NEGATIVE BEHAVIORS Requiring Problem-Solving That Does Not Fit Above:

1. Adjust Environment   2. Solve Conflicts   3. Listen to Feelings

---

REVIEW: Correction for Not-Minding Behaviors

How to Give a Command

1. **Give a choice** instead of a command if at all possible. If the child refuses to act on either choice, you must make the choice for him.

2. If you cannot give a choice, **describe** the situation.

3. Whatever kind of command you give, concentrate on using a **positive** tone of voice.

4. **The fewer words the better.** One word is often the best of all.

5. Give **lead time** if at all possible.

6. **Be reasonable** in the type and number of commands you give.

7. Be sure you can **follow through** with the correction. Otherwise, do not give the choice or command.

8. **Do not respond to self-indulgent behavior.** Do not get emotionally hooked by responding to arguments or accusations.

9. **Avoid turning this correction into a personal power struggle.** Give as little emotional attention as possible. Especially **avoid eye contact** with the child.

Physical Assist
Non-parents need special permission

1. State the choice or command only **once**.

2. If the child does not mind the first time, do something that physically involves you with the child. **Use the least amount of physical intervention necessary.**

Broken Record

1. **Tell the child what you want to have happen.** Give the command as many times as necessary in a calm, firm voice. Alternate commands with silence. **Avoid eye contact.**

2. **Use as few words as possible.** One word is often best of all.

3. The **physical assist** of placing your body close to the child may be helpful.

from *Caring Discipline: Practical Tools for Nurturing Happy Families & Classrooms*

Chapter 7 Discussion: PHYSICAL ASSIST AND BROKEN RECORD

1. Share this week's "Negative Behaviors" chart.

2. What percentage of the time do you expect children to obey you? Eighty percent? Sixty percent? One hundred percent? Talk together about what kinds of commands are reasonable. If you expect one-hundred-percent obedience, or perfection in any form from either the child or yourself, you will be disappointed. Do you expect perfection of your own behavior as a parent or teacher? Try to give yourself and the children the right not to be perfect. It is okay to be human. Making mistakes is how everyone learns.

3. Each person in the group needs to learn how to give the mild form of physical assist and the broken record correction since they are sometimes necessary for carrying out other corrections. Hopefully, two members of the group will volunteer to act out a not-minding situation using the physical assist and the broken record. Let each person who is willing have a chance to play an adult role so they will have some experience when they go home or back to the classroom to try it out with their children.

4. Role-play a situation in which the "adult" gives the broken record correction. The best way to experience how children will feel and how they will react to the broken record is to be a "child" yourself. It's usually more fun to role-play the part of the child because then you're free to act without thinking. So when it is your turn to be the responsible "adult," give yourself permission to make lots of mistakes. Making mistakes is how you will learn.

REMEMBER NOT TO SELF-SABOTAGE

The Correction for Self-Indulgent Behavior
Ignoring and the Either-Or Choice

Self-indulgent behavior is guaranteed to irritate even the most long-suffering teacher or parent. You can recognize self-indulgent behavior when children whine, argue, throw themselves on the floor and scream, accuse the adult of not loving them, threaten not to love the adult, clam up when they are spoken to, interrupt, pout, criticize ("Stop singing, that hurts my ears!"), bicker with other kids, cry even when there seems to be no real reason for it, tattle, constantly demand that adults do things for them, and on and on.

Preventing Self-Indulgent Behavior by Paying Attention at Neutral Times

More than any of the other misbehaviors, the goal of a child's self-indulgent behavior is to be the center of your attention. For this reason, the first step in stopping self-indulgent behavior is to *pay attention to the child in non-verbal ways at neutral times.* This alone, if carried out on a regular basis, is often enough to stop a child's self-indulgent behavior (if you are in doubt as to how to do this, please refer to Chapter Two.)

The Garden's Noise Preschool staff in Portland, Oregon uses the following method: every time a teacher gives a positive, non-verbal attention to a specific child at a neutral time, she moves a Popsicle stick from one jar to another. The goal is to move all ten sticks during the two and one-half hour session. The result is a rapid drop-off, often disappearance, of the child's self-indulgent behaviors. Making marks on a piece of paper works, too.

The Correction: Ignoring / Either-Or Choice

There are two parts of the correction for self-indulgent behavior. The first part of the correction, given when the child is just being irritating, is to ignore the behavior. Self-indulgent behavior that is ignored will drop away, if you remember not to sabotage yourself.

The second part of the correction is to be used when the child is not only being irritating, but also infringing on your rights. This second part of the correction involves setting up a situation in which you can again ignore the behavior by giving the child an Either-Or Choice. When self-indulgent behavior is ignored, there is no reason for the child to continue the behavior. Attention is what the child is trying to get from you. Behavior you give emotional attention to will continue, especially self-indulgent behavior.

FIRST PART: IGNORING

Ignoring is not an easy correction to use. Ignoring may seem like a passive, even cowardly, response, especially to all you A-type parents and teachers.

But ignoring is not a passive correction. It is one of the most difficult of the corrections to administer effectively because it requires that you give the child no attention at all. This means no eye contact, no facial response, in fact, no body language response whatsoever, and especially no talking. Remembering to do all this at a time when you might feel instead like giving the child a whack on the bottom is not an easy thing to do. Ignoring means to treat children as though they are invisible, as if they are not even in the room with you.

Many adults cannot believe what a powerful correction ignoring can be until they role-play a situation in which they act out the part of a self-indulgent child. During the first role-play, when they are given emotional attention by much scolding or cajoling and pleading from the "adult," these "children" find they have a wonderful time screaming and yelling and fighting. They break out into big smiles or gales of laughter when they experience how much fun it is to get an adult's emotional attention focused totally on them. During the next role-play, in which they have a chance to experience what it feels like to have the same behavior ignored, they scream and cry and complain while no one pays any attention to them. Gradually, as the other adults in the room continue to ignore the self-indulgent behavior, sometimes by taking refuge in the bathroom, the adults playing the part of the self-indulgent child feel their energy draining away, and the light of understanding dawns. As one mother put it, "I felt like a punctured balloon."

Ignoring self-indulgent behavior in a public place is one of the hardest of all corrections to pull off successfully because the adult usually is keenly aware of all those strangers eyeing the situation disapprovingly, waiting for the adult to *do something about that child.* As you can imagine, teachers have difficulty with this one. Hard as it is, you must resist the temptation to treat the child as you think other people expect you to. Stick to your own program.

Example A

A parent goes to the grocery store with her four-year-old daughter. The child picks up a candy bar. Mother says, "No, Melina. You can't have any more candy today." Melina protests loudly. Mother says, "No, Melina.

I mean it!" Melina promptly flings herself on the floor, screaming and kicking. Mother is embarrassed. She pulls Melina to her feet. Mother is angry but she tries to keep the peace, "Oh, all right. Just this once. But no more." Melina immediately quits crying and smiles happily. She has gotten the candy bar she wanted, plus Mother's undivided attention. Melina is in control of the situation, not Mother.

To use the ignoring correction, Mother needs to say, "No, Melina. You can't have any more candy today." Then go on her way down the aisle and say no more about it. When Melina whines, yells, and throws herself on the floor in a fit, Mother should pay no attention to her and continue on down the aisle with the shopping cart. You have probably heard stories of children holding their breath until they pass out during a tantrum. Rest assured that the instant a person passes out, the body will again resume the process of breathing. Breathing is controlled by the autonomic nervous system and it will not stop just because your child holds her breath. Have you ever heard of a single child, or adult for that matter, who killed himself by holding his breath? If you have any doubts, set your mind at ease by consulting your pediatrician.

If the incident happens right beside the check stand where Mother cannot move away from Melina, she will have to grit her teeth and ignore, in spite of the fact that ten people behind her in line are looking at her disapprovingly.

Example B

Another example of ignoring, this time in the classroom, was told by a resource room teacher. The teacher had a third-grade student named Karrie assigned to her room. Karrie came into the room looking sullen and angry. The teacher ignored Karrie's cross looks and did everything she could think of to help the child feel she was welcome and that she belonged. Finally the teacher put a math worksheet in front of her new student and explained it to her. Karrie sat back in her seat, folded her arms across her chest and said, "I'm not going to do it!"

The teacher, who has a very expressive face, arched an eyebrow and stopped to think for a moment. Which category of misbehavior was this? Should she treat this as a not-minding behavior, a routine not-minding behavior, or a self-indulgent behavior? She decided to treat the situation as self-indulgent behavior by ignoring it. She reminded herself that she was the latest in a million-year-old line of teachers. She put on her best nothing-can-be-done-to-change-the-way-things-are-look and ignored the refusal by describing the situation in a matter-of-fact way, "We do three of these papers every day." Then she moved away to help the next child. She told us she was prepared to come back later and try the Broken Record correction for not-minding if the first approach did not work. A little later she glanced over at Karrie who had begun working on her math sheet. No more was said about the incident and needless to say, the teacher gave her new student plenty of positive attention for working on her math assignment. This teacher laughed as she reenacted the scene for us. "I am so tough. I demand they do their very best, and they all seem to love me anyway. I think it's because now I know how to keep each of their emotional needs staircases strong."

If you are at home when the self-indulgent behavior occurs, and you can't stand to ignore the commotion a minute longer, leave the room. Go play the piano to drown out the noise, or go outside to pull a few weeds. If your child follows you, you can always go into the bathroom and lock the door. Your child may pound on the bathroom door or try to force the door knob. Continue to ignore it. If the child bangs on the door with something sharp and therefore is actually damaging the door, then you will have to give an either-or-choice. But usually that isn't necessary. Turn on the water, take a shower, pretend not to hear the ruckus.

Example C

A common self-indulgent behavior the classroom teacher must contend with is the unknown child who starts belching just when the class has settled down to a quiet study time. Most children, of whatever age, will first quickly glance at the teacher to check out her response before they decide whether to join in the belching or the laughter. To carry out this correction, the teacher ignores. But if the ignoring does not work and the belching and laughter begins to escalate, she can glance up briefly, catching some of the other children's eyes and convey a look of, "How childish. This kind of behavior is not worth noticing," and go back to her own work again. Hopefully, the teacher will not sabotage herself by giving the belching child the satisfaction of seeing that this is really bugging the teacher. (If this does not work, the teacher can always fall back on the either-or choice, or the classroom meeting, both of which will be discussed later.)

Example D

Another common example of self-indulgent behavior is the child who yells or whines or uses some other inappropriate tone of voice with parents or teachers. Describe the situation by saying, "I don't talk to people who yell at me" (or whine or boss or whatever voice the child is using with you). After you have stated your position, then ignore. After your one-time explanation, do not respond until the child uses a normal, acceptable tone of voice.

One first-grade teacher said she had a boy in her class who argued about everything. Since he also happened to be a good reader, she decided to make up some identical slips of paper, all of which said, "I am not going to argue with you." Whenever he started arguing with her, she gave him one of the slips and turned away from him. After a few times of this, she had only to make a move towards her desk to get one of the slips of paper and he stopped arguing.

Example E

A mother's three-year-old boy, Kit, constantly whined and complained. The mother decided to ignore her son whenever he whined. She told him, "I'm not going to pay any attention to you when you whine." That day he whined for three whole hours. The mother was nearly at the end of her rope but she didn't give in. At one point, Kit demanded, "Do you mean you're just going to stand there and ignore me?" The mother said, "Yes." From that day on the whining stopped. It has not resumed.

At first, as in the example of Kit and his mother, when you try ignoring self-indulgent behaviors, children will often *increase* their misbehaviors. They will not believe you are really going to ignore them. After all, you have always before (or nearly always) given in and given them what they wanted, your undivided, intensely emotional attention. Do not get discouraged.

The increase in misbehaviors is only temporary while they check out your new response. You will be doing them a favor by being firm and not giving in. If you let children whine and scold for two hours and then finally give in, they will have learned that if they whine and scold for two hours next time they want something, they will get what they want. The self-indulgent behavior will have become even more firmly entrenched. Ignoring can be an agonizing correction to carry out, but hang in there. If you ignore every time the self-indulgent behavior happens, you will have to go through a big scene only once or twice.

Example F

Another example of a self-indulgent behavior is the child who constantly interrupts and monopolizes adult conversation. Will was an eight-year-old boy who continually interrupted whenever his aunts and uncles got together. Will was a bright and outgoing boy who was unfortunately becoming the most disliked person in the family. The adults tried to ignore his efforts to control the conversation but would eventually give in and pay attention to him, either negatively, "Will you please stop interrupting," or positively, "Well, what is it you want to say?" Since they were mostly C-type adults, they tried being polite to him even though they often felt like throwing him out the door.

Will's counselor tried to change Will's behavior by suggesting to the family that they use a combination of ignoring Will (correction) whenever he interrupted and then immediately attend to him with smiles and warm eye contact when he was quietly listening to someone else (four to one positive social reinforcement). It helped. From then on Will was much more likely to listen and take his turn talking. One of his aunts commented, "Have you noticed that Will is not so bratty lately? He must be growing out of it."

Notice that the family used more than just the correction of ignoring: They also gave Will many kinds of positive nonverbal attentions for the behaviors they liked. *If they had only ignored him and not given him lots of attention at neutral and positive times, Will's behavior would have gotten worse, not better.* It is crucial that as soon as the child exhibits positive or neutral behaviors, you give him or her immediate positive attention. This is also an effective technique for using with a child who constantly tries to dominate the conversation in a classroom situation.

Example G

We have already discussed how to deal with fighting when you suspect it is primarily a problem-solving behavior. Now consider what to do if you suspect the kids are bickering and fighting mostly to get your sympathy and attention. Strange as it may appear at first, children often fight and argue to gain the sympathy and attention of their parents and teachers. Since the basic correction for self-indulgent behavior is to ignore it, adults often recoil in horror from the suggestion to ignore self-indulgent fighting. "Won't the big child hurt the little one?" If you do not dare leave two children alone, because the stronger one will seriously hurt the weaker one, then the fighting is not self-indulgent. It is aggressive. We will deal with the correction for aggression in Chapter Ten.

Self-indulgent fighting or bickering is often started by the younger or weaker of the children. When the older or stronger child retaliates, sometimes after having tried to ignore the goading for a while, the adult will often come to the rescue of the younger child.

Take a typical brother and sister self-indulgent fight. Melanie is five and Brian is eight. Brian has brought his friend Todd home with him to play. The two boys are playing with Brian's Legos in the bedroom. Melanie wants to be included in the boys' game but they do not want to play with her. This has been a problem in the past which Mother has earlier tried to help them solve. Today Melanie is again feeling lonely and left out. She ignores the ideas for making things go better for herself that have been suggested during other problem-solving fight situations and decides to instead try to enlist Mother's sympathy and at the same time make the boys miserable. She starts to call them names: "Brian is a big dumbbell. Stupid, stupid dumbbell!" Brian and Todd try to ignore her. Finally, Melanie runs into the bedroom and kicks over their elaborate Lego structure, strewing Legos all over the room. This is too much for Brian. He chases her from the bedroom, yells at her, and hits her from behind as she runs down the hall screaming for protection from Mother.

Melanie: "Mother! Brian is hitting me. Make him stop. I never did anything to him."

Brian: "She did too. She started it. She wrecked our Legos."

Melanie (crying pitifully): "They won't be nice to me. He hurt me."

Brian: "She's a brat!" (Tries to hit her again.)

Mother (decides that her earlier efforts at helping them problem-solve have not worked. She grabs Brian's arm): "Brian, you stop this hitting right now! I know little sisters can be aggravating but can't you be more patient with her? After all, you're older than she is. Melanie, you tell Brian you are sorry. Brian, you tell Melanie you are sorry. Now go back and play nicely. If I hear any more fighting, Todd will have to go home and you two will have to stay in your rooms until dinner time."

In the above example, even though Mother is trying to be fair to both parties, Brian feels unfairly punished. After all, he was minding his own business until Melanie started bugging him. And why should Todd have to go home? That's just what would make Melanie happy. Brian may infer from incidents like this one that Mother loves Melanie better than she loves him. Otherwise why would she always stick up for Melanie? Teachers, too, will recognize this kind of squabble. Teachers are often expected to get to the root of every child disagreement. And, like parents, they often fall into the trap of expecting themselves to have the wisdom of Solomon.

As has already been pointed out, the younger sibling, or the weaker child in the school relationship, is often the one who starts the fight, even though it is the weaker child who apparently gets the worst of it. It is safe for the younger child to start the fight if mother or dad or teacher can be counted on to intervene. In this way, the younger child not only becomes the center of the adult's attention, he or she is also protected from experiencing the natural consequences of the behavior. Even when the parent or the teacher tries to be fair by sending both children to separate rooms or opposite corners of the school yard, the older child still feels unfairly punished since, as he sees it, he was minding his own business until the younger child came along and bothered him. If this happens regularly, a cycle of resentment and anger builds within the older child until he is no longer fighting for attention or trying to solve the problem of being hassled, but is finally angry enough to want to take revenge on the younger sibling or school mate.

In the above example, Mother can extricate herself from the no-win referee position by treating Melanie's and Brian's fighting as self-indulgent behavior. If Mother has previously helped her two children learn problem-solving skills, she can feel confident Melanie and Brian are ready for this next step. The next time she and her children are in a neutral or positive situation, when they are watching television, driving in the car, or working with her in the kitchen, for example, she can explain her new approach to their fights.

Mother (in a friendly tone of voice): "You know, I have been thinking about that argument you had yesterday. I never know who actually starts it. You two are old enough now to do your own problem solving and settle your own arguments. From now on, I'll keep out of it."

Mother can also lay down some ground rules at this time. If the children have been hitting each other with objects or throwing hard things at one another, for example, she can say: "There's just one important rule about your arguments. There can be no hitting with hard things like bats or rocks. If you use hard things for hitting I will have to give that person a time-out." (Time-out will be explained in Chapter Ten.)

The basic idea you need to convey is that it is the responsibility of the children to solve their problems with one another. You can, of course, help problem-solve if they ask for your help, but do not offer unless they both want you to help. If you believe that these arguments are self-indulgent on the part of at least one of the children, stay out of it. The main idea is to covey the message that this is *their* problem, not yours. If asked, the adult is always available to help find solutions, but basically things are up to them.

Next time they fight, one or the other, probably the youngest, will come running to Mother. Mother can then carry out the correction of ignoring by saying, "I'm sure you two can talk this over and figure out a solution," and next proceed to emotionally withdraw from their arguments, and, if possible, to also withdraw physically. If Mother is alone with them in the house, she can withdraw to the bathroom and lock the door. It is a good idea to leave some magazines in the bathroom for something to do during such incidents. The kids may stand outside the door screaming and crying and pounding on the door, but she should continue to ignore them. This kind of behavior is closely related to a tantrum and should be treated as such. If one child hits another with a hard object, the fight has become aggressive and you can intervene with a time-out.

Do not assume, just because the youngest one cries "Brian hit me!" that this is an aggressive situation. As we have seen, Melanie may very well have done something to provoke the hitting. Brian's hitting may be his attempt to find a solution to the problem of his sister's self-indulgent behavior. Hitting may stop Melanie's self-indulgent behavior faster than any problem solving a parent or teacher can do. If, after you stay out of the fights for several weeks and Brian seems to be escalating the fighting with his sister, then it is time to assume his behavior is aggressive and stop using the ignoring correction. If the older child is so angry at the younger child that he is seeking to hurt her out of a need for revenge, it is time to protect the younger child. It is also time to try to figure out what is causing so much anger in the older child.

In the school setting, teachers do not have the option of treating hitting as a self-indulgent behavior. In the interests of creating a safe school environment for all children, no type of physical fighting can be ignored. All hitting must be treated as either a problem-solving or an aggressive behavior. Bickering between children at school, however, is a self-indulgent behavior and can be dealt with as such.

SECOND PART: GIVING THE EITHER-OR CHOICE

Now the second part of this correction. Every parent and teacher knows it is not always possible to ignore. Sometimes the child will engage in self-indulgent behavior in a way that interferes with your or other people's rights. It is impossible in a classroom with twenty-six other children to let one child make a lot of noise and disrupt the entire classroom atmosphere. If you are a parent at home alone with your child, you can leave the room, go to the bathroom or outside. But you cannot very well leave a classroom of twenty-six children unattended. In the home environment, if the children jump on your furniture, for example, or argue and yell when you are trying to talk on the phone or when you have visitors in the house, or when you and your spouse are trying to watch a favorite television program, they are clearly infringing on your rights. In these situations you need to use the second stage of the Ignoring correction, the Either-Or Choice, because when children infringe on your rights, you can no longer ignore their behavior.

Example A

If Melina, the child in the earlier grocery store situation, escalates her self-indulgent behavior and infringes on your rights or the rights of others by pulling groceries off the shelves or banging the cart into you or other people, one possible either-or choice could be, "You can either stop this behavior or we will have to go home." If Melina continues, say, "I see you choose to go home." If she refuses to go, use the physical assist. Leave your groceries where they are, pick Melina up, carry her out to the car and drive home. Do not lecture and scold her about the inconvenience this has caused you. Do not let her argue you out of it. Let your nonverbal message be that you are in this for the long haul. Be a force of nature with the whole power of the patient ocean behind you. This may be aggravating for you, but it is how she will learn. Try not to take it as a personal insult. Melina is not winning and you are not losing, nor is it the other way around. You are teaching her a new way to behave. Teaching behaviors takes time and patience. Most children like to go to the store. Going home early means Melina has missed the treat you usually buy her. Do not sabotage yourself by mentioning that to her. Children are smart. Melina will know and remember.

Example B

A family goes to a pizza parlor for dinner. Eleven-year-old Sharon complains that she does not like pizza, all they ever do is go to pizza or hamburger places, the other kids get to go for Chinese food, this food is no good, and this is a dumb family. Mom and Dad try to ignore all this but finally come to the conclusion that Sharon is infringing on their rights. After all, they are paying hard-earned money for this meal and they have a right to eat it in peace. Instead of trying to scold or reason with her or persuade her that her accusations are not true (which gives her enormous amounts of attention and is likely to increase her self-indulgent behavior), they can set up a situation in which they are free to ignore her again. If it is a small town and they can see the car from their booth, they can say, "You can stay here and quit complaining or you can go to the car with your pizza and eat out there until you are ready to come back without complaining."

Or, if it's a big city and the car would not be a safe place for her to be, Mom and Dad can say, "You can quit complaining or we will move to a different booth. You can join us when you decide to quit complaining." Then when Sharon continues to complain, Mom and Dad and the rest of the family can pick up and move to a different booth to finish their meal. If Sharon decides to join her family and does not complain any more, they should accept her back into the group *without comment* in a friendly way, as though nothing had happened. After she returns to the group, Sharon immediately needs lots of positive attention from her parents when they notice neutral or positive behaviors. If Sharon starts complaining again, they can point to the other booth and say, "I see you choose to finish your meal alone." After that, assume she has made her choice and do not let her return to your table. After you pay the bill and leave the restaurant, do not mention what happened. Talking about it will sabotage the experience and build a power struggle. Sharon is a competent human being. She does not need to be reminded.

Keep in mind that either-or choices are not intended to be punitive. You are simply setting up a situation in which you are free to ignore the self-indulgent behavior. The fact of the matter is that this time your dinner out will probably not be much fun. You might have to pretend to be having a good time with the other members of the family. Only by convincing Sharon that she cannot control the rest of the family and have all attention focus on her because of her self-indulgent behavior, will you teach her not to act this way. You are involved in a teaching process. Teaching new behaviors takes time. If you can carry out this correction consistently, and remember not to sabotage yourself, Sharon's behavior will change. The day will come when you can have fun when you go out to dinner together. But you must be willing to invest time and energy in the effort to change her self-indulgent behavior.

The main requirement for the either-or choice correction is for the child to go somewhere else so you can continue to ignore the self-indulgent behavior. "You can either choose to (stop the self-indulgent behavior)" or "You can go (be self-indulgent somewhere else)." The goal of the either-or choice correction is not to get the child to obey a command, but rather to set up a situation in which you can again ignore the child's self-indulgent behavior.

Example C

Jana and Paul, brother and sister, somehow got into an argument during a card game that soon escalated to hitting and yelling. Their father was satisfied that earlier he had given them plenty of practice in problem solving, so he decided to give them an either-or choice. "You two can either stop fighting or you can go outside and settle things out there." They ignored him and continued to yell and throw cards at each other. Dad said, "No. I said the argument must be settled outside." He took their arms firmly and walked them through the door and shut it behind them. (Notice the physical assist when the misbehavior switched to not-minding.) Jana yelled through the door at him that it wasn't her fault, that she certainly didn't start the fight. Paul yelled that it was too her fault. Dad ignored the yelling and went back to reading his newspaper. He was prepared to put Jana and Paul back outside if they came in still arguing and complaining. Eventually, things quieted down outside. Soon Jana and Paul came in the door and went back to the card game. Dad said nothing but he gave them some positive attention by giving them a warm smile and friendly eye contact as if to say, "I knew you two could handle it yourselves."

Example D

As a substitute teacher, I was confronted with a boy and a girl in a seventh-grade classroom who were suddenly involved in a wrestling match over a comb, right in the middle of a quiet study period. They pushed and shoved, each of them loudly complaining that the comb belonged to them. I used my best matter-of-fact Mother Nature voice, "You two can either stay here and take your seats, or you can go out in the hall to decide who owns the comb." The boy immediately blushed a fiery red and handed the comb back to the girl. He sat back down in his seat. "I guess it's hers," he said.

Example E

One morning our preschool class got a new student. Jeanette was a beautiful, delicate looking three-year-old. Every morning she broke into the most heart rending wailing when her mother left her to go to work. The mother was guilt-ridden about leaving her daughter. Each morning she apologized to the child, and to the teachers, for having to go to work. The entire staff tried to reassure the mother there was nothing to feel guilty about and that the best approach was to be matter-of-fact and cheerful as she went out the door. The mother tried her best, but each morning we had to practically push this teary-eyed mother out the door, leaving her little girl wailing behind her. Despite our attempts to comfort and reassure her each morning, Jeanette would continue to sob pitifully for thirty to forty minutes. After that she settled in to being a perfectly happy, self-assured child.

After observing all of this and satisfying herself that the little girl enjoyed the extra attention she got from her mother and from the staff rather than really being upset, the head teacher suggested, "Tell Jeanette she can choose to sit in the rocking chair to cry or she can choose to work at the paint easel. If she keeps crying say, 'I see you choose to cry.' Be very friendly, pick her up, sit her in the rocking chair, put a cuddly bear in her arms and say, 'Tell me when you are ready to choose something else to do.' Then go off and pay no more attention to her."

Desperate, we decided to try the new idea. The first day Jeanette cried for her full thirty minutes or so, rocking in the chair, hugging the bear and watching the activities at the nearby water table and paint easels. When she finally stopped crying and left her rocking chair for the water play table, one of the adults immediately smiled at her and said, in a friendly and interested tone of voice, "I see you choose to work at the water table now." No more was said to her about it.

The second day, Jeanette stayed in the rocking chair only a few minutes before she went over to the paint easel. One of the adults said as before, "I see you choose to work at the paint easel now." Again, no more was said about it.

The third day, when Jeanette started to wail as her mother disappeared out the door, a teacher asked, "Do you choose to sit in the rocking chair and cry this morning or do you choose to do something else?" Jeanette opened her mouth to cry, then stopped almost in mid wail and said, "I choose the paint easel." Jeanette never fussed again when she was left at the preschool and her relieved mother was finally able to be cheerful and calm when she waved good-bye.

Notice that no one tried to argue Jeanette out of her feelings. No one tried to interfere with her body functioning by telling her to stop that crying. She was given reasonable either-or choices and allowed to experience the consequences of each choice. Everyone involved— Jeanette, her mother, and the school staff—learned a valuable lesson. Each of us has the power to choose our own behaviors.

Example F

The student who constantly disrupts by talking, teasing, scraping his chair and desk across the floor, and throwing wads of paper at his neighbors is infringing on the rights of other students in the classroom in a way that cannot be ignored. This child is especially difficult to deal with in the elementary classroom in which the teacher has organized the desks in clusters so that the students are seated very close together. Ignoring on the teacher's part often will not help because the attention this child is getting is coming mostly from fellow students who either are tempted to join in the fun, or who scold and blame the misbehaving student. This situation calls for a creative either-or choice. Remember, the choice should be as non-punitive as possible. You only need to set up a situation where the self-indulgent behavior can be ignored. Following are some either-or ideas for this situation that have been used successfully by teachers. The situations given in this section take place in a school setting, but the quiet corner idea works equally well in the home.

Ask the custodian for one or two extra desks. In the farthest corner of the room, set up a "quiet corner." When children disrupt, they have the either-or choice of being quiet where they are or taking their work to finish in the quiet corner. When the work is finished, they may return to their own seats and try again. Quiet corners are not punitive places. The Lewiston, Idaho Head Start class calls their quiet corner "Henry's Chair." Henry is a rascally little critter in the "Little Critter" series by Mercer Mayer. Each year, the children are told the story of Henry, who is a lovable soul, but who keeps getting into trouble. Whenever a child begins to infringe on other people's rights, the teacher says, "You had better use Henry's chair for awhile." Each child is free to come back to the group as soon as he or she feels they can handle it. Children often go sit in the chair without anyone even telling them. "I think I better go sit in Henry's chair for awhile." Another little boy once pulled a chair right next to Henry's chair and sat there. When the teacher asked what he was doing, he said, "I'm keeping Henry company." At Fanno Creek Children's Center in Portland, Oregon they used a rocking chair. Another preschool classroom used bookcases to make a fenced off area with big pillows and books available.

If children continue to disrupt to the extent they cannot be ignored in the quiet corner, they can be given the either-or choice of staying where they are and working quietly, or going to another room and finishing the work there. If you use another room, try to find a place other than the principal's office or the hallway. The principal's office and the hallway are too interesting; too many people coming and going there who will sabotage you by scolding or reminding or by expressing interest in why the child is there. An upper grade classroom makes a good quiet corner backup. The older children need to be forewarned by their teacher that occasionally a younger child will come in to use a quiet corner. They should be asked not to give the younger child any attention, just pretend he or she is not even there. As soon as the child's work is finished, he or she is free to return to the original classroom.

Whenever possible, move the child to a higher grade level. This will avoid the pitfall of making the choice seem punitive. There is no doubt that sending a child to study with the younger kids would be perceived by most children as a demeaning and punitive choice. If the child is already in the highest grade level in the school, look for a neutral zone. A classroom on his own grade level sometimes works, or maybe the health room area would do.

The Robert W. Coleman Elementary School in West Baltimore provides a quiet room they call "the mindful moment room." Children are given instruction in how to use mindfulness meditation so they can use the mindful moment room as a place to calm themselves during times of stress. Andres Gonzalez, one of the organizers of the program, says that children are even bringing the value of meditation home to their parents. One parent reported, "I came home the other day stressed out, and my daughter said, Hey, Mom, you need to sit down. I need to teach you how to breathe."

All adults involved must remember not to sabotage. You want to convey the message that this either-or choice is a part of the natural order of things. This is not a personal, punitive move on your part. It is the way things are. Nothing can be done about it. The whole force of society is behind you. You are the latest in a million-year line of parents and teachers. The minute the child returns to his or her place, give immediate warm eye contact. Act as though nothing has happened. Give recognition for the finished work. Welcome the child back into the group with no mention of the self-indulgent behavior that caused him or her to leave in the first place.

Do not remove children to an isolated spot for longer than it takes to finish their assignment. Immediately give them a chance to come back into the group and try again. Do not isolate them from their classmates for days, weeks, or months at a time. Long-term isolation, which places disruptive children off to one corner of the room all by themselves, tears down their staircase of emotional needs. Isolated children lose their sense of belonging to the group. They no longer believe they are respected and liked by you and their classmates. Over the long term, the behavior of the isolated child will deteriorate, not improve.

When you use the either-or choice for a self-indulgent situation in which the child is infringing on someone else's rights, remember that the basic idea is to set up a situation where the child can choose to *leave your presence*. In this way, you can again ignore the child's behavior. If children are not infringing on anyone else's rights, they are even free to scream and yell. At home, children are free to scream if they go into their bedroom or outside. This is not an infringement on other people's rights (as it would be if children make the same kind of noise at the dinner table) and so you are free to ignore them once more. Let your whole attitude convey the idea that people, of any age, have a perfect right to be angry and frustrated. It is okay with you if they let out their feelings by yelling and screaming. But, on the other hand, you have the right as a parent, teacher, and human being to expect that children will respect your need for quiet during a special television show, or when you are visiting with a friend, or when you are explaining a lesson in the classroom.

Example G

An example of this lack of respect for others' rights is when the child whines, complains, and generally spoils the mealtime for the rest of the family. Like the situation in the restaurant, this kind of behavior is an infringement on other people's rights. You have the right to a peaceful mealtime. Use the either-or command, "You can choose to be quiet or you can leave the table" (go to your room, outside, or whatever). If the child continues to complain, say, "I see you choose to leave the table." If the child refuses to go, use the physical assist. Take the child's arm and walk him or her off to wherever the choice indicated. Concentrate on the idea that you are merely setting up a situation where you can again ignore the behavior. *If the child shouts and yells in his or her room, pretend you cannot hear it.* Remember, this is not a punishment, this is a teaching method. Ignore as many self-indulgent behaviors as you can when the behaviors are merely irritating. Only when the behaviors pass the boundary of interfering with your rights should you step in with the either-or choice.

Example H

A six-year-old boy began swearing at every opportunity in front of his mother and her guests, using advanced swear words that visibly embarrassed and horrified his mother. She tried everything she could think of, including spanking, to get him to stop. The boy's teacher finally referred the mother to the school counselor who, after visiting with the boy and his mother a few times, advised the mother to treat the swearing as a self-indulgent behavior that was infringing on her rights. Mother certainly had the right not to have to listen to language that was upsetting to her. The mother finally agreed to the counselor's plan, even though she found it very difficult.

The next time the boy started swearing, she said to her son, "You know I don't like to listen to swearing language, but if you really think you need to swear, you can choose to go to your bedroom, shut the door, and swear in there all you want. And then you can come back out here when you're through." The boy's face lit up at this exciting new development. He ran to his room, slammed the door and proceeded to swear at the top of his lungs. Mother could still hear every word of course, but she turned on the television and pretended to be totally absorbed in a news program. After a while, her son was silent. He came back out to the living room where his mother looked up, smiled, and said, "Are you as hungry as I am? Let's go fix dinner." Her son tried swearing in front of her one more time. Mother once more carried out the either-or choice without sabotaging herself. After that there were no more swearing incidents.

If children begin to break things in their room after they have chosen by their behavior to go there to be ignored, you can treat this new misbehavior as either routine not-minding or aggressive, depending on how extreme it is. We will talk about these corrections in the next two chapters.

On rare occasions an instance might occur when children get so carried away with self-indulgent behavior that they could be a danger to themselves. For example, if Julie starts flinging herself blindly around on a subway platform, you will have to take her firmly by the hand, or in some way physically restrain her, so she does not accidentally fall onto the tracks. Whenever the child is in physical danger, of course she must be physically protected by any nearby adult.

You probably noticed in the examples given earlier that when the either-or choice was given, not-minding behavior often occurred along with the self-indulgent behavior when the child refused to take either choice. As in the examples above, you may have to physically assist the child to leave the table, or use the broken record until he or she leaves the room. This is often the case, so be alert. *Switch from the ignore correction to the not-minding correction when the child disobeys.*

As with all corrections, try to carry out this one as though you were the patient wind, a moss-covered rock, or any other force of nature. Try not to get emotionally involved in the child's self-indulgence. Try to take the attitude of the young mother who had just told her three-year-old boy it was time to go home. He wanted to stay at Grandma's house a little longer, but Mother said, "No. We have to go now." He shouted at her, "I hate you!" His mother looked down at him calmly and said, "Well. I guess I can live with that," and she continued to walk towards the door. He followed along behind her pouting and scolding that she ignored. Both Mother and Grandma continued to cheerfully visit with one another as they walked down the front steps. By the time they reached the car, the boy was smiling and waving good-bye at his grandmother. I have never forgotten that mother's words, and her quiet shrug, "Well. I guess I can live with that." Yes, we *can* live with that because the truth is that our children will not hate us if we expect reasonable rules to be obeyed. On the contrary, they will love us all the more because we gave them the security of firm and reasonable guidelines.

Exercise

As in previous weeks, continue to use the "Negative Behaviors" worksheet on the next page to write briefly about the four misbehaviors and the three problem-solving behaviors as you observe them. If you attempt to carry out any of the corrections, write about these, too. Also continue to watch for those self-sabotages.

WORKSHEET

NEGATIVE BEHAVIORS
The Four Misbehaviors and Three Problem-Solving Situations

NOT-MINDING (Not Doing What Is Asked)

SELF-INDULGENT (Attention-Getting)

ROUTINE NOT-MINDING (Will Not Do Routine Tasks)

AGGRESSIVE (Deliberately Hurting)

NEGATIVE BEHAVIORS Requiring Problem-Solving That Does Not Fit Above:
1. Adjust Environment   2. Solve Conflicts   3. Listen to Feelings

---

from *Caring Discipline: Practical Tools for Nurturing Happy Families & Classrooms*

WORKSHEET

EXERCISE

When to Ignore and When to Use the Either-Or Choice

IGNORE Examples of self-indulgent behaviors that strongly irritate you:	EITHER-OR CHOICE Examples of self-indulgent behaviors that not only irritate you, but are infringing on your or someone else's rights:

from *Caring Discipline: Practical Tools for Nurturing Happy Families & Classrooms*

REVIEW: Correction for Self-Indulgent Behavior

Remember, you may not need to use these corrections if you are paying attention to the child at neutral times on a regular basis.

1. **Ignore** if the behavior is merely irritating. Remember to ignore both verbally and nonverbally,   — or —

2. If the behavior is infringing on your rights, give the **either-or choice**:

   "You can either choose to … " *(stop the self-indulgent behavior)*
   — or —
   "You can go … " *(be self-indulgent somewhere else).*

3. You may have to use the **broken record** or **physical assist** if the child switches to a not-minding behavior. Remember to keep ignoring the child's self-indulgent behavior as you carry out the broken record or physical assist correction.

4. As soon as the child makes the choice to stop the self-indulgent behavior, be pleasant and cheerful with him. Do not mention it again.

REMEMBER NOT TO SELF-SABOTAGE

DO NOT: Procrastinate
Forget to give attention at neutral and positive times
Talk about misbehavior
Give negative scripting

DO: Be aware of your own hidden unmet needs

---

from Caring Discipline: Practical Tools for Nurturing Happy Families & Classrooms

Chapter 8 Discussion: IGNORING AND THE EITHER-OR CHOICE

1. Share the past week's "Negative Behaviors" worksheet. Which of these behaviors bothers you the most when you see it in your children?

2. Did you sabotage yourself in any way this week?

3. Did anyone try the physical assist or broken record correction this week? Were you able to carry it through without sabotaging yourself? How did it feel to be in this Mother Nature, nothing-can-be-done-about-it role? If any person has a hard time being this firm with a child, listen to him or her talk about why being firm is difficult to do. Go easy on giving your opinions or advice. The rest of the group can help best by just listening so that the other person can "think out loud" about it.

4. Each individual take five minutes to fill out the "Exercise" worksheet on the previous page. Share your lists with one another. Do you have similar tolerance levels for self-indulgent behaviors, or are you quite far apart as to the irritating behaviors you can endure without resorting to the either-or choice?

5. Check back with the guidelines given at the beginning of the book for conducting these weekly discussion groups. Is your group having difficulty with any of the guidelines?

CHAPTER NINE
The Correction for Routine Not-Minding Behavior
Making Choices and Living With the Consequences

Children who avoid or refuse to do the daily chores of their lives are engaging in routine not-minding behavior. Not finishing school work, not cleaning their room, continually leaving the bicycle out in the rain, leaving their snack mess in the kitchen, not following basic playground rules, not being responsible for feeding the pet, not taking out the garbage, "sneaky" behaviors like getting into off-limit items and stealing are common examples. The child knows the behaviors that are expected, knows certain behaviors are to be done on a regular basis, knows he or she will encounter strong negative attention from adults if the jobs do not get done, yet does not follow the rules or do the tasks until pushed. This kind of misbehavior causes parents and teachers to shake their heads and wonder, "Why on earth is that kid so irresponsible?"

By not doing the ordinary tasks of life, the child gets incredible amounts of negative attention from caring adults. The child's routine not-minding behaviors make him or her the focus of vast numbers of social interactions, both verbal and nonverbal. The adults try to gain control of the situation by reminding, scolding, reasoning, threatening, and punishing. The child tries to gain control of the situation by not doing what the adults want done. In order to keep his or her sense of independence and integrity intact, the child refuses to be "bossed around." The adults, in turn, give the child a constant barrage of negative attention.

Children caught in this dilemma believe that if they finally give in and do what the adults want, they will lose their inner integrity and independence. These children begin to feel justified about their irresponsible behavior. Some children even come to believe everything is the fault of the adults and blame them for all problems. These children convince themselves that if adults would just leave them alone, things would turn out okay. The irresponsible child is like a glacier adults have to push through life. The adults are exhausted and angered by their efforts. The child is sullen, uncooperative, and angry at the adults. It is a downward spiral from which the child cannot extricate herself without help from you.

We have already talked about offering a choice as part of giving a command, and giving an either-or choice as part of the correction for self-indulgent behavior. For the logical consequence correction, however, choices become not just a part of the correction, but its central core.

Natural Versus Logical Consequences

In learning how to use the logical consequence correction, it is important to understand the difference between "natural" and "logical" consequences. When the natural consequence occurs, life itself provides the consequence without anyone having to plan it ahead of time. For example, if a child goes out without a coat and it starts to rain, the child will get wet. If teenagers drink and drive, they are likely to have an accident, or will perhaps get arrested and lose their license. If a child does not do schoolwork, the natural outcome will be failing grades. If teenagers are sexually active without taking proper precautions, they are apt to become teenage parents or contract a sexually transmitted disease. If children eat too much candy, they are likely to get a stomach ache. If you stay up to watch the late movie on television, you will be tired when you get up next morning to go to work.

These natural consequences are the basic experiences of life from which all thinking creatures have for millions of years learned how to grow up strong and competent. Natural consequences teach us how to survive in our world. In all these natural situations, no one has to plan a real life experience for the person involved. The natural consequence follows from choices the person makes. Natural consequences arise naturally, from either the laws of nature itself, or from the culture in which the person lives. The major problem with natural consequences is that they are often delayed until the consequences are extremely severe and, sometimes, even life threatening. A consequence is natural, but too severe, for example, if children are allowed to fail at schoolwork until they fall so far behind they have to repeat a grade. No parent or teacher wants a child to be dealt with in as harsh a way as the natural consequence may eventually provide.

Logical consequences, on the other hand, are real life situations that an adult plans for the child ahead of time. The situation needs to be as natural as possible, yet with consequences that are not really harmful or life threatening to the child. Even though the logical consequence should cause discomfort to the child, it is not as severe as a natural consequence might be. *The logical consequence is also different from a natural consequence in that it always provides a way out for the child. At any time, the child can improve the situation by making a different choice.*

Logical consequences need to be perceived by the child as reasonable and fair, as part of the natural order of things. The inherent logic of the situation, the life experiences themselves, will do the teaching. If you sabotage yourself, especially by talking about the misbehavior, the consequence will most likely be perceived by the child as punishment or personal revenge on your part. Any such perception will fuel a power struggle between you and the child. If you or any adult helping you sabotages in this way, the logical consequence correction will not work.

Remember, you have all the parents and teachers who have ever lived on this earth behind you. You are the growing tip of a branching tree of humanity whose roots reach down a million years. Your task, like our ancestors, is to teach children about the outer reality of the world and still keep their spirits strong and independent. You have the authority of society and generations of elders behind you. There is no need to sabotage your authority by scolding, lecturing, and otherwise venting your emotions at the child.

Giving Children Choices

The basic prevention plan: Give children daily opportunities to make, and to live with, their choices. The basic idea is to set up a situation that gives the child an opportunity to experience the consequences of his or her choices.

Practice in making choices and living with the consequence of choices is the foundation of developing responsible behavior patterns. Once children learn what "yes" and "no" mean, what "this one" and "that one" mean, they have begun the process of decision making. Teaching children responsible decision making is a long-term effort. Choice by choice, consequence by consequence, like water dripping on a stone, or building a self-esteem staircase brick by brick, children learn to take responsibility for their own behaviors. In the process, children are empowered and strengthened from the real life experience of living with the consequences of their choices.

1. Give your child practice in making fun choices

Encouraging children to make their own choices will be hard for some A-adults because they often automatically assume adults should make most decisions for children. But even a two-year-old can choose between, "Do you choose orange juice or apple juice for lunch?" or "Which of these two books do you choose for me to read to you?" One mother said she always allowed her preschoolers to choose which of two outfits to wear for the day. It helped speed up the dressing process each morning. As they got older, they chose clothes all by themselves. "They didn't always match, but they were so proud." As children grow older, you should increasingly provide more and more areas of their lives in which they can make choices. Remember that every choice a child makes and lives with is another brick installed on his or her competency/respect stairstep.

2. Never give a choice if there is no choice

Sometimes it is not possible to give children a choice. If that is the case, do not confuse them by giving them a choice when there really is no choice. "Do you want to go home now?" or "Let's go home now, okay?" Okay? implies that you are giving a choice between staying where you are or going home. Use the word "choose" instead of "want" or "okay?" It will help you keep the difference between choosing and wanting clear in your own mind as well as teaching children that they are actively "choosing" instead of passively "wanting."

A grandmother was changing her two-year-old grandson Nate's diapers. It was time for his nap. Grandma was chatting with a friend while she changed his diapers and casually said, "It's time for his nap now." Nate heard this matter-of-fact description of the situation and he continued to smile up at his grandmother. Then Grandma said to him, "Let's go to bed for a nap now. *Okay? Okay?*" Nate immediately stiffened his body and started to scream. You can see that when she acted as though the nap was inevitable, Nate accepted it, but when she gave him a choice (okay?), he chose not to go down for a nap.

If there is no choice, simply describe the facts of the matter. "Now it is time to go home." The sun goes up and the sun goes down. Nothing can be done about it. In the same way, "Now it is time to go home." If an adult initially offers, "Want to go to bed now?" and the child says, "No," the adult is left in the uncomfortable position of having to switch tactics, either cajoling or forcing the child into going to bed. If the adult insists on bedtime as a personal and emotional issue, "I said you are going to bed right now!" it invites rebellion and a power struggle. If instead, from the very beginning, the adult uses the inexorable, unemotional needs of nature and society as the reason for going to bed, "Now it is time to go to bed," the personal power struggle can often be avoided. No one, not even mother and dad, or teacher, can go against the natural order of things.

3. Keep the choices limited and appropriate to the child's age

"Do you choose chicken noodle or tomato soup today?" is enough choice for a three-year-old. "What do you want for lunch?" is not an appropriate choice. It is hard enough for adults to decide what they want for lunch. A three-year-old will not be able to choose among so many possibilities and will probably end up changing his or her mind. At that age, the child who is given too many choices will likely end up frustrated and crying at whatever you finally do serve for lunch. As a child grows older, you can expand the concept of choices, for example, it would be appropriate for a ten year old to help decide *when* the weekly chores should be done, or to help choose *which* of three different vacation options the family could take that year.

4. Once the child makes the choice, let the child live with the consequences

Some preschoolers will, at first, get a bit drunk on their new decision-making powers and continually change their minds. They are just testing to see how far their power goes. For example, when you give the choice between apple and orange juice, the three-year-old may choose orange juice and then abruptly push away the orange juice and say, "No. I want apple juice." It is important for you to treat this refusal as a self-indulgent behavior. Say only one time, "No. You chose orange juice," and then pay no more attention to the demands for apple juice. If the child tantrums at this point, for example, if he or she throws the orange juice on the floor, assume the choice has been made for no juice at all. Remember not to sabotage yourself by scolding as you clean up the mess. (Or, as many an A-parent has told a C-parent, you can give the child a rag to clean up the spill himself.)

C-adults are often tempted to leap in and rescue the child from the logical consequences of the situation. They think, "Well, this child is only three years old, and, after all, I am an adult who shouldn't act as petty as a little kid." It is not petty to teach children they must live by their choices. If you allow children the opportunity to experience the consequences of their small choices, you will be saving them from suffering the serious and long lasting consequences they are capable of precipitating in their teen years. If you insist that children experience the short-term consequences of their behaviors now, they will gain the experience needed to avoid long-term and calamitous natural consequences in later life.

C-adults are also prone to let the child have "one more chance," especially if the child is properly contrite and promises, "I won't do it any more." Allowing children to evade consequences because they are cute or because they say "I'm sorry" in a sincere tone of voice only teaches them that if they learn to be charming enough they can always do pretty much as they please. This is a sure-fire formula for raising irresponsible adults. *Allowing children to do whatever they want, as long as they apologize sweetly afterwards, teaches them to cultivate charm instead of responsible behavior.* A charming but irresponsible adult has not learned basic survival skills for living cooperatively within the human family. We have all met adults like this. No one likes living with them, because they go through life expecting others to suffer the consequences of their own poor choices.

Example A

Sometimes, unknown to you, children will make an unwise choice and then at the last minute expect you to save them. Your fourteen-year-old daughter, Elsa, may come to you at dinner time and plead, "I need to go to the library tonight to do a report for English class. It's due first thing in the morning. Will you take me to the library tonight? Please!?" Of course it is okay to help your daughter if it is no problem for you and you want to go to the library anyhow, but, if your daughter has made a habit of this kind of thing and if you have a prior engagement, or if, in any way, taking her to the library means you will wind up feeling resentful, it is better to say no. It is fine to show sympathy for her plight, just as you would do with any other friend, but do not place yourself in the position of suffering the consequences of her shortsighted choices. You can say, "Gosh, I'm sorry, but I have choir practice tonight" (if that is the case) or "I am just too tired tonight. I'd planned to clean up this kitchen and then go straight to bed." If your daughter chose to watch television or go visit her friends earlier in the week rather than do her schoolwork, she needs to experience the consequences of her choices. If she continues to wail and plead, treat it as a self-indulgent behavior and ignore it.

The only exception to allowing children to live with the consequence of their own behavior is if their choices have produced a natural consequence situation that is in some way life threatening or has the potential for damaging their future. If the natural consequences of the choice are especially severe and long lasting, of course you should not say, "Well, I feel really badly about it but you made your own bed and now you will have to lie in it." An example of this is if Elsa got pregnant. If that happens, like any loving parent you need to step in and move heaven and earth to help Elsa do what needs to be done. We all make mistakes. If children make a really big one, they deserve all the help they can get from caring adults.

Perhaps the hardest part of letting a child live with his or her choices is remembering not to scold, lecture, remind, or in any way let the tone of your voice say, "I told you so." It is absolutely crucial for the success of teaching children to "own" the consequences of their choices that they perceive the logical consequence as a fact of life, as a part of the natural order of things. If they see the consequence as a punishment that you are personally dishing out to get even with them, it will set up a destructive power struggle between the children and you. If you want children to become independent, responsible persons, you need to learn to sidestep the power struggle and, as someone put it, "Take your sails out of their wind." Hence the advice, at the risk of boring you, is repeated: *Do not mention it again.*

Setting Up a Logical Consequence for the Child

Choices and consequences form a basic prevention plan for keeping a child from ever developing irresponsible behaviors in the first place. But what if the child has already established a specific routine not-minding behavior? If the basic prevention plan is not enough to change an old behavior pattern, here are some guidelines showing you how to use logical consequences as a correction.

1. Decide which routine not-minding behavior you want to

change

You cannot change everything at once. Choose the one routine not-minding misbehavior that troubles you the most. It may be that the child is never ready for school on time, or perhaps never finishes schoolwork on time even though the school has done testing and found him or her to be capable of doing the work, or maybe the child will not give the dog food and water on a regular basis. Focus on only one routine not-minding behavior at a time.

2. Choose the situation you want to change. Enlist another adult, if possible, and make a plan

Planning a logical consequence requires flexibility, creativity, and, sometimes, a sense of humor. The possibilities for designing logical consequence plans are endless and depend somewhat on your own personality, the child's personality, and whatever seems comfortable to you. It is important to brainstorm ahead of time with your spouse, another teacher, or a friend to decide on what your specific plan will be. If you are not sure what you are going to do ahead of time, the consequence may turn out to be more punishing than logical. Sometimes, of course, the consequence may occur to you on the spur of the moment and you will not be able to resist "just doing it."

Example A

One mother expected her son to do a few morning chores before he left for school, among which was to set the table for breakfast. One morning he sat down as usual, not having set the table, and started reading a book. His mother took the pancakes off the griddle, saw there were no plates on the table, and on impulse, without saying a word to him she flipped the pancakes onto the bare table. Then she went back to the stove and started the next batch of pancakes at the same time as she continued to talk to her husband about something else. The boy sat staring at the pancakes for a second, then got up, and went to the cupboard for the plates. Next day, he put dishes on the table without being asked. His mother resisted the temptation to laugh although she said it was all she could do to keep a straight face. This kind of spur-of-the moment consequence is fine, especially if you are the kind of person who feels comfortable just winging it, but most situations require some preplanning.

Example B

Preplanning would certainly have helped the father who one morning impulsively decided to give his six-year-old daughter a logical consequence. His daughter, Jayla, constantly avoided getting ready on time for the school bus. This particular morning, the father, who remembered to give Jayla ten minutes lead time, finally said cheerfully, "Time to go," as he picked up his daughter and her lunch sack, and carried her out to the bus stop where he deposited her, kicking and screaming, on the school bus. Jayla arrived at school, by this time nearly sick from sobbing, still in her pajamas, and greatly embarrassed. Jayla's indignant teacher told the principal, and the principal called Children's Services to report child neglect. The father spent a lot of time explaining the situation to some very suspicious school and child protective services personnel. If the father had only involved the child's teacher or bus driver with his plan ahead of time, someone would have realized the father needed to also send along Jayla's school clothes so that at any time she chose, she could improve her situation.

Example C

There are times when it is not just helpful, but absolutely necessary, to have the support of another person. Take, for example, the case of three-year-old Mimi, who had a tantrum nearly every time her father took her to the grocery store. The father finally asked a friend to help out. The next time he took his daughter to the grocery store and when she began her tantrum, he left his groceries in the aisle, picked Mimi up, carried her to the pay phone and called his friend, who was waiting by the telephone at her nearby home. "Will you come get Mimi? She doesn't know how to act here at the store." The friend promptly came to get the child and matter-of-factly took her home, being careful not to give her too much attention. The father finished his shopping. When the father got home, he pretended he had forgotten all about the incident, but he brought no treat home for his daughter. (She usually got a treat when she went to the store with her father.) Both the father and his friend were careful not to self-sabotage by laughing or talking about it in front of Mimi. *All logical consequences must be carried out as though they are nothing special, as though they are natural events like eating and sleeping,* and certainly not a cause for humor. If the father and his friend continue to be successful in not sabotaging themselves, Mimi will learn that if she wants to go shopping, she must change her behavior.

Even though you may have spent considerable time and effort planning a logical consequence, it is okay if the consequence comes as a surprise to the child. After all, life's natural consequences usually come as a surprise.

Example D

An example of a logical consequence that was totally unexpected by their children was told by a couple whose children used abominable table manners nearly every evening. Dinner time was a miserable experience. The parents were constantly reminding, scolding, and punishing. One evening they decided on a bold surprise consequence. They said nothing to their kids about their plan; everyone sat down at the table and things went from bad to worse. As usual, the kids yelled at each other, chewed loudly with their mouths open, reached across the person next to them, and spilled food. Finally, Dad stood up and said, "I don't like to eat at the table with you kids when you act like this. It makes me lose my appetite. I'm going to take my food and eat in the bedroom. Want to come with me?" he asked his wife. "I sure do!" she said, and off they went, taking their food with them. There was a stunned silence at the table. The parents finished their meal on a card table in the bedroom where they carried on a lively conversation about what had happened that day at work. The kids silently finished their meal in the dining room. After that, table manners were noticeably improved. The parents remembered not to sabotage themselves by talking and laughing about it in front of their children, although they had a wonderful time relating the incident to their parenting class.

You can see there are elements of the either-or choice correction in the above examples. It is true that the parents in both situations could have given their children a firm either-or choice ("Either you stop fussing or you can go home" and "Either you stop that behavior or we are going to eat in the bedroom"), but it would then not have had the element of surprise and naturalness that these had. Parents and teachers are often delighted and amazed when they find out how much fun these consequences can be. Parents often start laughing when they talk about the logical consequence plans they have been trying at home. And all this hilarity from parents who were in tears a week or so earlier! The laughter comes from the relief we feel when we discover that discipline doesn't have to be so grim. Logical consequences take much of the burden off dedicated adults, because they are so much simpler and so much easier than the old way of pushing the child ahead of you through life.

3. Ensure that the child, not the adult, will feel uncomfortable

If children can begin to experience discomfort because of a choice they made, their misbehavior will have been magically moved from a misbehavior that gave the adult a problem to a situation in which the child is having a problem. If you will look at the *"Caring Discipline Overview"* chart on page 322, you can see that the negative behavior listed in the misbehavior box as "Routine not-minding" can, with the help of a planned logical consequence situation, be shifted down to the box entitled "Child Has a Problem." Once the negative behavior becomes the child's problem, he or she may sometimes need help from you in sorting out his or her feelings about the matter, but mostly the child will have to deal with the problem by making some different choices. In other words, if you have set up a true logical consequence situation, the child, not you, should be the one feeling unhappy about the situation. It is now the child who has the problem, not the adult. It is the child who will have to start thinking about how to make some different choices so the situation can improve.

In the case of the mother who flipped the pancakes on the table, she no longer had the problem. Her son did. Or, in the case of the parents who went to their bedroom to eat, the children left to eat alone at the dining room table had the problem. The parents were having a good time in the bedroom. Remember the child who had a tantrum in the grocery store? Her father shifted the problem to her when he sent her home with his friend. Think back to the example of the girl who expected her mother to drop everything at a moment's notice to take her to the library; her mother gave the problem back to her daughter by saying, "Gosh, I just can't do that tonight."

Example E

Here is a logical consequence plan told by a school bus driver who has learned to turn the problem of noisy, out of their seat kids over to the kids themselves. Early in the fall, the first time the noise gets to the discomfort level for him, he pulls off the road and just sits there. He does not say anything to the kids. He pulls out a magazine and pretends to read it. Eventually someone asks when they are going to leave. He says, "It isn't safe to drive with all this commotion. I'm not going until things settle down." Before long, the bus grapevine has passed the word along and things begin to quiet down. Nobody wants to just sit in a school bus. When things are quiet again, the bus driver pulls back into traffic. He never mentions it again and he continues to be pleasant to the kids. He has to do this only a couple of times a year. He has one of the quietest bus loads of kids in the school district. Parents have also successfully tried this tactic with their children. One father and mother parked the car and went to sit on a grassy knoll to read their books while they waited for the kids to quiet down.

Example F

Here is a different logical consequence in which a mother turned what had been her problem over to her two teenage sons, ages thirteen and fifteen. Several times a week Deborah took Barry and Brian in her car to various sporting and school events, returning to pick them up when the event was over. Lately, they were becoming more and more rowdy in the car, telling dirty jokes in off-stage whispers amid uproarious laughter, swearing, and leaning out the window to yell insults at passersby. Deborah asked them many times to stop, telling them it was embarrassing to her. They ignored her and continued the behavior. After talking to a friend about it, she came up with a logical consequence plan.

The next Saturday afternoon, as she was taking them to a school event, Barry and Brian began to sing an off-color song at the top of their lungs. Finally, they rolled down the window at an intersection where their mother had to pause for a red light, and stuck their heads out the window in order to serenade numerous pedestrians with the bawdy lyrics.

"Okay," Deborah thought to herself. "This is it." Without saying anything to her sons, she drove to the nearest park-and-ride bus terminal. (She had scouted out the closest terminal the day before.) She pulled into a parking spot in the park-and-ride lot and said, "You boys will have to get out and take the bus. I don't want to drive you anymore when you behave like this. Here's some money for your fare."

Barry and Brian just laughed. "Hah! You can't make us. Don't be such a prude, Mom!"

Deborah did not respond except to get money for their bus fare out of her purse and put it on the dashboard. Then she got out of the car taking the keys with her. She walked over to sit on a bench at the bus pick up. Barry and Brian sat in the car, confident they could outwait her. To their surprise, ten minutes later their mother boarded a bus and went home.

Several hours later, a subdued Brian and Barry showed up at home. Deborah had to ask a friend to drive her to the bus terminal to pick up her car later that evening. The relationship between mother and sons improved after that experience. Although Deborah was prepared to do it again if need be, her sons never gave her the opportunity. She never mentioned it again and neither did they.

4. The consequence should follow logically and naturally from the misbehavior

Every logical consequence situation should give the child the gift of experiencing what it is like to live in the real world. Consequences that do not follow logically from the social or natural order of the situation will be perceived as punishment and invite a power struggle.

A mother, when she first began learning to give the logical consequence correction, told this story. Her nine-year-old daughter, Maggie, was invariably late getting up, late getting dressed, and often late for the bus. The mother always took her daughter to school after scolding and lecturing her on the trouble this was causing. On Halloween the mother came up with a consequence. Halloween morning she told her daughter, "If you miss the bus today, there will be no trick or treating for you tonight." At our meeting the next day, the mother told us, "Maggie got up yesterday and made it to school on time, but today I couldn't get her out of bed again." There was a round of sympathetic laughter and one parent asked, "Yes, what are you going to do for the other 364 days of the year?"

Whether or not a child is allowed to go trick or treating one night out of the year has nothing to do with being on time at the bus stop every school day. The consequence of not being allowed to trick or treat because the child missed the bus had nothing to do with the natural or logical order of things. On the other hand, here are three examples of logical consequences, all having to do with getting to school on time, which arise naturally and logically out of the situation.

Example G

One mother said it was like fighting a war to get her first-grader ready for school. This mother was under tremendous pressure to get to work on time. She had been warned about being late twice by her boss, but the more she pushed and urged her son to get dressed and out to the bus stop, the slower he went. She formulated a plan with a neighbor who was always up and at home each morning. After the plan was ready, the mother told her son, "From now on my boss says I have to leave for my job at 7:30 a.m. I will set the timer so you know that it is almost time to go." (She set the timer to give him a ten-minute lead time.)

Next morning when the timer rang, her son continued to play with his trucks. Ten minutes later she said, "Gosh, time for me to go." Trying to be cheerful and matter-of-fact, she picked up her son, who was still in his pajamas, gathered up his lunch and school clothes and deposited them all on the front porch, locking the door behind her. (Notice the use of the physical assist.) "Mrs. Riley said you could finish getting dressed at her house if you want to." Hoping she was still being cheerful and mat-ter-of-fact, Mother drove off waving to her son as she went. The neighbor watched out her kitchen window as the boy frantically gathered up his clothes, hid behind a bush while he changed, and scurried off to the bus stop. From that day on, he got dressed on time without any nagging from Mother. The neighbor and Mother both remembered not to self-sabotage by telling the story in front of the boy or to anyone else who might repeat the story or laugh about it within his hearing.

Example H

Another mother, who did not work outside the home, continually nagged her daughter, Crystal, to get ready in time to catch the school bus. But in spite of scoldings and an occasional spanking, she usually ended up taking her daughter to school in the car. Mother finally devised a plan and asked for the teacher's help in carrying it out. She asked the teacher not to pay much attention to Crystal if she was late to class. She did not ask the teacher to be punitive, just to be busy, too busy to have much time to orient the girl to what had happened during the first part of the morning. This mother was determined to try to withdraw emotionally from feeling more responsible than Crystal was over whether or not she was late for school. Knowing that the teacher approved of the plan helped set her mind at ease.

The next time Crystal missed the bus, Mother said in a friendly voice, "Oh, gosh, did you miss the bus? That's too bad. Well, I can't take you right now, but as soon as I finish doing my morning chores, I am going to the grocery store and I could drop you on my way." Notice that Mother was sympathetic about her daughter's problem. It is perfectly all right to be sympathetic with children when they have gotten themselves into an uncomfortable situation. In this way, you let them know that you care about them, but it is still *their* choice and *their* problem. In spite of Crystal's crying and carrying on about being late, Mother took her time about getting her chores done. The girl arrived an hour and a half late to find the class already involved in a project, with a teacher too busy to give her any personal attention. Neither teacher nor parent ever mentioned it to her again. When the mother told this story, she laughed and said, "It worked and it was so easy!"

Example I

In this example, a mother was afraid to let her daughter, Mysha, go to the bus stop alone because there had been a report in the neighborhood of a man stopping along the road and trying to entice small children into his car. As in all the other examples, Mysha did not get ready in time without continual reminding and scolding from her mother. The two of them always made it to the bus stop in time but not until Mother was exhausted and angry. The plan she formulated for this situation was for her to say, "I will be ready to go to the bus stop in five minutes." Then in five minutes, Mother was to put on her coat, say cheerfully, "see you at the bus stop," and leave the house. The first time Mother put this plan into operation, Mysha was out of the house just a few minutes behind her and from then on was ready when her mother was. Mother was a very talkative woman, but she managed not to sabotage herself by mentioning it to Mysha, and the problem evaporated.

Each of the examples given above not only takes the problem away from the adult and gives it to the child, but each situation also arises naturally and logically from individual circumstances. Each example also involves the element of the unexpected and contains, at least from the adult point of view, a touch of humor. Discipline does not have to be grimly serious. It can be creative, even fun. But never forget you must *not laugh or talk about the situation in front of children so that they will overhear you telling someone else what happened. Also, do not repeat the story to anyone who will repeat it back to the children.* Assume the role of a force of nature that does what needs to be done and then forgets; otherwise children will feel their integrity threatened and you will have begun a needless and painful power struggle.

None of the children in the situations above had a self-indulgent tantrum in response to these logical consequences. If you are concerned that your child would "go to pieces" if you tried anything this unexpected, continue to concentrate first on changing his or her self-indulgent behaviors before you move on to correcting the routine not-minding behaviors. Unless there are some very unusual background circumstances, like a recent death, divorce, or other severe loss in the family, "going to pieces" is almost always just another self-indulgent behavior. If you are convinced that going to pieces is not a self-indulgent behavior, but a serious terror response, you need to take your child for private counseling.

5. Be cautious about taking away a privilege

Losing a privilege, like not being able to leave the yard, or forfeiting an allowance, or not being allowed to go out for recess, is often used as a consequence for routine not-minding behaviors. The consequence of losing a privilege has the advantage of being easy to think up, but it often becomes exceedingly difficult for the adult to enforce. It also often violates the principle of taking the problem from the adult and giving it to the child. For example, if a teacher tells two children who have had a fight that they may not play together all week during recess, then all week long the teacher must take on the duty of prison guard to see that the children do not play together. This is a lot of work for the teacher and not much of a problem for the kids. Even worse, the teacher can give the job of prison guard to whoever happens to be on recess duty, thus shifting the problem to another adult and leaving the kids free to play a game with the unfortunate person on recess duty called, "Are they playing together or aren't they?"

If, on the other hand, you are convinced that losing a privilege makes sense because it arises directly from the misbehavior, set it up so that *you* act instead of having to force the child to act. You want the consequence to be uncomfortable for the child, not for you. For example, if the child has misbehaved the last time you took him to the grocery store, you can say, "I won't take you to the store with me next time I go." Not taking the child to the store with you next time you go is within your power and easy for you to carry out. But if, instead, you say, "You can't go to the store until next Saturday," you will cause yourself a lot of aggravation always checking to see that your child has not sneaked out to the corner store. You will have given yourself the extra job of being a prison guard.

In the same way, it would not make sense for a parent to tell a sixteen year old who already has a driver's license, "You may not drive next weekend," because the teenager may have friends with cars who will let him drive when the parent is not around to see. However, the parent can say, "I will not loan you my car next weekend."

Any consequence you can think up will be most effective if the adult concentrates on what the adult can do without becoming a prison guard and forcing the child to do something. The idea is *not to force* the child to behave. The idea is to set up a situation that makes the child uncomfortable enough *to see the sense of behaving in a different way.* "I will not loan you my car" and "I will not take you to the store" lose the child privileges that are logical and are relatively easy for the adult to carry out.

Example J

A grandfather tells this story of an effective loss-of-privilege consequence that his mother gave him when he was a child (notice that the loss-of-privilege consequence is a logical outcome of the situation). When he was seven years old, his mother told him that she was not his servant and if he treated her like a servant by leaving his clothes lying around the house, he would have to pay her one penny for each item of clothing she put away. His allowance was five cents a week. His mother was not a verbal person, and he does not remember ever being reminded or scolded about it. That first week he left three items of clothing on the floor and paid her three cents, but he never had to pay her again. That was sixty-five years ago. And his wife says he still hangs up his clothes.

6. Loss of privileges should be short-term

Losing one turn or one recess, one hour or one day, is enough time for the loss of a privilege related to a logical consequence. The teenager can handle two or three days, or one weekend. If you go past this point you will find it hard to carry through, and not carrying through on a logical consequence only convinces the child that "Dad never means anything he says."

The longer you have to enforce the consequence, the harder it will be to keep from getting upset and sabotaging yourself by talking in some way about the misbehavior. It is impossible to let the incident be in the past when you are in the position of continually having to enforce the consequence. When you sabotage yourself by talking about the misbehavior, a power struggle begins, or, if a power struggle is already present, it will intensify.

A mother at first resisted the idea that grounding her fifteen-year-old son to the house for two days would be more effective than the two weeks grounding she usually gave him. Her son, Charlie, was continually coming in past his curfew time. He would no sooner finish having to stay home for two weeks than he would go right out and come in late again. The power struggle between Charlie and his mother was intense. He constantly argued with her and bombarded her with sullen looks.

Since, in her mind, things could not get much worse anyway, Mother finally decided to try a shorter consequence time. The next time Charlie's two-week consequence was over, Mother told him that from now on when he stayed out past his curfew time he could not go out again for two days. His only response was to raise his eyebrows. (Besides shortening the time of the consequence, she also tried to stop reminding her son about what would happen if he stayed out late. Not sabotaging herself by talking about it was now easier for her to do because she knew she only had to enforce the consequence for two days.) The next weekend she heard her son talking to a friend on the phone, "If we can't get back by eight o'clock, I'd better not go. It wouldn't be worth having to stay home two nights just for that." At her next parenting class meeting the astonished mother asked, "What happened?" What happened was that the power struggle disappeared, at least in this area of their lives, when the son was presented with what he perceived as a more reasonable consequence, and when the mother was able to stop sabotaging herself by not reminding and arguing with her son about it.

Another problem with using long-term consequences is that long-term consequences prevent a child from immediately trying out and learning new behaviors. A common example of this is the parent who insists that once children decide to participate in some organized activity they must continue all year. Many eight-year-olds are in Little League, soccer, Cub Scouts, church choir, take piano lessons, and are also expected to do homework each evening. One third-grader in particular was an exceedingly responsible child, but showed every sign of an adult type of depression. He rarely smiled, life seemed to hold no joy. This child did not have one single week night with even a fifteen minute unorganized time to just sit or play. When his teacher shared his concerns with the mother that her son be allowed to drop a few of his activities, she protested, "But he wanted to do all those things. He is the one who decided to take these things. And we have always taught him that once he starts something he has to finish it."

Waiting for the end of the school year is too long for an eight-year-old boy. Luckily, this mother sat down and really listened to her son. When she realized the burden he was carrying, she did him the kindness of adjusting his environment by changing her expectations of him. She told him, "I think you just bit off more than you can chew this year. It is okay with me if you drop one activity now, and then in a couple of weeks, if you are still feeling bogged down, you go ahead and drop another one." The boy chose to drop Cub Scouts, and this alone seemed to be enough. He soon stopped looking so depressed and started smiling again. He felt in control of his life once more. He was no longer trapped for the next six months; he had some choices.

It is certainly fair to insist that your child go to Cub Scouts, for example, for six to eight weeks before quitting. He needs time to find out what it is really like. But more than that is too much. Wait to buy a lot of special equipment or clothing until you are certain the child really enjoys the activity. It's okay if your child expects life to be fun. Children who grow up in homes where adults have fun playing their own musical instruments are usually the kids who keep at their own music lessons. The pre-puberty years are a time for playful exploration. They should not be a time of grimly signing long-term contracts to play soccer or golf or to be a Girl Scout. There is no good reason for becoming an expert at anything when you are eight or nine years old. Watch children play together.

Sometimes they stay at one activity for a long time. Other times they run from one activity to another. This variety is a natural expression of how children explore and learn about their world. Give children the gift of exploring the world at their own pace.

Here are more examples of logical consequences. You can see that the creative possibilities are endless.

Example K

Eight-year-old Ali kept forgetting to feed his dog each evening. The dog dish was in the kitchen. It was easy for Ali's mother to see whether or not the dog had been given food and clean water. Weeks of reminding, scolding, and finally even threatening to get rid of the dog had made no impression on her son. Finally, Mother told him, "From now on you can't have your dinner until the dog has his." For all of this mother's adult life, she had served herself only after the rest of her family was settled at the table. It made sense to her that you do not eat until those you are responsible for get something to eat. That evening at mealtime, the dog dish was still empty. Mother said nothing until it was time to serve the meal. (In this family, Mother dished up each plate at the stove and each member of the family took their filled plate to the table.) When Ali came to the stove to wait for his food, she shook her head and said, "The dog." She then ignored him while she continued to dish up for the rest of the family. He groaned and complained a bit, which she continued to ignore. He finally went to feed his pet. This happened only a few times before her son began to feed the dog without being constantly reminded.

Example L

First-grader Billy was an only child. Since he had two doting parents who were totally involved with helping him to do everything, Billy believed he wasn't very competent. He often complained the work was too hard. Billy constantly asked for help from his teacher and any other adult who came into the classroom. After several weeks of this, the teacher decided that

Billy was actually very bright and well able to do the work himself. The teacher told him, "Billy, you will have to finish the work yourself before you can go out to recess." The rest of the morning she proceeded to ignore his sighs, moans, and complaints. Recess came and all the other children went out to play. He tried to leave too, but she said matter-of-factly, "As soon as your work is done." He sat back down and cried softly. She sat down to work at her desk and tried to ignore his sad sniffles. Soon it was quiet. She eventually got so involved in her own work she was surprised to look up and see him at her desk with the finished paper in his hand. "It's all finished," the teacher said in a pleased tone of voice. She gave him a big hug. He grinned and hugged her back before he ran outdoors. The paper was perfect. He was able to do it. He had learned something important about himself, that he was indeed a competent person.

Taking away a recess is a logical consequence in that we all have to get our work done before we can play, but taking a recess away from an elementary school child on a regular basis can also tear down his or her self-esteem staircase, so be cautious about using this consequence. If you find you are often taking away the child's play period, the consequence is not working. It is time to try something else.

Example M

The following example was told by a middle-school teacher. She had a few students who consistently came to class without pen, pencils, and books. They would ask to be excused to go to their locker and get supplies, then straggle back to class having missed the first ten or fifteen minutes. She first tried the logical consequence of having them stay in class and just sit there not being able to do their schoolwork. This was ineffective because they were perfectly happy to sit and do nothing. No discomfort for them there. Next she told the class that from now on anyone who forgot their supplies could go back to their locker but she would record the time they left and the time they returned. They would then be expected to stay after class to make up their lost time. The next teachers of the day were not too keen about late arrivals to their classes, so the teacher had to clear this plan at a faculty meeting. Just as in a family, things work better if all involved adults know what is going on. A logical consequence for late arrivals at the next class was to again have the student stay and make up lost time before leaving.

You can see that this kind of consequence is a potential prison guard situation. How is the teacher going to force students to stay? It happened that at this school, the staff had already set up a Saturday school for students who needed to make up lost time or missing schoolwork assignments. They had people available to round up kids who needed rides or who did not show up as scheduled. The staff had a clear concept that consequences should not be punitive. They made an effort to make their Saturday school into a warm and welcoming place, even providing snacks for the kids. (The adults were surprised and pleased to find that, for some students, it actually became a popular place to study. Kids were getting the personal help and attention teachers were not able to give them during the week.) Parents, teachers, and administrators all took turns working on Saturday mornings so that no one adult had to spend too much off-duty time there. As this teacher told us, "Contributing one Saturday morning every three months is no big deal." In the process, she gained the benefit of having a backup whenever she needed to apply a logical consequence for missing schoolwork and lost time. As it happened, none of her late arrivals refused to stay to make up time. Over the long run, the problem dissolved. Perhaps just the fact that all students knew Saturday school existed gave her the backup she needed.

Backup systems in schools are exceedingly important. Just as in a family, every teacher needs to have other adults available to help brainstorm logical consequence plans and to provide backup for the plan. Too often teachers are expected to handle discipline problems all alone. As in the Saturday school example given above, it is much more effective when administrators, teachers, and parents can work as a family, brainstorming and planning together.

Example N

In any situation involving body functions, as, for example, when an older child wets or messes his or her pants, the adult should never try to force the child. All body functions belong solely to the person who lives in that body. But if the child is developmentally ready (many boys, for example, do not achieve control of their bowels until the age of three) and after the adult has eliminated any potential environmental causes, including allergies or other physically based reasons, and still things have not improved, treating wetting and pants messing as a routine not-minding behavior can be very effective.

A family had four boys who were born very close together, four children in five years. All four boys needed to be diapered before going to bed. The oldest boy, Dion, was five years old and in kindergarten, but continued to wet the bed. He wore diapers every night and woke up wet every morning. The parents tried everything they knew including limiting Dion's drinking water after dinner. They checked with the doctor to be sure Dion didn't have a physical problem. Nothing helped. (Many years later the family discovered that Dion had a smaller bladder than normal.) The parents understood that boys especially were often slow to get bladder control and so they managed to be successful at conveying a sense of calm and not making a big deal out of it. Dion would sometimes complain about wearing diapers to bed, but he always accepted the situation when his mother told him, "I'm sorry, Dion. One of these days you will be able to wake up when you need to go to the bathroom, but until then, this is the only way we can keep your bed dry." (Notice this mother treated her son as she would have treated any friend with a bed-wetting problem, while at the same time she was matter-of-fact about the need to reduce her work load by keeping the bed dry. She did not sabotage by shaming him or talking in other ways about the problem.)

Then one morning, Dion's three-year-old brother Tavon woke up dry. Tavon was dry again the next morning, and the next! The parents were amazed and delighted. They didn't want to hurt the oldest boy's pride anymore than it already was, so they tried very hard to stick to giving describing praise, "Tavon was dry when he woke up this morning!" "Tavon was dry *again* when he woke up today!" Of course their tone of voice conveyed their joy at the situation. Years later this mother still remembers the whole family standing by Tavon's bed and admiring his dry diaper. Dion seemed pleased for his brother Tavon, but, after all, he was the oldest child and accustomed to being first at everything. There must have been quite a lot of discomfort in that. Four days later, Dion woke up dry. More joy, and more describing praise from the parents. "You woke up dry!" "Dion got himself to wake up in the night to go to the bathroom and that's hard to do!"

The situation above was unique to a particular family, as is any case involving wetting or pants messing. For that reason I hesitate to give much specific advice here about the problem except to say that after the age of three and one-half, wetting and pants messing during the day (given that your child has no basic physical or developmental problems) is basically no different from any other routine not-minding behavior. The idea is to set up a situation where the child will experience discomfort instead of the adult. For example, there is very little discomfort for a child wearing disposable diapers when he or she wets or messes because disposable diapers have been ingeniously designed to absorb large amounts of water, thus keeping the child's skin warm and dry. So the first step is to stop buying disposable diapers and either buy or borrow some cloth ones that will be more uncomfortable because they are wetter and colder. You will also need some plastic cover-ups, preferably the kind with an elastic leg opening because they tend to feel a bit scratchy. If your child asks for the disposable kind of diaper, just say, "Those other kind of diapers are getting to be too expensive, and anyhow, pretty soon you won't need diapers at all."

Don't be in too big of a hurry to change your child's diapers when he or she asks. You can say pleasantly, "Okay, honey. I'll get around to it as soon as I can," and then keep busy doing other things before you get around to changing the diaper. Remember the goal is to set up a situation that will help the child to experience enough discomfort to see the sense of remembering to use the toilet.

It is absolutely crucial that you keep any situation involving wetting and pants messing from turning into a power struggle. Do not let on that you hate to change dirty diapers, or scold, or remind, or shame, or sabotage in any way. Don't talk and laugh about your new plan with Grandma or anyone else. Treat your child as you would any other friend who has a problem with remembering to use the toilet. Keep calm, convey a quiet attitude of "This is what needs to be done and this is no big deal." Convey the idea this is just a temporary situation, which it is. If the child wets the bed, you can expect him or her to take the wet sheets and toss them in the wash. At this age, children are too young to make their own bed but they can put the wet sheets in the washer. Do not expect children to change their own soiled diapers: This will only fuel a power struggle and result in an even bigger mess for you to clean up.

If you find it is impossible to treat pants wetting and messing as a routine not-minding behavior without a lot of emotion and sabotaging, look for a family counselor who can guide you through the process. And don't despair. A few years from now, you'll laugh about all this.

Exercise

Using the "Negative Behaviors" worksheet on the following page, continue to write down any misbehaviors or negative attempts at solving problems that you observe your children doing this coming week. Also, write down which corrections you are beginning to use. Using the chart each week is helpful for refreshing your memory when you join in the weekly group discussions.

If you are interested in some ideas for working with children who are involved in stealing, or who habitually do not do schoolwork that they are capable of doing, you will find detailed discussion of these routine not-minding behaviors in the Special Case sections at the end of this chapter.

WORKSHEET

NEGATIVE BEHAVIORS

The Four Misbehaviors and Three Problem-Solving Situations

NOT-MINDING (Not Doing What Is Asked)

SELF-INDULGENT (Attention-Getting)

ROUTINE NOT-MINDING (Will Not Do Routine Tasks)

AGGRESSIVE (Deliberately Hurting)

NEGATIVE BEHAVIORS Requiring Problem-Solving That Does Not Fit Above:

1. Adjust Environment   2. Solve Conflicts   3. Listen to Feelings

---

from *Caring Discipline: Practical Tools for Nurturing Happy Families & Classrooms*

REVIEW: Correction for Routine Not-Minding Behaviors

PREVENTION PLAN: Give Children Daily Opportunities to Make, and Live With, Their Choices

1. Give the child practice in making **fun choices**.

2. **Never give a choice if there is no choice.**

3. Keep the choices **limited and appropriate** to the child's age. "Either this or that … " is enough for a preschooler.

4. Let children **experience the logical consequences of their choice.**

BASIC CORRECTION FOR AN ESTABLISHED BEHAVIOR: Set Up a Logical Consequence Experience for the Child

1. Work on changing **one routine not-minding behavior at a time.**

2. **Make a plan** for the child. If possible, find another adult to brainstorm with you. Find backup help from another adult if needed.

3. The logical consequence plan should ensure that **the child, not the adult, will experience discomfort.**

4. Logical consequences **should be experienced by the child as part of the natural or social order** (not as a punishment).

5. **Be cautious about taking away a privilege** as part of a logical consequence.

6. Any loss of privilege should be **short-term.**

REMEMBER NOT TO SELF-SABOTAGE

Chapter 9 Discussion: MAKING CHOICES AND LIVING WITH THE CONSEQUENCES

1. Share your "Negative Behaviors" worksheet notations. Are you having any problems recognizing which negative misbehaviors are which? Did any problem-solving situations arise?

2. Did anyone have any particular problems with the ignoring correction? Give some examples of what happened this past week with the either-or choice.

3. Has the anger level dropped for anyone in their relationships with their children? Has anyone experienced a lessening of a power struggle?"

4. Talk together about how giving children fun choices and helping them to live with the consequences of their choices fits in with Maslow's staircase of needs.

5. Is everyone clear as to the differences between logical consequences and punishments?

6. Think of a routine not-minding incident and, following the guidelines in this chapter, ask the group to help you plan a logical consequence. When you think up your initial ideas, feel free to brainstorm, be creative, and have fun. Afterward, you can be serious, look at the ideas, toss out the ridiculous ones, and choose a situation you feel comfortable with. Do you need a backup person to help with the plan? Finally, ask yourselves, "What can go wrong?"

7. Regarding the Special Cases at the end of this chapter, has anyone had a problem with children stealing or not getting schoolwork done? What kinds of corrections or punishments did you try in the past? Are the ideas presented similar or different from what you have tried before?

8. Regarding the list of Secondary Reinforcers described in the Special Case on Schoolwork, discuss whether or not you are comfortable using secondary reinforcers with your children. Can you think of more secondary reinforcers to add to the list?

Special Case: STEALING
A Logical Consequence Plan for Dealing With Stealing

Parents who catch their children stealing are often devastated. Not to be able to trust one's own child to leave off-limit items alone sends many parents into a panic. Teachers, too, are greatly troubled by the child who steals. Stealing goes against some of the most cherished values of our property oriented culture. As a consequence, parents and teachers often manage to thoroughly sabotage themselves in dealing with stealing misbehaviors. They do lots of spanking, grounding for extreme lengths of time, lecturing, advising, warning, even bursting into tears. When it comes to stealing, the basic rule of carrying out the correction and then not mentioning it again seems almost impossible to do. "How will children learn right from wrong," parents and teachers ask, "if I don't let them know just how terribly wrong it is to steal?"

Children already know that stealing is wrong. You must take this leap of faith and try not to lecture about it. The old ways of lecturing, hitting, scolding, crying, shaming, and advising did not work, so what have you got to lose? Remember what was said earlier about the ineffectiveness of teaching ethical values and morals during negative behavior times? Children will either close their inner door and let your words slide off or they will actively rebel against the talking you do during these times of stress. Giving energy and emotional attention during times of misbehavior will set up power struggles and make matters worse. As upsetting as stealing is, try treating it essentially as you would any other routine not-minding behavior. Here are some guidelines to help you through the process.

1. Check very carefully into the situation before you proceed

Stealing often happens when the child attempts to solve a real life problem. Maybe the child was hungry so he stole his neighbor's lunch. Maybe the child could not afford a special trinket currently popular with the other girls, so she took one from someone else.

At a later time if necessary, you can go behind the scenes to ensure that from now on this child has enough food to eat, or to set up an opportunity for this child to occasionally earn a special trinket. But for the present, treat the theft as you would any other routine not-minding misbehavior and deal with it. Whatever the underlying reason for the theft, stealing cannot be allowed.

If you suspect the accusers might be mistaken, give the child a chance to tell his or her side of the story. Do this in a concerned, not an accusing, manner. Really listen. If you have no doubts at all about the matter, as for example, if you yourself find a cache of fishing lures still in their store wrappings stashed under the mattress, or you witness the child taking a toy from another child's desk, then do not discuss it beforehand but proceed directly to the next step.

2. Be honest and direct with the child

Be honest with the child. Describe the facts as you know them. Do not ask questions you already know the answers to. Immediately state what you know or believe to be true, for example, "I just found out from your teacher that you stole Dirk's lunch money."

Many parents and teachers are tempted to put the child on a witness stand and force him or her to tell the truth. For example, "What do you know about Dirk's lunch money?" and "Where were you when it happened?" and "Do you mean to tell me you don't know anything about it?" *Do not ask for or expect a confession.* Resist the temptation to play detective or lawyer. Do not ask questions designed to trick the child into a confession. Do not say, "It will go easier on you if you tell the truth." This puts children in a situation where they may feel forced to solve the problem by lying to you.

The day I ate a whole plate of cookies my grandmother was saving for dessert is still vivid in my memory. My indignant grandmother confronted me and my older brother with the nearly empty plate. "Who ate these cookies?" she demanded. My innocent brother denied it. I was backed into a corner. If I admitted my guilt, I was certain my grandmother would lose all respect for me. I was the apple of my grandmother's eye. I was not afraid of physical punishment because she never punished us physically. But she did emotionally punish us by withdrawing love and shaming. I was terrified of losing my grandmother's love and respect. In my eight-year-old mind, telling Grandma the truth could not possibly make things easier for me. I dearly loved my big brother. I did not want to get him in trouble, but, in an instinct of self-preservation, I looked up at her and said, "I don't know." My grandmother believed me and sent my brother to his room for the rest of the day, after telling him at some length he should be ashamed of himself for being a liar. Even though some years ago I finally apologized to my brother for that incident, to this day I still feel guilty about that lie. But, I know that given the same circumstances, from my eight-year-old problem-solving point of view, I would probably do it again.

3. You do not have to prove the child's guilt. It is enough that you are sure beyond a reasonable doubt

Children may vigorously deny that they stole something, but if you believe beyond a reasonable doubt that they did steal, go ahead and proceed with the correction. They may deny it, argue, tell you they hate you, accuse you of being unfair, of not loving them, or even threaten to run away. Do not allow yourself to be baited into an argument. Treat these protests as self-indulgent behavior and ignore them. If you are absolutely convinced the child did it, say only once, "If I am mistaken, I am sorry, but I think you stole the money."

4. If the child has stolen an object, he or she must personally return the object or its equivalent to the rightful owner

Returning an object to the rightful owner is not a pleasant experience for either parent or child, but it is an absolute requirement for helping your child to stop stealing. Children must experience this basic consequence of stealing. It may be embarrassing for you but rest assured you are not alone. Many children try stealing at some point in their lives. Most adults who have raised kids themselves understand this. They know it is the responsible parent who cares enough and is gutsy enough to march a child back into the store or school or neighbor's house to return the stolen object. By so doing, you will earn the respect of every sensible adult. Do not return the object for your child, as some C-adults are tempted to do. Be sure the child returns the object *in person* with you at his or her side.

If the stolen object has already been eaten or broken, children can use or earn their own money to replace it. If the object has been damaged in any way, choose a treasured object of comparable value belonging to them and have them return both the damaged object and their own possession to the person they stole from. If children steal a second time, insist they give up a possession of equal value even if the stolen object has not been harmed. If the victimized person does not want the child's possession, ask him to take it and contribute it to someone else who could use it.

5. Do not sabotage yourself

Try very hard not to sabotage yourself by spanking, scolding, crying, or worrying out loud about what is to become of the child, will he end up like cousin Robert in prison or whatever. Go ahead and look as grim as you feel, but be matter-of-fact. It is important not to shame or demean the child. Let your nonverbal attitude give the message that you are a force of nature, like the patient ocean or a granite boulder. Say firmly and calmly, "I can't let you steal. You will have to return it." Let your body language convey the message that there is nothing else that can be done. This is the way things are.

Give the child as little attention and social interaction during this process as possible. If you do much talking, you will end up sabotaging yourself. After you return home, go about your usual routines. Do not mention the stealing again. Immediately begin to give positive attention, both verbal and nonverbal. Do your regular bedtime routine of reading in bed together or whatever you usually do at bedtime. Let the incident be in the past. Concentrate on giving those four to one positive attentions. Let your nonverbal behavior convey the message, "All that is over and done with. This is a new day." The experience of returning the object will have been an extremely painful experience for the child. Children need to know you do not think they are "bad." Respond to their neutral and positive behaviors with positive attention so that they clearly understand it was their behavior you disliked, not them.

At this point, concentrate on using nonverbal communication: Make friendly eye contact, smile sometimes from across the room, ruffle his or her hair as you pass by, give a loving hug. Stealing is just another misbehavior. The fact that your child stole something is not the end of the world. It does not mean you are a failure as a parent or a teacher. It does not mean he or she is a bad kid. Stealing is only a mistake which many of us make on the way to learning how to behave as responsible persons. Making mistakes is to be expected. It is an integral part of learning. If the child seems withdrawn and depressed the day after the incident, bring the subject up at a positive or neutral time. Say in a kindly way, "You must be feeling badly about what happened. Everyone makes mistakes sometimes. You have done what needed to be done to make it better. Today is a new day. Yesterday is over and done with." Give the child a hug, listen if he or she wants to talk about it. Then let it go.

6. If the child is innocent, apologize and explain to those involved

If it happens that you later find out the child did *not* steal, immediately apologize to the child, and then do whatever you possibly can to see that the child's innocence is made clear to everyone else involved. Go with the child personally to everyone in the situation and tell them you made a mistake. But you do not need to be awash in guilt. You did the best you could with the information you had. Part of the child's learning is that each person's credibility is built brick by brick, over a long period of time. Children need to learn it is a fact of life that when a reputation for stealing or lying is established, it takes time for trust to build again. If you are matter-of-fact in treating the theft as just another misbehavior and if you do not sabotage yourself while carrying out this correction, the child can handle an occasional mistake on your part.

REVIEW: Special Case—STEALING

1. **Check very carefully into the situation before you proceed.**

2. **Be honest and direct with the child.** Do not put the child on the witness stand by asking questions to which you already know the answers.

3. **You do not have to prove the child's guilt.** It is enough that you are sure beyond a reasonable doubt.

4. **If the child has stolen an object, he or she must personally return the object or its equivalent to the rightful owner.** Do not return the stolen object for your child, as some C-adults are tempted to do. Be sure the child returns the object *in person* with you at his or her side. If the stolen object has been eaten, children can use or earn their own money to replace it. If the object has been damaged, choose a treasured object of comparable value belonging to the child and have him or her return both the damaged object and their own possession.

5. **Do not sabotage yourself.** Let your body language convey the message that this is what must be done to set things right. Be a force of nature, like the patient ocean, or a granite boulder.

6. **If it happens that you later find out the child did not steal, immediately apologize to the child.** Go with the child personally to everyone in the situation and tell them you made a mistake, but you do not need to be awash in guilt. If you treat the theft as just another misbehavior and if you do not sabotage yourself while carrying out this correction, children can handle an occasional mistake on your part.

Special Case: SCHOOLWORK
A Logical Consequence Plan for the Child Who is Falling Behind in Basic Academic Skills

This schoolwork plan is intended to be used only with the elementary school child who is having severe problems in completing schoolwork and as a result is falling far behind his or her peers in maintaining basic academic skill levels. (You will find a schoolwork plan for teenagers in Chapter Twelve.) *Schoolwork is academic work that the child is supposed to complete while at school.* Homework is extra academic work assigned to the child to be completed at home. This is not a homework plan. I have a strong bias against overloading elementary school children with homework. This contract plan deals only with schoolwork that should have been completed at school.

This plan is also not recommended for children who are generally doing average work and getting "B" or "C" grades. If you are worried that getting "C" grades in school will endanger your child's future, relax. It is okay if your child is an average student. School is a temporary situation, and, in many ways, it is also an artificial environment. Many capable children who do only average work in school because they cannot see its relevancy to their lives will eventually blossom into "A" and "B" students when they enter college or find what they perceive to be more meaningful work to do in the larger world outside the classroom. *The basis of a successful adult life is the sense of being a competent and respected person, and an ability to live in responsible and loving relationships with other human beings, not just getting A's and B's in school.*

Especially by the time children enter their junior high school years, as long as they are doing average "C" work and are becoming *well-grounded in basic skills like math, writing, reading, and critical thinking,* let them manage their own schoolwork. Encourage them, help them to build a strong emotional needs staircase, let them know you are proud and happy for them when they do well, let them know you are interested in the joy of learning for its own sake, but let them worry (or not worry) about the temporary end product of high grades.

However, if you have a child who is definitely having problems in maintaining basic skill levels because he or she does not do the assigned schoolwork, and *if you are convinced that not doing the schoolwork has become a direct threat to the child's competency needs*, then the child needs your help. If that is the situation, you can try this contract plan. It is described from the point of view of the parent, but teachers and school counselors can also initiate this kind of contract.

A contract is not easy for adults to carry out. Long-term contracts involving consequences such as secondary reinforcers (like earning stickers or a popcorn party) are the most structured and time-consuming of all the logical consequence approaches. This plan has worked for many children, but it takes commitment and the willingness by all involved adults to stick with it, sometimes for months, so be sure you and the teacher are willing to put forth that kind of effort before you attempt it.

Before beginning to work out a schoolwork plan for a child, parents and teachers need to discuss ahead of time whether or not the schoolwork is at the child's ability level. Children cannot be expected to do work that is beyond their ability. Besides that, many extremely bright children have attention deficits or "Hunter brain traits" which make it difficult for them to learn in the usual ways. If you suspect this may be true, you have the right to request that a professional evaluation be given to your child by special school personnel to find out if your child is learning disabled. By federal law, every public school is required to create an Individualized Education Plan for every special-needs child. Parents and teachers must agree together on this Individualized Education Plan, or IEP, as it is called. If your child is eligible for an IEP, make sure that both the homework process and the schoolwork process is included in the plan.

If your child is tested and found to have some kind of learning disability, DO NOT PANIC. Studies have shown many kids outgrow the problem before their high school years. Also, many children respond to changes in the environment, as we discussed in Chapter Six. In the meantime, these children need special tutoring help that focuses on keeping their competency stairstep strong.

Albert Einstein, the genius who formulated the theory of relativity, was apparently an "Edison" gene child. One of his elementary school teachers made one of the greatest misjudgments of all time when he advised Einstein's parents not to waste money sending Einstein to secondary school because he was not intelligent enough. As the world now knows, just the opposite was true. So called learning disabled children are of average, or higher than average, intelligence. They are not stupid, and they are not slow learners. But, unfortunately, they often don't fit into the ordinary classroom situation because, as we discussed in Special Case: Understanding the ADHD Diagnosed Child, their brains process incoming information differently than most other children.

For example, some children are categorized as learning disabled because their brains cannot screen out incoming information in a way that allows them to focus on just one thing at a time. As a result, these children seem to be in a continual whirl of motion, jumping from one thing to another. They sometimes cannot concentrate on their written schoolwork for more than a few minutes at a time. Some can cope with only ten minutes of written work at a sitting. These children can sometimes be successful if they are allowed to answer most schoolwork orally, using a tape recorder. Maybe it would be better for them to write out ten math problems instead of thirty, and then get up and move around while they are talking into the tape recorder about the rest of the problems. Maybe they need special paper with darker lines and wider spaces. Because these children are often extremely bright, teachers and parents sometimes jump to the conclusion that since these children are not stupid, they must be lazy. "If Cheri would only work harder, she would get good grades." Many of the schoolwork problems of the attention-deficit child can be solved by adjusting the child's learning environment.

Learning disabilities come in all varieties, sometimes in very unexpected and individual packages. Even experienced professionals do not always recognize the difference between sleep deprivation or a true difference in brain processing function, so get competent professional advice if you are in doubt.

When you are finally satisfied that not doing schoolwork is truly a routine not-minding behavior and not a lack of ability to do the work, go ahead and begin to draw up a plan.

A CONTRACT PLAN INVOLVING SECONDARY REINFORCERS

1. Visit your child's teacher

Visit your child's teacher to share this schoolwork plan. In the vast majority of cases, your child's teacher will be delighted to help you in this effort. Give the teacher a copy of this book to ensure that both of you are operating on the same wave length. A counselor can also initiate this program with parent and teacher, but only if she has enough time. Remember that acting as a case manager for a program like this is time-consuming.

2. Tell your child, at a neutral or positive time, that you are going to help him or her change old habit patterns

Don't give your child a choice in this matter. State the facts in a friendly tone of voice. "I sure don't like it when you don't get your schoolwork done. The teacher doesn't like it, and I know you hate it when everyone nags at you about it. I've got a plan to help you change the old habit." Present your plan as something that will make life happier for both of you.

3. Provide a positive secondary reinforcer to reward your child for a positive behavior change

Secondary reinforcers are objects like stickers or fun activities. Until now, you have focused on giving children the primary reinforcer of your personal attention. The secondary reinforcer is something you give in addition to personal attention. You will find a list of suggested secondary reinforcers at the end of this section. Choose a few ideas from the list or create some of your own.

One middle-school substitute teacher brings a small gift, beautifully wrapped, to each new class assignment. Every time a child completes an assignment, the child gets one free guess as to what is in the box. The child who makes the correct guess gets to keep whatever is inside. The prize is always an inexpensive little fun gadget of some kind.

Almost every parent has used secondary reinforcers at one time or another, whether it is giving children dessert only after they eat their meat and potatoes, or a dollar for every A or B on their report cards. Giving food as a reinforcer is treading on shaky ground because you do not want children to equate food with attention and love, although some middle-school teachers have been amazed with the results they get from a box of Milk Duds. A simple sticker or a fun activity with mom or dad is preferable to money or candy. Whatever you decide, use money or food reinforcers with caution. You eventually want to be able to drop the reinforcer. *Both money and food are difficult to drop once you start them.*

Offer a choice of reinforcers to the child. Say, "I know how hard it is to change old habits so I'd like to do something nice for you each day when you get your schoolwork done. What would you like to earn for every day your teacher sends home a note saying your work is finished?" Get out a pencil and paper and make a list together. Be creative. Let your child offer ideas. Together you can brainstorm some fun things he or she can earn. This is the part of the contract children love.

Some parents resist the use of secondary reinforcers on the grounds they are somehow unethical. "Sounds like bribery to me." It is true that you will eventually want to get rid of the secondary reinforcer. Your ultimate goal, after all, is to help the child internalize the pride and satisfaction of a job well done. However, the secondary reinforcer does serve an important function in the early phases of the behavior change program because it is so tangible. The child can touch, taste, or play with it. It is immediately apparent. It helps to catch the child's attention and makes the difficult process of habit change into a fun game. It functions as a kind of exclamation point to the primary reinforcement of paying attention to the child at positive times. It also provides a structured way to remind the adult to give more positive attention to the child.

As adults, we like to give ourselves a treat when we manage to change damaging old habits. Many a woman has bought herself a new dress when she lost twenty pounds, and many a smoker has treated himself to a special night out when he has succeeded in not lighting up a cigarette for two months. Why is it so bad to do the same for children? Children's damaging old habits are hard to break, too. Why not celebrate with children when they are successful? Most children, if given the choice, will choose an activity time with mom or dad rather than an object, even if the object is food or money. This is not surprising since loving attention from a parent, or other admired adult, is what children crave.

The secondary reinforcer should be something special, something the child would not ordinarily have the opportunity to own or to do. A troubled five-year-old kindergarten boy, Daniel, was willing to work very hard on improving his behavior with the other children after his teacher hit upon the reinforcer of one marble for each day he did not hurt another child. Daniel loved those marbles and seemed determined to acquire the entire sack full. Five marbles and five days later of not hitting other children, Daniel's grandmother bought him a whole sack full of marbles. "I didn't realize he loved marbles so much," she told the teacher. Daniel's grandmother valued Daniel's approval more than she valued his need to grow into a strong and competent human being. Daniel immediately fell into his old ways and his teacher never found a secondary reinforcer that had the power of those marbles for him.

As the weeks go by, keep checking in with your child about the list of secondary reinforcers, "Is there anything about our plan we should change this week?" Secondary reinforcers like stickers become boring fast and need to be varied periodically in order to continue to be of interest to the child. Make a weekly appointment with the child to go over the program and see how it is going. Do this at neutral or positive times. Make it a friendly, problem-solving meeting. Remember not to dwell on the failures or to lecture. After every meeting, put the appointment on the calendar for the next week to insure you do not postpone things until a crisis comes along. It is difficult to be friendly, and oriented towards problem solving, at crisis times.

The most common cause of failure of this type of program happens when adults neglect to carry through their end of the bargain. When the child's behavior begins to improve, parents and teachers frequently forget or postpone carrying out their part of the plan. It is tempting to stop a secondary reinforcer program as soon as the behavior improves. Teachers are so busy at the end of each school day they often forget to give the child the promised positive note to take home once the behavior is improving. When things are going along better, we tend to turn our attention to the area of more concern. The squeaky wheel really does get the grease. For obvious reasons, the negative message sent home when things are not going well is easier to remember. Parents and teachers should prepare for this eventuality by planning ahead of time for the parent to call the teacher at home if the child says the teacher forgot. Teachers are human, too, and it is possible that this time, the teacher did forget.

4. Give secondary reinforcers to the child when the desired behavior happens

Another important point to keep in mind is that the secondary reinforcer should be given to the child as close to the desired behavior as possible. The younger the child, the less time should elapse before reinforcing the improved behaviors. A rather extreme example of this need for frequent reinforcement was the first-grade boy, Bobby, who could not stay in his seat and attend to his work for more than a few minutes at a time. His teacher bought a digital kitchen timer that could be set to quietly beep every few minutes. The teacher started out by setting the timer for three minute segments during math time. He chose math time because that was the hardest time of the day for Bobby to sit still. The beep reminded the teacher to smile or touch or in some way give positive attention to Bobby whenever the beep occurred at the same time Bobby was in his seat. The teacher gradually lengthened out the time between beeps until the child was sitting and working for nearly the entire math period. This method failed when, after having had a moderate amount of success after the first week, the teacher turned his attention elsewhere. The child then reverted to his old behavior pattern and the discouraged teacher did not want to try the program again.

The temptation for a tired parent or teacher is to postpone giving the reinforcer until tomorrow or the weekend when the adult hopes there will be more time and energy available. Unfortunately, if you do this, the child will lose his enthusiasm for the plan. If the adults keep putting things off, why not the child? Be sure you don't promise a reinforcer that takes too much energy or time. Keep daily reinforcers short and sweet. You are both supposed to have fun with this. Do not promise to play a game of checkers if you hate checkers.

Young children need positive and immediate reinforcers. Some parents and grandparents promise distant reinforcers like a trip to Disneyland next summer. The lure of Disneyland next summer is a useless secondary reinforcer. It does more harm than good. Since it is almost certain that a far off Disneyland trip will fail to get children to do their day-to-day chores, their families will wind up blaming them for not being able to go on the trip. Or, if the family does go to Disneyland in spite of a child's poor performance, that child will have learned that no one means what they say anyhow so he or she can safely continue to be irresponsible about schoolwork.

Reinforcers should not be expensive. As you will see from the list of ideas at the end of this chapter, cheap can be fun. If you can afford to go to Disneyland next summer, wonderful. Wait until a few weeks before it is time to go and say, "I think we can afford to go to Disneyland this year. We are all such neat people, I think we deserve it," or you can say, "We have all been working so hard and doing such a good job, I think we should treat ourselves to Disneyland." You would no doubt have gone to Disneyland even if they were not doing a good job, but there is nothing wrong with emphasizing your pleasure at their efforts. Let them know you notice and appreciate their work. But do not offer it six months ahead of time as a reward contingent on good behavior.

5. Don't stop the secondary reinforcer too soon. The desired behavior should be displayed for three weeks

Before you quit or decrease the secondary reinforcer, children should have demonstrated the desired behavior for three solid weeks in a row. Many children will begin to wean themselves at this point and forget to collect the reinforcer. It is wonderful when a child shows more interest in the social reinforcer than the secondary reinforcer, but until those three weeks are up, always offer it just the same. It is a mistake to assume you can forget about the plan after the child has shown good progress for a week or so.

If you quit at the end of one week, the child will usually slip back into the old negative behaviors once again. An important part of the value of using the secondary reinforcer is that it also provides a structured way to remind you, the adult, to pay more attention to the child at positive and neutral times. If you stop using the secondary reinforcer too soon, you will not have had enough time to change your own old habit pattern of not giving this particular child enough positive attention.

6. Give loving, positive attention when you give the reinforcer

Whichever kind of secondary reinforcer you use, make sure you give your child loving, enthusiastic attention just before you give the sticker or token. People internalize behavior and attitudes through the primary reinforcer of gaining attention from admired fellow human beings, not from the stickers and tokens per se. The secondary reinforcer is useful for a while, but do not depend on it too much. Its major purpose is to catch your child's interest and cooperation while you work on building their staircase of needs by giving them the primary reinforcer of your loving attention.

Many parents and teachers ask if it is okay to take away a reinforcer for negative behaviors, instead of giving a positive reinforcer for positive behaviors. An example of this is the teacher who gives a child ten stickers at the beginning of each school day, and then, throughout the school day, takes one sticker away every time the teacher sees a negative behavior. The problem with using negative reinforcers is two-fold: first, it gives frequent and powerful attention for negative behaviors, and secondly, it is usually perceived as punishment by the child which in turn helps to tear down the child's staircase of needs, often adding more fuel to the power struggle. For these reasons, it is best to stick with giving positive reinforcers for positive behaviors.

7. Provide a logical consequence for times your child exhibits the old irresponsible behavior

If you and the child are involved in a plan that provides the child with a fun secondary reinforcer, you cannot change the plan without first consulting with the child. You and the child have made a contract with one another. You have made a promise to the child and you must keep your word. But the child has also made a promise to you. The contract should provide for a logical consequence in the event the child does not keep his or her part of the bargain.

For the teacher, the most difficult part of this contract is to send a note home every single day. It is important for the teacher to carry this out, because the first time a note does not come home, you will wonder whether your child actually finished the work. Maybe your child threw the note away, or maybe the teacher forgot to send it. Maybe your child is "forgetting" to bring the note home as a way of problem solving a difficult situation. It works best if you expect a note every single day. You and the teacher can provide your child with a special manila envelope for bringing home notes and unfinished schoolwork. If your child does not have a backpack for carrying books and papers, buy or borrow one.

Sending a note home each day is asking a lot of the teacher because the note needs to be written at the end of the school day which is often a hectic time in the classroom. Expect that sometimes the teacher will forget. Teachers are not, and should not be expected to be, perfect. Forgetting to write the note is one of those things that occasionally happens so create a backup plan to use at these times. Maybe the teacher can give you his or her home number or email address for your child to check the assignment (it is best if children are responsible for making their own contacts) or, if this doesn't work, it is sometimes possible for the school to temporarily loan you a second set of school books to keep at home. This way, you can give some reasonable substitute assignment on your own.

You also need to talk with your child about the logical consequence of doing the work at home if the work has not been done at school. Decide together on a regular time for doing unfinished schoolwork. Children need a little time to play and relax right after school, but they should not be allowed to do anything special before their schoolwork is done. For example, no television or going to a friend's house. Remember that you must not sabotage yourself with talking about the unfinished schoolwork. When the child comes in the door with a note saying there is work to be finished tonight, do not talk about it. Do not scold by saying, "Well, now you don't get to play checkers with Dad tonight," or whatever fun thing the child was to have done.

Set aside a special spot in your home for your child to do his schoolwork. If the child does not have a desk in his or her room, the kitchen table will work just fine as long as the television is off and the rest of the family are busy doing their own thing so the child is free to concentrate on the schoolwork. One family put a plastic cloth on their unused formal dining room table to use as a permanent schoolwork/homework center for the entire family.

Your son or daughter will also need a regular time to sit down to work. If the two of you have agreed upon 7:00 p.m. as schoolwork time, you can say, "It's seven o'clock." If your child ignores you or refuses, you can use a loss-of-privilege consequence like no television viewing until the schoolwork is done. You can use the Broken Record. Or, as one parent did, you can say no more about it and wait until your child is asleep, then wake him or her and say, "I'm so sorry to wake you, honey, but that schoolwork isn't done yet." Ask some other adults to help brainstorm a logical consequence to fit your situation that you can feel comfortable about. Remember to say as little as possible about the schoolwork. Be a quiet, inexorable force of nature. Act, don't talk.

Sometimes children need your help with directions or understanding a concept. But if you suspect your child is constantly asking you questions to get your attention and to avoid doing the work, put a limit on the number of questions he or she may ask during a work session. Perhaps three opportunities to ask questions would be reasonable for your child. Let your child know ahead of time that he or she will be able to ask for your help only a specific number of times. It is up to the child to choose when help is needed. Keep your involvement friendly and sincere but keep it to the minimum required. When your child is finished and brings the work to you, check it over, and unless it is obviously a sloppy job, say, in a pleased tone of voice, "Looks like you are all done." Leave it to the teacher to do the actual, in-depth correcting. If the teacher feels it is not good enough to accept, the teacher can send it back again the next day.

Remember not to give the secondary reinforcement to the child for completing unfinished schoolwork at home, but once the schoolwork is finished, be pleasant and enjoy your child's company. Doing schoolwork is not a punishment. *Having to do the schoolwork at home is just a logical consequence of not having done the work at school.* Remember how important it is to give children those four-to-one positive attentions the minute you see neutral or positive behaviors. Once the old behavior patterns are broken and children have developed more independent, responsible behavior patterns, you will not need to pay so much attention to giving them the careful structure of a logical consequence, but they will always need your loving attention.

A word of caution: If you decide to try a plan that uses secondary reinforcers, the other children in the family or classroom may feel left out and consequently worsen their behavior unless you somehow include them. You can put the other children on a similar program, but this is unnecessary and is at least twice as much work. Often the child earning the secondary reinforcer is happy to earn the reinforcer for siblings or classmates also. Include some such arrangement when you first work out the agreement with the child. Ask, "Would you like to earn a chance for you and Carrie to make a tent to eat dinner in?" or "Would you like to earn a chance for the whole class to have a popcorn party?" In this way, all children in the family or classroom benefit from the one child's improved behavior and are apt to be supportive instead of resentful.

8. Parents and teachers can use reinforcers for a group of children

Teachers and parents can also reinforce positive behavior for a group of children. An example would be putting a marble in a jar every time the adult sees someone in the group behaving in a helpful way. When the jar has a certain number of marbles in it, the entire group receives a popcorn party or a special video movie or whatever. No one is left out, by the way, not even the kids who did not earn a single marble. Being left out of a popcorn party because he or she did not earn a marble would be perceived by the child as a punishment which would erode the self-esteem staircase. (Unless, of course, the child had actually destroyed the popcorn machine or engaged in some such incident directly related to popcorn parties. In this case, being left out of the popcorn party would be a logical consequence of wrecking the popcorn machine.)

Suggested Secondary Reinforcers

A. **Single items**: a sticker, a pencil, a bag of popcorn, a warm fuzzy ball, a piece of bubble gum.

B. **Single items that can be collected as part of a group**: one marble, one jack, one bead, one of a set of stickers, one card, one piece of a puzzle, one chance on guessing what is in the prize box.

C. **Activities to do with mom, dad, or other adult** (Set a time limit of 15 to 20 minutes or whatever you are comfortable with):

 1. Play checkers, Chutes and Ladders, hopscotch, or cards.
 2. Go for a walk.
 3. Color in a coloring book together.
 4. Help cook something for dinner.
 5. Practice playing basketball, or throwing and hitting the softball.
 6. Pop popcorn and watch an extra half hour of television together.
 7. Get a lesson on a grown-up card game or magic trick.
 8. Work on or wash the car together.

D. **Activities to do alone** (Set a time limit of 20 or 30 minutes):

 1. Work with hammer, nails, and wood scraps.
 2. Stay up an extra half hour past the regular bedtime.
 3. Mix up bubbles with a mixer in the sink. (May need some adult supervision.)
 4. Water play in the kitchen sink or bathtub.
 5. Make a tent out of a card table and blankets. (Can invite others in for a visit or snack.)
 6. Use special clay or paints or a special coloring book.

from *Caring Discipline: Practical Tools for Nurturing Happy Families & Classrooms*

REVIEW: Special Case—SCHOOLWORK PLAN

1. **Visit your child's teacher to share this schoolwork plan** and to ask for his or her help. A counselor can also initiate this kind of program with parent and teacher.

2. Tell your child, at a neutral or positive time, that **you are going to help him or her change old habits.**

3. Sit down with your child and together **come up with ideas for positive secondary reinforcers** to reward him or her for positive behavior changes.

4. Secondary reinforcers should be given to the child as **close to the desired behavior as possible.**

5. Whichever kind of secondary reinforcers you use, **make sure you give the child loving attention** just before you give the reinforcer, for example, of a sticker or token.

6. **Do not stop the program until behavior is at the desired level for at least three weeks.**

7. **Provide a logical consequence** for times your child exhibits the old, irresponsible behavior. Do not sabotage yourself during this process.

8. You can also use secondary reinforcers to reinforce positive behavior for a group of children.

REMEMBER NOT TO SELF-SABOTAGE

The Correction for Aggression and Loss of Self-Control

Time-Out

Aggressive behaviors are actions that deliberately try to hurt, either physically or emotionally. Children are being aggressive, for example, when they destroy objects in a room, bite, spit in people's faces, fling themselves around the room knocking things over and bumping into people, or bang their heads against a wall. It is aggressive behavior when children seem to lose all inner controls by going into a rage and hurting themselves or others. Aggressive behavior can also be carried out in a more controlled way, for example, if the child deliberately tries to humiliate or hurt someone's feelings, or tickles someone for sustained periods of time, or tells a lie in which the goal is to get even and hurt another person.

The term "aggressive behavior" as used in this book does not apply to the boisterous, competitive, rough-housing type of behavior so often exhibited, especially by boys. A father, who was tired of his wife's complaints that her four pre-puberty sons were driving her crazy as they bounced around the house during the summer, ordered a whole truckload of sand to be dumped in their back yard. He then went to a farm supply shop, bought a huge tractor inner tube that he blew up to just the right size for jumping. The four boys kept busy all summer making roads and other construction projects in the sand, using the back yard hose for irrigation projects, and having contests to see who could bounce who off the inner tube first. It was the most peaceful summer the boys' mother could remember since her sons had been born. Not every family has such an option; for more ideas on adapting the environment to a boy's need for large muscle activity, read Michael Gurian's fine book, *The Wonder of Boys,* in which he defines the special environmental needs of the male child.

The basic correction for aggressive behavior is the Time-out. Time-outs are different from the either-or choice that was described earlier as part of the ignoring correction. At first blush, the either-or choice and the time-out seem similar. If you tell a child, "You can either be quiet during this TV program or you can go be noisy in your bedroom," it seems much the same as saying, "Go to your bedroom and take a five-minute time-out." But they are not the same. There are important differences. The child who makes the either-or choice to go to the bedroom rather than stay by the television and be noisy, is free to leave the bedroom whenever he or she chooses a different behavior. That is, as soon as the child is quiet, he or she is free to come back to the living room. But children may not leave time-out whenever they choose. They must abide by the time frame laid down by the adult for the time-out procedure. That is, they must stay quietly seated for the amount of time determined by the adult.

Time-out is a much more controlling correction than the either-or choice because there is no opportunity for children to have any choice in the amount of time they must stay in time-out. It is the correction most likely to fuel a power struggle if the adult fails to carry it through with a "I am a force of Nature" attitude. For this reason, *try using all the other corrections and preventive measures before you use the time-out. Think of time-out as a last-resort correction.* In fact, as you use the other ideas in the book, you will find yourself having to use time-out less and less. A Head Start teacher recently said that after using the ideas from her *Caring Discipline* class, she had to use the time-out correction only three times in a three-month period compared to having earlier used it nearly twice a day.

Like the other three corrections, time-out is not a punishment. Its purpose is to stop the misbehavior, get the adult back in control of the situation, and the child back in control of himself.

Time-Out

Here are the guidelines for administering the basic Time-Out.

1. Time-out is not appropriate for the child under two-and-a-half to three years old

For the very young child, for example, an eighteen month old who is whacking big brother with a shovel, the best tactic is simply to say, "No hurting other people," as you pick the child up and carry him or her to another room of the house, perhaps placing the child in the high chair or a play pen with some toys. (Do not forget to give big brother a hug to help ease the pain and the injustice of being whacked.) If a young child bites you or pulls your hair, say in a strong voice, "No. People are not for biting." If the child does it again, once more say, "No." And put the child down. The consequence of being put down is a powerful reminder that if you want to be with people, you cannot hurt them. Or, maybe your toddler is teething and needs something to chew on.

2. Act the first time you see the aggressive behavior

You learned the value of not procrastinating in the section on self-sabotage. Aggressive behavior especially should be dealt with immediately because every child needs to know that deliberate hurting is never allowed.

3. Time-out should be short

For the preschooler, sitting quietly for three to five minutes is usually enough to stop the behavior and calm things down. For older children, one minute for every year of their age is a reasonable rule. Making the child sit quietly for unreasonable lengths of time is punitive and will escalate a power struggle. Children quickly need another chance to try a different way of behaving. Excessively prolonged time-outs result in increased power struggles that sabotage the learning of responsible behavior.

4. Time-out should happen in a place where there is nothing interesting to do

A child's bedroom is generally not a good time-out place because it is filled with interesting things to do. The bottom step of a stairway in the front hall is good. Or you can use a chair in some part of the room out of sight of the television, where there are no books or toys. Keep in mind this is *not* a shaming, punishing exercise like sitting in a comer with a dunce cap on your head. The idea is to find an uninteresting place for the child to sit. If you are in a public place, the child can stand by a wall or sit on the floor. Sending a child to the principal's office is the worst possible place for a time-out because there are always interesting things going on there. The basic idea is that there should be no social interaction and nothing interesting to do. Time-out means just that: taking time out from all other activities.

5. Use as little talking as possible

Say, "Time-out." Remember the effectiveness of one-word or two-word statements.

6. As soon as the child is seated, quietly set a timer

If you do not already have a timer, buy or borrow one. Set the timer and put it down near the child. Say, "You must sit quietly for five minutes." Then walk away and continue to carry out your normal routine.

7. If the child fusses or does not sit quietly, use the Broken Record

If the child argues, complains, or bangs the chair around during the time-out period, go back to where the child is seated, reset the timer and say, "No. I said sit quietly for five minutes." Remember to keep calm, settle into your body, and imagine yourself as immovable and patient, a moss-covered rock. (See Broken Record, Chapter Seven.)

Teachers, agency personnel, foster parents and childcare providers should have special permission and training before using either of the following two Physical Assist techniques.

8. If the child does not stay in the chair, use a Physical Assist

If the child does not stay seated quietly or attempts to run, use a physical assist. Go stand behind the child, with the palm of one hand on his or her shoulder while the palm of the other hand presses down at the base of the child's neck, securely holding the child down in the chair. Say, "No. You must sit quietly." *It is important for you to practice this physical assist with another adult before you try it with a child.* Pressing down with the open hand just below the child's neck should feel secure and calming to the child. If it does not, you are probably digging in with your fingers or pressing down too hard. *Keep experimenting with the other adult until you have taught each other how to do it.* Do not use more force than necessary. Do not hurt the child. Release your hold as soon as you feel the child stop the struggle. Try to get into your "I am a force of Nature" mode. Be as centered and as calm as you know how to be. Let your nonverbal body language convey the fact that this is something that must be done, and there is nothing anyone can do to change it.

When the child is quiet and stops struggling, restart the timer and walk away. Occasionally, a child will fight the time-out procedure for a long time. Be prepared to stick with this an hour or all evening if necessary. If you do not sabotage yourself, children will generally only test you at such an intense level one or two times. If you are firm and consistent, they will feel safe with you. If they know what the limits are and they know the limits are fair, they will not continue to test them.

One last admonition: Using the physical assist by holding the child in a time-out place can turn into a power struggle if you let yourself become emotional about it. Keep in mind that you are using a teaching method, that you are acting as a force of nature like a wide river or a steady breeze. It is not easy, but you can do it. If you find yourself using the time-out correction more and more, instead of less and less, you and the child are caught up in a power struggle. You need to go to another adult who is familiar with these corrections to help you figure out how you are sabotaging yourself.

9. If the child loses all self control, use the physical restraint

When I was working as an intern at the Children's Psychiatric Day Treatment Center at the University of Oregon, I had to put an extremely aggressive ten-year-old boy in time-out. As sometimes happens with very angry children, he exploded with rage. The only way I could make him stay in time-out was to wrestle him to the ground and sit with my back against the wall, holding him on the floor in front of me between my legs. I crossed his arms in front of his chest, held his back against my front, and held on. He was strong and I had to hold on to him with all the strength I could muster. When he relaxed, I relaxed my hold. When he started to struggle, I tightened my grip. We sat there on the floor for over an hour until he finally sat quietly for five minutes. It was one of the longest hours of my life. But from that day on, he was my friend, and he never seriously disobeyed me again. I was astonished at his positive reaction. He did not seem to feel demeaned, probably because, interspersed between our long silences, I also made an attempt to respect and listen to his feelings. "I know this is hard for you. It is hard for me too."

A mother told her parenting class about a time she used this kind of physical restraint with her daughter. The daughter was an attention-deficit child who, for various reasons, had had a long and stressful day. By evening, she had totally lost control of herself, screaming and lashing out at everyone around her. This sensitive mother finally stepped in, and told her daughter, "I am going to hold you until you can be in control of yourself again." The mother took a position on the floor with her struggling daughter similar to the one described above. Almost immediately the child collapsed sobbing in her arms and calm was restored.

A Head Start teacher tells how amazed she was when, as she began holding an out-of-control child in this way, the child immediately began to suck her thumb and curl up in a fetal position.

Priscilla, who worked as a Head Start Family Visitor, told how one day when she was making a home visit, she had to forcibly hold a boy in this same way. The boy, Tommy, had gone into a rage. He was tipping over furniture and smashing things while his mother stood helplessly by. After Priscilla had calmed Tommy by forcibly holding him down on the floor, the boy's mother quite seriously brought up the possibility of placing him in a foster home. Priscilla was amazed when Tommy faced his mother's rejection calmly. He moved to stand beside the person who had so recently held him down on the floor. "That's all right. I'll go live with Priscilla."

Feeling safe is one of the most basic of human needs. Do not hesitate to hold children securely if they explode out of the boundary of self-control. Let children gain the security they need from the strong and matter-of-fact way your body holds them. *Never hold the child on your lap.* Hold the child so he or she is sitting on the floor in front of you between your legs. Your own physical size and strength is obviously the limiting factor that will determine the size of child you can hold in this way.

Ask another adult to role-play this situation with you in the role of the child. (See page 238.) Only then will you understand how safe and secure it feels to be held in this type of physical restraint. No child feels good about losing his or her inner control. Even though it happens only rarely, you will feel more confident if you are prepared for the rare instances you need to help a child regain inner control.

10. When the time-out is over, do not mention the negative behavior again

Time-out is not a punishment. It is a way to temporarily help you stop the misbehavior and help the child get back in control. Once the incident is over, begin giving positive attention for neutral and positive behaviors. In the same way you would give children a chance to get right back into a canoe if they tip it over, so children need to be given the chance to immediately resume normal behaviors in order to experience success in their interactions with you. As soon as they are exhibiting positive or neutral behaviors, let them know by your positive attentions that you care about them. It was their behavior you did not like.

Look for the Underlying Cause of the Aggression

If children are frequently acting out in aggressive ways, you can be certain they are responding to some deep hurt which they perceive has been done to them. Children who continually lash out at the world in aggressive ways are acting on an instinctual premise that they must protect their inner core of integrity. They have come to believe that their best defense is a strong offense. It may not be clear to you right now, but invariably, every child who frequently feels compelled to manipulate or hurt others is doing it from a need to secure himself or herself from further physical or emotional hurt. In order to help the child, you need to know how the child perceives his or her world. *Listen to the child.* The next chapter will give you ideas on how to do that.

Besides listening to the child, talk to other adults who know the child. Talk about the problem with your spouse or partner. Talk it over with the teacher or members of your family. If you are a teacher, talk it over with the child's parents. Ask each other the question, "What has hurt Marty so much that she feels the need to hurt and manipulate others?" If you can discover what it is, you will better know what kinds of specific positive attentions you can give Marty to help her feel safe enough, and loved enough, so she will not have to keep lashing out at other people. If you look deeply, every aggressive child in some way feels there is at least one of Maslow's needs that is not being supplied for him or her. The problem is that children cannot verbalize their unmet needs. Often parents and teachers cannot figure it out without help. The value of going to a good family therapist is the help in finding the answer to that question. If after you have tried everything suggested in this book, and nothing changes, it is time to look for such a person. Chapter Twelve will give you ideas on how to find the right family therapist.

It is sometimes hard to figure out whether a misbehavior is self-indulgent or aggressive. Trust your own inner feelings. If your gut reaction is one of shock and hurt because you believe the behavior was meant to really harm or manipulate, or if you sense the child is not just having a temper tantrum but has lost control of himself, use the time-out. If you are experiencing extreme irritation with the behavior, and believe it is primarily a bid for attention, treat it as a self-indulgent behavior.

Teens: A Special Case

The type of time-out described above is not appropriate for the pre-teen or teenager. Their larger size and near adult development obviously calls for a different strategy. As is true for all ages of children, parents and teachers need to concentrate on looking for the underlying cause of the aggression. Chapters Two through Five have given you the tools you need to be able to discover and deal with the underlying problem causing a child of any age to either erupt in outwardly aggressive ways, or turn inwards in self-destructive behaviors. Chapter Eleven will teach you how to lead a family or classroom meeting to problem-solve common concerns on a regular basis. Chapter Twelve is geared specifically to teenagers and will give you ideas for how to work with an aggressive teenager who does not respond to any of your earlier efforts. Chapter Thirteen will teach you how to work with other adults on a regular basis to problem-solve specific problems that arise with your children or students.

All of this takes time and effort. If the power struggle with your teen has been building for a long time, there are deeply hurt feelings on both sides. It will take not only time and effort, but courage, for you to try new ways of approaching the problems between you and your teen. But only by doing so can you take charge of the relationship and begin to stop the process of hurt, rejection, and anger that both adult and child are feeling. The fact you are still willing to read a book like this one is proof that you have not given up. As long as you don't give up and are willing to learn some basic methods for communicating with your child, there is every reason to have confidence that you can change the downward spiral now happening between you and your teenager.

Exercise

Continue to use the "Negative Behaviors" worksheet for recording a sampling of misbehaviors and problem-solving behaviors that you observe in your children or students.

This chapter completes the explanations of the four basic types of misbehaviors. Review the summary chart, "The Four Misbehaviors and Their Corrections," on page 236. Be sure the concepts make sense to you and that it is clear when to use the corrections and when to intervene in helping the child solve problems.

WORKSHEET

NEGATIVE BEHAVIORS

The Four Misbehaviors and Three Problem-Solving Situations

NOT-MINDING (Not Doing What Is Asked)

SELF-INDULGENT (Attention-Getting)

ROUTINE NOT-MINDING (Will Not Do Routine Tasks)

AGGRESSIVE (Deliberately Hurting)

NEGATIVE BEHAVIORS Requiring Problem-Solving That Does Not Fit Above:

1. Adjust Environment   2. Solve Conflicts   3. Listen to Feelings

---

from *Caring Discipline: Practical Tools for
Nurturing Happy Families & Classrooms*

THE FOUR MISBEHAVIORS AND THEIR CORRECTIONS

Misbehavior	Correction
Not-Minding (will not do as asked)	Physical Assist or Broken Record
Self-Indulgent (attention-getting)	Ignore or Either-or Choice
Routine Not-Minding (will not do routine tasks, is irresponsible)	Give children daily opportunities to make, and live with, their choices
	Set up a logical consequence situation so children can experience the consequences of their choices
Aggressive (deliberately hurting self or others)	Time-out and Physical Assist or (rarely) Physical Restraint

Non-parents need special permission

Child Has a Problem	Adult Helps the Child By:
1. Child cannot live up to adult expectations, even when he tries	1. Adjusting the environment
2. Child has a conflict with someone	2. Teaching assertiveness and negotiation
3. Child is troubled	3. Listening to inner-reality feelings

from *Caring Discipline: Practical Tools for Nurturing Happy Families & Classrooms*

REVIEW: Correction for Aggressive Behaviors
The Time-Out

1. The time-out is a **last-resort correction** to be used when everything else has failed.

2. **The time-out is not appropriate for the child under two-and-a-half to three years old.**

3. Act the **first time** you see the aggressive behavior.

4. **A short time-out is best:** 3–5 minutes for preschoolers. One minute for every year of age for older children.

5. The time-out place should have **nothing interesting** for the child to do.

6. **Use as little talking as possible.** Do not sabotage yourself.

7. As soon as the child is seated, set a timer, and **quietly walk away.** Use the Broken Record, if needed.

Non-parents need special permission to use #8 and #9:

8. If the child does not stay in the chair, use a **physical assist.**

9. On the rare occasions when a child loses all self control, you can use the **physical restraint** procedure.

---

10. **When the time-out is over, be pleasant with the child** and do not mention the negative behavior again. Time-out or physical restraint is not a punishment. It is a way to temporarily help you stop the misbehavior and a way to help the child get back in control of himself.

11. **Look for the underlying cause,** especially if the aggressive behaviors are frequent or severe. "What has hurt the child so much that he or she feels compelled to lash out at others?"

REMEMBER NOT TO SELF-SABOTAGE

from *Caring Discipline: Practical Tools for Nurturing Happy Families & Classrooms*

Chapter 10 Discussion: CORRECTION FOR AGGRESSIVE BEHAVIORS

1. Share and discuss your comments on the past week's "Negative Behaviors" worksheet.

2. Did anyone try offering some fun choices to their children last week? Did anyone try a logical consequences plan?

3. **Practice the time-out procedure:** Everyone take a turn being the child and adult in a situation where the adult is holding the child in the chair. Have the "child" struggle while the "adult" practices the physical assist of placing the palm of one hand on the child's shoulder and other at the base of the neck. Do this until you find a position that feels most secure and convincing for the child. The goal is to give the child a sense of security. It will help all you C-adults to know that, when a child is out of control, he or she can feel safe again knowing the adult is in control. Try to convey the sense that "I am a force of Nature and this must be done." Use the minimum pressure necessary. Avoid digging in with your fingers. Avoid any sense that you are punishing the child.

4. **Now, practice the physical restraint procedure:** Take turns playing the part of the child. Hold the "child" *on the floor* in front of you. *Do not hold the child on your lap.* The child needs to feel the firm support of the floor under him while feeling your body giving support by enfolding him in your arms. Remember you will probably have to hold the child's arms by crossing them against his or her chest. Experiment with different ways to hold the child's arms if the child tries to bite you. Be aware of the need to keep your head clear if the child is tall enough to hit your chin with the back of his or her head.

5. Discuss the difference between the either-or choice and the time-out. Is everyone clear on the difference?

6. Look at "The Self-Sabotages" chart again at the end of Chapter Three. Is there one that you feel has been especially powerful in sabotaging your relationships with your children?

Chapter ELEVEN
The Family and Classroom Meetings

If you have experimented your way through this book, trying out each new concept as you went along, you have acquired some new and effective tools for dealing with discipline. By now you are beginning to feel "in charge," at least some of the time. And, if you are like most parents and teachers, you are also feeling relieved at knowing that you can take charge in a way that encourages each child to blossom as a strong and unique individual.

This chapter will show you how to use what you have learned to organize and facilitate classroom and/or family meetings. The value of meetings are three-fold. First, regular meetings provide children the opportunity to learn the art of problem-solving, negotiation, and compromise. Second, when children get involved in problem-solving for the group, it lifts some of the burden of responsibility off the adult. Third, these meetings will not only help strengthen the child's staircase of needs, they will also enrich and strengthen the family or classroom group.

Today powerful forces are pulling families and classrooms apart. Each individual goes off to a different place to spend a major part of their twenty-four hour day. In many families, the individual members have no idea what happens to the other family members during their work time. This is why so many parents feel such sadness when they leave their child alone at school for the first time. They know that from now on there will be a large part of that child's life unknown to them. To make matters worse, many families are so busy in the evenings, they no longer sit down at a table to eat and visit together. The family or classroom meeting can be a precious time of getting to know one another better, and of strengthening emotional bonds, as well as a time for working on problems.

A family in which the father had always been expected to solve most of the family problems started holding regular family meetings after the father got a job driving a long-distance truck. With the father gone over half of the time, the mother and grandmother turned to a weekly meeting as a way to involve the whole family in providing the discipline they had earlier expected the father to give. To their pleasant surprise, the meetings turned out not only to provide the means by which they could deal with the problems of living together, but they also enriched the relationships between the generations. The grandmother used the opportunity to begin sharing her experiences of growing up in Mexico with her daughter and grandchildren. As a result, the children became well acquainted with their family history in a personal way they might never have realized without the leisurely and regular meetings their mother and grandmother provided. The father also began to participate in the meetings when he was home, sharing with them his experiences on the road, and seemed quite comfortable with this new way of dealing with family problems.

One of the major objections many adults have to holding classroom or family meetings is their basic assumption that, if no unanimous solution can be found, then the issue must be decided by vote. After all, we live in a democracy so the democratic way must be to vote and let the majority decide. Consequently, many adults refuse to hold meetings with children because of their fear of being outvoted by the kids. Understandably, adults are nervous about giving children an equal vote. The thought of being outnumbered by their children and students is scary. As one father said, "It's crazy to give a five-year-old an equal vote with a parent. Kids don't have the background or the responsibility that adults do. We don't let anybody vote in this country until they are eighteen. No five-year-old is going to have an equal vote in this family." So it may surprise and please you to learn: *There is no voting allowed at family or classroom meetings.*

While the custom of voting is the best available system for a nation, voting in the more intimate family or classroom setting can tear the group apart. Whenever there is a vote, someone wins and someone loses. People who lose are likely to feel misunderstood and put down. The losing minority often resists the will of the majority, sometimes in very subtle ways. The result is that the family or classroom begins to fracture and split into factions.

Take the case of twenty-eight sixth-graders who voted 20 to 8 in favor of a new classroom rule. The result was twenty children who obeyed the rule and eight children who continued to resist, either openly or behind the teacher's back. Even worse, subsequent classroom meetings became forums for argument in which one section of the class tried to persuade their classmates to vote for the "right" point of view. The outcome was that everyone was so busy defending their own position, hardly anyone could hear what the other people were saying. One has only to listen to political discussions at the state and national level to find extreme examples of the polarization that happens when no one is really listening to the other person's point of view.

The next important concept to remember is this: *The process of searching for a solution is more important than actually finding a solution.* Many adults and children assume that the primary purpose of the family or classroom meeting is to find a solution to a specific problem. But even more important than finding a solution is the process of searching for the solution. The meeting will have been a success if the process has given each person a chance to speak and to be heard. The group does not have to find a unanimous solution to the problem. Remember Maslow's staircase of needs. The opportunity to talk and be listened to gives each person the emotional support needed to strengthen his or her staircase.

People of all ages who have their needs met for belonging, security, being-love, and competency/respect are much more likely to be cooperative and trusting of other members of the group. By providing for at least some of the emotional needs of its individual members, the meeting will help both the group and the individuals in it stay vital and strong. In marriages that break apart, in families where children run away, in schools where students drop out, the bonds that held the group together have been weakened. When the group is somehow no longer supplying the basic emotional needs for each individual, members will withdraw either physically or emotionally.

Following are two examples of meetings, each with an entirely different problem and involving different age groups. The first was a family meeting with only four people involved, the second was a series of meetings that took place in a middle school with more than twenty people involved. Neither situation resulted in a solution with which everyone could agree, yet both meetings were successful. Both meetings had an adult in charge who managed to concentrate on the *process* of solving the problem, rather than persuading everyone to agree on a specific solution. No solution was forced on any group member, and yet the problem was resolved, or, it might be more accurate to say, the problem no longer seemed like such a problem anymore. To paraphrase John Dewey, "We don't usually solve our problems so much as we just get over them."

Family Meeting Example

A mother had two sons, Mustafa, age four, and Abdullah, age six. Abdullah stayed home from school one day with a cold and a slight fever. When it was time for her to take Mustafa to his preschool class, Mother said to Abdullah, "It's time to put your coat on so we can take Mustafa to school." Abdullah protested, "I don't need a coat. I'm hot. I'm real hot."

As you can imagine, an argument followed, with the mother trying to reason with Abdullah about how she did not want him to go out in the cold rain with a fever and no coat. Finally, in desperation, she used the physical assist and forcibly put the coat on her son while he screamed and cried. Once in the car, Abdullah kept taking his coat off causing her to stop several times to put it back on. By the time they returned home, they were both angry. Abdullah alternated between being cross and sullen all the rest of the day. Finally, in the late afternoon, Abdullah demanded, "I want a family meeting!"

Mother agreed that a family meeting would be a good idea. They decided to have the meeting after dinner when Dad would be home. After dinner, they popped some popcorn, divided two cans of soda and sat down around the table. Abdullah started out by telling them he was old enough to know whether or not to wear a coat and it's nobody else's business anyway. Mother again explained why she could not let a sick child go out without a coat. Abdullah insisted he had the right to decide whether or not he had to wear a coat. After all, it was his body. Everyone got a turn to give an opinion, even four-year-old Mustafa who was mostly interested in munching on the popcorn. Mother and Dad tried their best to listen to Abdullah's inner reality by looking at him intently as he talked and saying, "Gosh," and "Hmm."

But there was no way Mom or Dad could ever agree that Abdullah had the right to go out in a rainstorm with a fever and no coat. Dad tried describing the situation, "So you didn't think it was fair for Mom to force you to wear the coat. And Mom, you didn't dare let him go without the coat because you were afraid he would get even sicker." Both Abdullah and Mom nodded their heads in agreement. Dad finally threw up his hands. "I don't have any ideas. It just seems like two people who have entirely different points of view." There was a long silence while they sipped their sodas and ate their popcorn. Finally Mother said, "Well, I don't know what to say. I can't change my mind and I guess Abdullah can't either. Let's just quit talking about it for awhile. Maybe one of us will get an idea for something to do about it later on." Dad said, "Does anybody want to play Chutes and Ladders before it is time for bed?" In this way, the meeting adjourned. No solutions were found. Mother and Abdullah still disagreed about a proper course of action.

The interesting outcome of this meeting was that Abdullah's disposition immediately returned to his normal, sunny self and he never mentioned the incident again. The next day, when it was time to take Mustafa to preschool, Mother said, "Time to get ready to go." And Abdullah, still sniffling from his cold, put his coat on without complaint.

By listening to Abdullah's inner reality, by using describing words to talk about a negative, high stress situation, and by not insisting that all parties come to an agreement and find an immediate solution, both Abdullah's and Mother's emotional needs were met. Even Dad's and Mustafa's needs for belonging and competency were met because their opinions were asked for and respected. In the process, Abdullah was able to hear his mother's genuine concern for his health, and consequently his honest inner self made the responsible decision to wear his coat.

Classroom or School Meeting Example

A middle-school principal gave a school counselor an urgent morning phone call asking her to spend a day at his school. The regular counselor was unable to come to school because of illness, and the principal needed someone to try to prevent a student from being badly hurt by some of the other students.

Joe, a ninth-grade student, had been killed in an automobile accident several days earlier. Another ninth-grade student, David, had been overheard to say, "It's no big loss to the world that Joe got killed. He was a son-of-a-bitch anyhow." David's remark was overheard by some indignant students who spread it throughout the school. David's comment was eventually reported to Joe's friends and to Joe's seventh-grade sister. The girl was devastated. The remark added cruelly to the pain she was already feeling over the death of her brother.

Joe's friends were upset and angry. They decided to take revenge. They made a plan to catch David when he got off the bus after school that day and "kill him." This plan was in turn reported to the principal, who got on the phone to call the counselor for help. The principal did not think Joe's friends would actually kill David, but was convinced they were angry enough to seriously hurt the boy when they caught him alone off the school grounds.

The principal spent considerable amounts of time that morning going into classrooms, and bringing back various groups of students to meet with the counselor as she asked for them. The major groups that met to talk were Joe's grieving friends, a group of respected students who were neutral but sympathetic, and David and his friends. Joe's sister was not included in any of the groups since she asked not to be involved. All that morning, the counselor met with small groups of students, asking them to state the problem, listening to feelings, asking for ideas.

First, the counselor met with Joe's friends. They were understandably upset, extremely hostile and unforgiving towards David. Lee, who had been Joe's best friend, was especially in a cold rage against David. During this meeting, the counselor totally concentrated on listening to their inner-reality feelings of pain and anger.

Next, the counselor met with David and his friends. David was well aware of the threats against him. He was now very sorry, very frightened, and was feeling completely hopeless that any solution could be found. David knew his teachers and his parents could protect him today and tomorrow, but at some future time, Joe's friends would find a way to punish him.

The next group to meet was the concerned group of neutral students. At this meeting, one person came up with the idea that David could write Joe's sister a note of apology and also spend his own money to buy her a teddy bear for her stuffed animal collection. The neutral group agreed this was a good idea because it would be similar to bringing flowers to a funeral and would mean more than just a note of apology. When the counselor presented the idea at a meeting of David and his friends, David eagerly agreed.

Next, the neutral student group met with the counselor and the dead boy's friends. They presented the teddy bear idea as a possible solution. All Joe's friends, with the exception of Lee, thought the teddy bear idea was a good one. As in earlier meetings, Lee sat sullen and hostile, refusing to participate. The counselor asked him, "Would it be okay with you if I told David you think giving Joe's sister a stuffed animal and a letter of apology would be a good idea?"

Lee looked straight at the counselor, hostility shining from his eyes, and said, "You can tell him anything you want."

The counselor shook her head. "No, I don't want to say anything that isn't true. Would it be okay if I tell him you are so hurt and angry you don't even want to talk to him at all?"

Suddenly, tears welled up in Lee's eyes. Each person in the group also felt tears welling up in their own eyes, as they realized the intensity of pain Lee was feeling for his lost friend. Lee said nothing, perhaps he could not have spoken without breaking down and crying, but he nodded his head in agreement. The rage had left him, leaving his grief stark and clear for everyone to see.

Joe's other friends went to Joe's sister and told her what David was planning to do as an apology to her. She felt supported and protected by her brother's friends and was relieved they had tried to find a peaceful solution. The principal called David's parents to ask for their help in taking their son to buy the teddy bear. The counselor again met with David to tell him that most, but not all, of Joe's friends had agreed to the idea, and that Lee in particular was still so hurt and angry he did not even want to talk to David. A subdued David said he would write the apology and buy the teddy bear that evening.

When the students got on the bus that afternoon, no one knew for sure whether the situation had been defused. After all, Lee was a key leader of the group and he had not agreed to any solution. Lee had only agreed that the counselor could tell David he was so hurt and angry he did not want to talk to him. There was great relief on the school staff when the two adults who had volunteered to monitor David's bus stop reported that there were no unpleasant incidents that afternoon. Nothing violent happened to David that day, or for the rest of the school year.

As in the earlier situation involving Abdullah and his coat, we see the healing power of respecting every person's emotional needs. No solution was imposed on any member of any group. Nobody voted for or against the teddy bear/apology idea. There were no winners and no losers. The adults hoped things would be all right for David at the end of that school day but had no way to know for certain. Lee had made no promises to leave David alone. What the counselor did know was that in each group that met that morning, everyone, including David and Lee, had a chance to talk and be listened to. Each person's inner reality had been respected. Doors to communication that had been slammed tight were reopened. Undoubtedly, the turning point came when the counselor respected Lee's inner-reality feelings by saying, "I don't want to tell him anything that isn't true. How about if I just tell him you're so hurt and angry you don't even want to talk to him at all?"

Guidelines for Holding Family or Classroom Meetings

Here is a basic list of guidelines for setting up and leading a meeting. Keep in mind the importance of trying not to persuade anyone in the group to accept any particular solution. As leader of the meeting, you will have plenty of opportunities to use the skills learned in earlier chapters, especially listening to inner-reality feelings, using describing language in negative situations, and not sabotaging yourself by talking, talking, and more talking.

1. Schedule a regular meeting time

Most families and elementary classes have time for at least one weekly meeting. High school classrooms, in which students meet for only an hour a day, will probably have to meet less often. For example, some high school classes hold a meeting every other Friday. The main idea is that the meeting times be regular and predictable.

As a child, Larinda hated family meetings. Meetings in her family were held only during crisis times. Crisis times happened when her father got drunk and angry at his wife. He would start the meeting by yelling at everyone to get into the living room. He would then proceed to lecture his assembled children in a loud and angry tone of voice on why he was right and why their mother was wrong. The father's goal was to persuade his children to take his side against the mother. Mother rarely got a chance to speak because Dad would shout her down. "Who do you think is right? Your mother or me?" No child wants to be torn between taking sides with Dad against Mother, or with Mother against Dad. No wonder Larinda remembers those so-called family meetings with such anguish. The meetings Larinda described were political meetings designed to defeat and humiliate her mother.

Waiting for a crisis time to call a meeting always increases the possibility that the stresses of the immediate situation will turn the meeting into a negative experience for everyone. Weekly meetings held on a regular basis help insure a calm and supportive atmosphere in which differences of opinion are more likely to be listened to. Before holding your first family meeting, ask each member of the family when would be the best time to meet. From the very beginning, each person needs to know that this is their meeting and they will have a say in deciding when the meetings are held. Thereafter, before the closing of each meeting, ask the family, "Shall we meet at the same time next week? Will this be a good time for everyone?" Then write the date on a calendar which you display in a prominent place, such as the refrigerator door.

Classroom meeting times are more easily structured because the total school schedule is more predictable than the ordinary family situation. But even in a school situation, you need to be flexible. For example, if one child is unexpectedly scheduled into a special reading class during the regular Friday meeting time, the teacher can discuss the need for a change, "From now on, Eric will be going out of the room during our regular class meeting time. We'll need to change the time so everyone can be here. How about meeting just before lunch on Friday? Does anybody see a problem with that?" In this way, the teacher shows respect for her student's opinions regarding a new meeting schedule, while at the same time she emphasizes the idea that each individual is essential to the meeting.

2. Establish a relaxed and upbeat atmosphere for the meeting

Talking and listening flows better when people are feeling relaxed. In the classroom a favorite relaxing technique for younger students who have a hard time sitting still is to allow them to draw pictures at their desks while they are participating in the discussion. In smaller groups, children can choose whether they would like to color or work with clay while they talk and listen. Any adult who is part of the group can also participate. Clay is the best choice for the adult because children often become focused on what the adult is drawing instead of listening to the conversation. Never make anything special with the clay. Only roll it and squish it to establish a relaxed atmosphere. You want children to focus on the discussion, not on the art work. If anyone chooses just to sit, that is okay. If your room has a carpeted floor or pillows in a reading corner, children could choose whether to stay at their desks or sit on the floor. This might be the time to give a popcorn treat. Turn off those bright fluorescent lights. The dimmer, natural light has a calming effect on many children. In the upper grade classroom, arranging the desks in a circle helps establish an atmosphere of equality and informality.

At home, a special treat like popcorn, soda, or a Popsicle sets a friendly mood. Do any simple thing that helps convey the idea of a relaxing, friendly time.

3. Use an opening ritual

Ruth, who grew up in a Jewish family, remembers regular family meetings from her childhood. She recalls that she looked forward each week to these family meetings and that they made her feel very important. The meetings always opened with a reading from the Bible. (The practice of opening the family meeting by teaching a value system could be adapted to any faith. Any religious or secular philosophy could be used according to each parent's belief system.) After the opening reading, each child was asked to tell about something interesting that had happened in school that week. Only after these opening rituals were concluded were family problems then discussed with each child being asked their opinion. She remembers these meetings with great affection and now holds similar family meetings with her own children.

Rituals should be done on a regular basis so they help set the mood for the meeting to follow. Rituals can be as simple as tinkling a quiet bell, turning off the fluorescent lights, or passing out the popcorn. One family lit a fire in the fireplace on cool evenings just before the meeting began. You could light candles. In a family where the television is usually turned on, just the act of turning off the television can become a part of the ritual. One family opened the meeting with a short reading which anyone in the family was welcome to bring. Usually, it was the mother or father who brought a fragment of poetry or philosophy to read to the group, but occasionally one of the children would bring the reading. Hearing their child share some important belief, some learning discovery, or some beautiful lines of poetry were unexpectedly powerful emotional times for the parents.

Another kind of ritual you can use to open the meeting is for each person to share something that made him or her happy during the week, as well as some difficult experience that happened during the week. As in every other kind of ritual, adults must also participate in this sharing. It is important that the events being shared by the adult have nothing to do with the children's behavior. This sharing exercise is meant to give your children a peek at the life you lead when you are apart from them. In this way, they will get to know you better as a human being, not just as Mom, or Dad, or Teacher. As you share your life with them, you will find they will share more of their life with you.

4. Involve everyone in setting the agenda

An agenda is a list of the things to be done at a meeting. It is crucial for the success of the family or classroom meeting that every individual be encouraged to suggest items for the agenda. If teachers and parents are the only people to decide what gets talked about, the children will very quickly decide they do not want to participate. This is why so many children resist the idea of a family or classroom meeting when they first hear about it. They assume the adult will set the agenda items and that all topics of discussion will center on the adult telling the child what to do. Since no one likes to be a captive audience and have to sit through a lecture telling how to live a life, the normal kid says, "No thank you!"

The simplest method for getting everyone involved is to use a blank sheet of paper. Title the paper, "Topics for Discussion." Fasten it to a clipboard or to the refrigerator door. Tell everybody, "Here is where you can write down anything you want to talk about at the next family meeting." If there is something you want to talk about, write it on the list also. During the week, if anyone comes to you with a complaint about someone else, you can listen to their inner-reality feelings by saying, "Hmm," or "Gosh, what a problem." You could also suggest, "If that's something you'd like to talk about at the next family meeting, you could write it down on the list." If people are using the list for name calling or other inappropriate language, be sure to immediately write down on the list, "What shall we do about people who do name calling when they write down topics to discuss?" and then, if the problem continues, make the name calling issue a high priority topic for discussion at the next meeting. If the children are only writing down problems, be sure you occasionally include one fun topic to discuss, for example: "Where shall we go on vacation this summer?" Or, "Does anyone want to tell about something that happened in this classroom recently that made them feel happy or proud?"

After the opening rituals are finished, you can pass around the list of suggested topics for discussion and ask if anyone wants to cross a topic off the list. Probably some of the topics will no longer be a problem to the person who wanted to discuss it earlier in the week. "Oh, that. You can cross that one off. We settled it already." Sometimes, in both the classroom and family settings, difficult topics will arise that require more time than you can give in one session. The group may have to decide which topic to talk about first, and how much time to give each topic. If need be, use a timer to see that each topic gets equal time.

Setting the agenda for the classroom meeting can be accomplished by setting up a covered shoe box with a slot in the top. Encourage your students to fill out a simple form to be deposited in the box whenever they have an idea for something to discuss. The form should have three parts: "A Topic I Would Like to Discuss," a line for the name of the student, and a line for the date.

Asking students to sign their notes has several advantages. It allows the teacher to know who is having the problem. Sometimes the teacher may decide it is a problem best discussed privately. The signed note will give the teacher enough information to know who to talk with about the problem. The signed note also encourages accountability for any statements made about another person. The privacy of the notes in a box also prevents children in the classroom from having their feelings hurt over any name calling that might take place on a more public agenda. On the day of the classroom meeting, the teacher can take the agenda suggestions out of the box and decide how to present them to the class. In this way, the teacher can act as a buffer to insure that any particular child is not attacked by others in the room.

5. Keep focused on the general problem

Sometimes many specific individual problems will be related. Take, for example, a fourth-grade classroom in which six children write down six different incidents about someone teasing them. The teacher can ignore the specific names of who was teasing whom, and state the problem as a general one. For example, instead of saying, "Mattie said Geoff pushed her in the lunch line, and Craig said Nancy ran off with his coat during recess, etc.," the teacher can lump these related problems together by saying, "There are quite a few people who had a problem with someone bugging them this past week." The problem then becomes the general problem of "bugging" and not Craig, Nancy, Mattie, or Geoff. Emphasizing specific names of people makes it easy to end up with the meeting turned into a blaming session, where the "good" guys blame the "bad" guys and the "bad" guys blame everybody else. Throughout the discussion, you can help by refusing to focus on specific names and instead respond by always coming back to the more general problem, for example, when Craig says, "I don't know why Nancy is so mean," you can turn this statement back to the general problem by saying, "It's hard to understand why some people do so much teasing." Try to keep the group focused on the problem, rather than on any particular individual.

At home, where you are dealing with fewer children, you are freer to use names more often, but the principle is the same: Try to downplay focusing on any particular individual in favor of focusing on the general problem.

6. Watch out for hidden agendas

As leader, you need to be aware of unwritten, or hidden, agendas. A hidden agenda is the list of items no one actually writes down but that people instead carry around in their heads. Hidden agendas often happen when people come to the meeting determined to either find or prevent a particular solution. For example, the mother who wants to discuss the problem of people leaving their coats and books all over the living room when they come home from school may have a hidden agenda of trying to persuade her children to adopt the solution to the problem which she has already decided would work the best. (Her solution is to fine everybody five cents for every coat or book she picks up.) If Mother comes to the meeting convinced she has already found the correct solution, it will be almost impossible for her to listen her children's ideas. Since children are smart, they will soon realize their mother is not able to listen to ideas other than her own. The children will then develop a hidden agenda of their own, "Why should I have to lose my allowance? It's not such a big deal to leave a few books around. I'll be darned if I'll agree to her idea."

The hidden agenda item which children often bring to a meeting is to avoid being blamed for anything. By focusing on avoiding blame, they also effectively sabotage the process of finding a solution. "I'm not going to admit it's my fault. Other people do it all the time. I'm not going to take part in this dumb meeting."

The need for hidden agendas tends to disappear as everyone, both adults and children, begin to have faith in the power of the group to respect the rights of every individual as it searches for solutions to problems.

7. Use brainstorming to think about possible solutions

Here is a three-step brainstorm process you can use to look for a solution for any problem the group needs to discuss. You can use this brainstorm process at every age level, from elementary school age up to senior citizens. Although a solution is likely to emerge, do not *expect* a solution to come out of the process. Neither you nor the group is a failure if no solution is found. Take a leap of faith and trust the process. The group meeting will be successful if the group is able to explore many sides of the problem, and, if, at the same time, the inner-reality experiences of each person are respected.

STEP 1. Describe the problem

Give each person a chance to state the problem as he or she understands it. To start, describe what you think the problem is. For example, in the classroom teasing problem you could say, "Six different people had a problem with being teased. So it sounds like the problem to talk about is: What can you do when someone teases you?" Then open it up to the group by saying, "Does anybody else have another way to state the problem?" This gives the people who have the problem a chance to clarify or change the focus of the problem. In the small family group, you will have time to go around the group and ask each person specifically to state the problem. In the large classroom group, you will have to limit it to only those who volunteer.

Expect that some members of the group, especially those who are fearful of being blamed for the teasing, will at first try to sabotage the process. The person who has been doing much of the teasing may make outrageous statements like, "*She* calls it teasing, but she's just a big cry baby!" or "I get bugged all the time and I don't whine about it!" Try some describing and some inner-reality listening. Even the person who teases gets teased sometimes, too. You can say, "You hate to get teased, too, but you keep quiet about it." Or, if you cannot think of anything to say, just nod your head and say, "Hmm." Make frequent friendly eye contact with the persons in the group who are fearful of being blamed. Assume that no one in this entire group likes to be teased. Assume that even teasers get teased sometimes.

When everyone agrees on what the problem is, restate it, and write it down so that during the subsequent discussion you can refer back to it. At the family meeting, someone can act as secretary and write it on a piece of paper. At the classroom meeting, you or a class secretary can write it on the chalkboard. Do not go on to the next step until everyone agrees as to what the actual problem is.

STEP 2. Brainstorm possible solutions

Now invite everyone to come up with possible solutions to the problem. Make a list of each of the ideas on the chalkboard or the secretary can keep a list on a piece of paper if there is no chalkboard available. Expect that a few people are going to come up with outrageous solutions like, "Make the teasers go to a different school," or "Make them stay home for two days every time they make someone cry." All ideas, no matter how silly, must be written down on the list. This is not the time to find flaws in the ideas presented. If someone argues, "Well, that won't work. The principal won't let us send anybody to a different school," you can interrupt and say, "Next we'll talk about whether or not the ideas will work. Right now, all ideas are welcome."

The list can be written in shortened form but should contain the major idea—for example, "different school," and "stay home." Some of these outrageous ideas will be offered as a joke, so if you recognize the humor, be sure to grin a little as you write it down. The rest of the group will see your smile and begin to learn that brainstorming is a creative process that can be fun.

Include your own ideas on the list, for example, "Maybe it would work if the person being teased would try to pretend the teaser was invisible." You will be amazed at the creative ideas a group of children can engender. Feel free to offer your ideas as long as you, and the children, recognize that your idea is just one more piece of the brainstorming process, no more and no less important than any other person's idea.

When you and the group are satisfied you have a fairly complete list, go on to the last step.

STEP 3. Attempt to choose a solution

Even though it is okay if a solution is not found, it is important to sincerely explore all possibilities for a solution. Start at the top of the list. Take each idea in turn and ask the group, "What about this one? Do you think this would work?" Your leadership role for this part of the process is to help the group think out loud and to clarify their various options. You do not, and should not, have to make the decision. The entire group must make a unanimous decision about whether or not to choose a particular solution.

Many children are accustomed to having adults make all major decisions for them. They will often come up with solutions that shift all responsibility to the parent or teacher; for example, "We could come tell the teacher when someone teases us and she could make him stay in for recess." Even though you may be inwardly thinking there is no way you would ever agree to this idea, go ahead and list it on the chalkboard. But during this third step in the process, as you come to the idea that the teacher should be the judge, you can say, in a thoughtful way, "I wouldn't feel comfortable having to be the judge who everyone comes to about being teased. I wouldn't know who started it. I can't go along with this idea." If you do not want to be the judge, say so. Respect your own inner integrity and feelings just as you would respect those of any other member of the group.

After the group has gone down the list crossing off any ideas that would not work and circling the ideas that seem to have possibilities, go back to all the circled items and one by one, ask, "If we do choose this one, what could go wrong?" Things usually do go wrong with almost any new proposal. It is a valuable lesson in planning to try to anticipate as many glitches as possible. A fourth-grade group that I led in a similar brainstorming discussion finally selected out two possible solutions to the problem of being teased. The first was to play in a different area of the playground from the person who teased you. Not everyone agreed that playing in a different area of the playground was a good idea for them personally. Many students felt they had the right to play wherever they wanted. They were not going to let some teaser scare them away. But, and this was the point of universal agreement, they did agree it would be an okay solution for anybody who wanted to try it. When I asked, "What could go wrong?" someone immediately said, "The teaser might just follow you everywhere on the playground."

If the teaser did follow them around, they decided to use the second solution, which was to try to pretend the teaser was invisible. That way, people who teased would not get any enjoyment out of seeing they were making you miserable. When the group was asked what could go wrong with this solution, many children said they did not know how long they could keep up pretending when the other person was being really mean to them. Everyone agreed it is hard to ignore teasing. Then, a third proposal surfaced. Someone said, "If that happens, how about going over to talk with the grown-up on recess duty. You wouldn't have to tattle, you could keep on pretending the other person was invisible and just talk to the grown-up about other things. Then I bet the teaser would go away." Everyone agreed that might work. The meeting ended with an agreement to talk about the teasing problem at a later time if these three ideas did not help.

This discussion took a long time, almost forty-five minutes. But the incidents of teasing, or at least the complaints about being teased, dropped way off after this meeting. *It would be fine if the group had not found a single acceptable solution to try. It is the thoughtful and respectful process of involving every person in the group when looking for a solution which raises self-esteem and improves behavior.*

8. Practice the skills you learned about listening to inner reality and describing outer reality

The family or classroom meeting provides a perfect situation for practicing listening and describing skills. In fact, without your listening and describing skills, you risk being baited into power struggles with at least one of the group participants.

Naomi had four children who left their clothing and books strewn all over the house when they came home from school. Naomi hated coming home from work each day to this mess. Usually, she could not stand to look at the clutter so she would pick everything up and then scold her children about it at dinner time. Naomi decided to discuss this problem at the family meeting which she and her husband had recently begun to hold on a regular basis. She presented the problem to her kids, using good describing language, "When I come home from work, I see coats and books in the living room and dining room and after school lunch snacks left out on the kitchen counter. I'm tired at the end of the day. I get even more tired when I come home to a messy house. I need some help in figuring out a plan for keeping things picked up."

Her thirteen-year-old daughter said, "Why can't the baby-sitter pick things up? She's getting paid for taking care of us." And Naomi's ten-year-old son added, "Why should I have to work on this problem? I never leave my stuff around." Imagine Naomi's feelings at hearing her children trying to sabotage this meeting which she had put so much effort into planning. Before she could stop herself, Naomi sabotaged herself by giving an outer-reality lecture to her daughter on the need for everyone to be responsible for their own things, while the son got another outer-reality lecture from his father on the obligations of being a member of a family where everyone should be concerned for everyone else. All doors to communication promptly slammed shut. The meeting deteriorated into heated argument and ended with a pair of discouraged parents who began to question the value of family meetings.

If the mother and father had been able to bite their lips for just a moment, and think of a describing or inner-reality response, the meeting might have gone differently.

EXAMPLE A: Daughter's attempt to sabotage

"Why can't the baby-sitter pick things up? She's the one getting paid!"

Describing response: (Describe what the daughter said by repeating her exact words.) "You think the baby-sitter should pick things up." Try to look thoughtful and keep calm. Turn to the rest of the group and ask, "Anybody else have any ideas?"

Inner-reality response: "Hmm." Be quiet for a few moments while you try to think about it from her point of view. Turn to the rest of the group and ask, "Anybody else have any ideas?"

EXAMPLE B: Son's attempt to sabotage

"Why should I have to work on this problem? I never leave my stuff around!"

Describing response: (Describe what the son said by repeating his exact words.) "You never leave your stuff around so you think you shouldn't have to work on the problem." Try to look thoughtful and keep calm. Turn to the rest of the group and ask, "Anyone else have any ideas?"

Inner-reality response: "Hmm." Be quiet a few moments while you try to think about it from his point of view. Maybe you could add, "You don't think it's fair." Then turn to the rest of the group and ask, "Anyone else have any ideas?"

You can use either the describing or the inner-reality response to sidestep a child's attempts to disrupt the meeting. *Remember that when children are nervous about being blamed for the problem, it is common for them at first to attempt to sabotage the process. Don't give up.* They will become more cooperative when they discover that you are focusing on solving the problem, not on placing blame.

Naomi's parenting group role-played this situation with Naomi playing the part of her thirteen-year-old daughter. At first, Naomi played her daughter's role as an extremely hostile child. But after she experienced the inner-reality and describing responses from the person playing the adult, she couldn't keep up her hostility. "It's amazing," she said, "but I don't feel like arguing anymore. I think I'm ready to start problem-solving."

When a child makes some apparently outrageous and self-indulgent remark, the indignant adult can hardly resist giving the child a logical, outer-reality response in return. Even though it is tempting to tell the child how the real world actually works, talking about outer reality during negative times of high stress closes the door to any further meaningful communication. If you can keep reminding yourself that the child's outrageous statement is only an attempt to protect herself by deflecting blame onto someone else, you will stand a better chance of keeping calm. Describe what the child said, or just say, "Hmm," then go right on and turn your attention to the next person. In this way, you can effectively ignore the child's behavior if it is self-indulgent. On the other hand, if the child's comments are really based on troubling inner feelings, do not try to argue him or her out of their feelings. Your goal is to ignore any self-indulgent behaviors while still respecting the inner integrity of the child. This is not an easy balancing act to pull off, but you can do it with a little practice.

The only way to learn how powerful the inner-reality and describing responses are is to practice them. The family and the classroom meetings provide a safe, regular way to increase your listening and describing skills. Reading about them will only give you a clue. You must dare to risk. You must dare to practice. That is how I learned to use them, and that is how you will learn to use them, too.

9. Rotate leadership of the meeting when children request it or when you think they will benefit from it

Probably the most efficient use of the limited school day is to stick with the teacher as leader. Yet, it is a valuable experience for each child to have a turn learning to use this type of problem-solving leadership style. If you decide to try student leadership of classroom meetings, wait until your students are familiar with the way you conduct the classroom meeting before you begin to rotate their leadership turns.

Parents, too, should wait before suggesting that their children take turns being the group leader. Children need to become familiar with the way the meeting is conducted before they try it. If a child asks to be the leader the very first time you hold a meeting (as one six-year-old put it, "*I* want to be President") tell the child yes, he or she can soon have a turn being leader. Make it clear to the child that adults will have the first turns since they are the people who have been studying how to do it. Children can learn how to lead the meeting by watching how mother and dad do it. After the first few meetings you will have established a basic framework. The children will know, for example, that the first thing the family does is to light a candle and open the meeting with a reading, and the second thing is to talk about the topics for discussion list. You will also have had time to set a tone of friendliness and respect for each person's ideas. By the time a child's leadership turn comes along, he or she will have at least some idea how to proceed.

If you rotate leadership, rotate the leader each week. *Do not elect the leader. There should be no voting for any reason.* If you need some way to select which volunteer starts the rotation process, toss a coin or draw names out of a jar. As children grow into their middle school years, the regular experience of having been a group leader, and of having learned interpersonal relationship and problem-solving skills by observing how you participate in the group will be invaluable in their personal lives.

Of course, the parent or the teacher will have to continue to exercise informal leadership in all the areas mentioned in this chapter which are beyond the capabilities of a child. Whether or not you rotate formal leadership of the group, you will be amazed at how much your children will learn from observing and copying your behavior in the group. How you interact will be how they think a group leader should interact. If you are able to listen to their inner reality, they will begin to listen to yours. If you demonstrate how to brainstorm ideas, they will learn how to do it, too. Children learn from everyday experiences of living with adults and observing how they interact with other people. By watching how you participate in the group, children will learn effective leadership and human relationship skills without ever having to read a book like this one.

Exercise

Study the *Caring Discipline Overview* chart before going to your next discussion group. Do you see how family and classroom meetings fit into the "Child Has Problem" box? Do you see how all the major concepts you have learned in *Caring Discipline* fit into this overall pattern?

Caring Discipline Overview

CHILD'S STAIRCASE OF NEEDS *

Self-actualization

As the staircase strengthens, behavior improves.

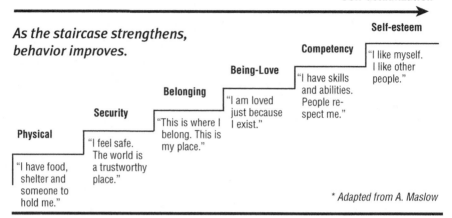

Self-esteem
"I like myself. I like other people."

Competency
"I have skills and abilities. People respect me."

Being-Love
"I am loved just because I exist."

Belonging
"This is where I belong. This is my place."

Security
"I feel safe. The world is a trustworthy place."

Physical
"I have food, shelter and someone to hold me."

* Adapted from A. Maslow

CHILD'S BEHAVIORS: Behaviors You Give Emotional Attention Will Continue

Positive	Neutral	Negative
1. Adult gives nonverbal attention (eye contact, touching, smiles) 2. Adult gives verbal attention (describing praise)	1. Adult gives nonverbal attention (eye contact, touching, smiles)	1. Not-minding (Physical assist, broken record) 2. Self-indulgent (Ignore and either-or choice) 3. Routine not-minding (Choices and consequences) 4. Aggressive (Time-out)
Pleases you—a joy for you	Child doing his or her own thing—not a problem for you	Angers or irritates you —a problem for you

THE FOUR SELF-SABOTAGES

1. Procrastination

2. Talking and talking about the misbehavior. Act, don't talk. Carry out the correction and do not mention it again.

3. Forgetting to give 4–1 attention (4 parts positive to 1 part negative)

4. Negative scripting

Child Has Problem

Adult helps by:
1. Adjusting the environment
2. Teaching problem-solving and assertiveness skills
3. Listening and accepting the child's inner reality

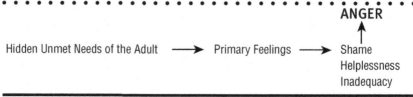

ANGER

Hidden Unmet Needs of the Adult ⟶ Primary Feelings ⟶ Shame
Helplessness
Inadequacy

---

from *Caring Discipline: Practical Tools for Nurturing Happy Families & Classrooms*

REVIEW: Guidelines for Conducting a Family and Classroom Meeting

1. Schedule a regular meeting time.

2. Establish a relaxed and upbeat atmosphere.

3. Use an opening ritual.

4. Involve everyone in choosing topics for discussion.

5. Keep focused on the general problem.

6. Watch out for hidden agendas.

7. Use brainstorm techniques to think about possible solutions:

   Step 1: Describe the problem

   Step 2: Brainstorm possible solutions

   Step 3: Attempt to choose a solution

8. Practice your listening and describing skills.

9. Rotate leadership of the family or classroom meeting after the children become familiar with how the meeting is conducted.

It's always gratifying to find a solution, but it not necessary. It is the thoughtful and respectful process of involving every person in the group in searching for a solution that improves behavior.

REMEMBER NOT TO SELF-SABOTAGE

Chapter 11 Discussion: THE FAMILY AND CLASSROOM MEETINGS

1. Before you try leading a meeting at home or at school, practice with your discussion group:

    a. Write out a "Topics for Discussion" list for your pretend family or classroom meeting. Choose a couple of topics that are presently a problem for your real family or class.

    b. Decide who will play the role of parent (or teacher) and who will be the children. When you play the part of a child, choose to be a child you know well. Try to get into the feeling of how you think that child would behave and feel in a similar situation. If you only have two people in your group, that is enough. It takes only two people to make a family.

    c. First, choose one of your topics and use it to practice the three-step brainstorming technique described in this chapter. If the "adult" gets stuck, he or she should call for a break while the group re-reads the material and discusses what happened. Then back to the role-play.

    d. After you have gone through all three steps, stop to discuss what happened during the role-playing. What was the hardest part about the brainstorm session for the "parent" (or "teacher")? Did the "children" feel listened to? Did anyone catch themselves having a hidden agenda? Did anyone use a describing or inner-reality response?

    e. Practice a family meeting from beginning to end. This time change roles so that the person who played a child role has a chance to play the part of the adult.

    f. Keep practicing with your discussion group until you feel comfortable enough to start holding meetings at home or in the classroom. Remember, the only way to learn this is to do it. The discussion group is a safe place to learn by making lots of mistakes. If you do not make mistakes, you will not learn.

from *Caring Discipline: Practical Tools for Nurturing Happy Families & Classrooms*

2. Look at the *Caring Discipline Overview* chart. Which of the concepts illustrated on the chart are most confusing to you? Which have been most helpful? Which idea is the hardest for you to put into practice? Has anyone noticed whether any of these ideas also work for grown-ups?

CHAPTER TWELVE
Helping the Aggressive and Self-Destructive Teenager

The most important life task for any teenager is to become an independent adult. The urge to become a competent adult member of human society is a basic drive that ensures the survival of our species. Much of the behavior that adults interpret as aggressive and self-destructive in teenagers is in reality a reflection of their teenagers' muddled attempts to become competent, respected adults.

Expanding beyond the family to become a member of the larger community is a normal and healthy progression into adult life for all human beings. In some cultures, teenagers are formally initiated into a widely shared and respected adult life style. Our culture, on the other hand, has no meaningful formal ritual to mark the passage into adulthood, with the possible exception of getting a driver's license. Even graduation from high school is not a commonly shared ritual since many of our teenagers drop out of school in the high school years. Western culture has no positive vision of adulthood commonly shared and experienced by every man and woman. The transition into modern adult life is not a clear or easy one.

The problem is compounded for many teenagers because our society not only has no clear message about just how to become a respected and competent adult, it also sends powerful messages that promiscuous sex, rudeness, and violent behaviors are an accepted part of adult life.

The media relentlessly sends the message that violence is an acceptable way to solve problems. Video games desensitize our youth to killing by using the same video simulation techniques the Army uses to teach young men how to kill. Incidents of violence are given far more emphasis on the nightly news than events that highlight character, civility, problem-solving, and compassion. We have more guns than adults in this country; sixteen thousand guns are manufactured every day in the United States. The situation is so bad that one wit suggested it is time to replace the torch held in the hand of the Statue of Liberty with a gun.

Guns are now so widely used in the United States that more and more parents are asking, when their child is invited to sleep over at a friend's house, does the hosting family have a gun? Is it kept in a secure place out of the reach of children?

Sexuality and human relationships are other areas of great confusion and conflicting messages. The media bombards our teenagers with the message that promiscuous and early sex is highly desirable. As a society, we are squeamish about seeing a baby feeding at her mother's breast, a situation rarely, if ever, shown in the movies or on television. Instead, women's breasts are featured in countless situation comedy programs and commercials as valuable ornaments useful only for attracting men. Males are valued for having "cute butts" and being "sexy." Television and movie scripts depict people of all ages apparently afflicted with diarrhea of the mouth, spewing out coarse sexual and bathroom witticisms. A barrage of put-downs towards both sexes is woven into the majority of situation comedies. The press rummages through and publicizes the private sexual affairs of famous people with obsessive fascination. Sports figures who lack basic civility and kindness are idolized. The rich and the famous are envied no matter how shallow or empty their value systems. No wonder teenagers are confused about how to become a fully functioning adult in this society.

And yet, in spite of growing up in an often non-supportive culture, our teenagers continue to represent the very best attributes of being human: their idealism, their faith that the human condition can be improved, their refusal to go along with what they perceive to be hypocrisy, a deep conviction that the world should be fair, and their powerful enthusiasm for life, make living and working with teens an exhilarating, if occasionally frustrating, experience.

Despite the difficulty of raising a child to adulthood in a confused and conflicted society, the values and love of each caring parent are deeply rooted in the child. Teachers, also, are important role models and mentors for children, providing guidance and direction throughout the formative years. I once attended a workshop in which the speaker asked the group to share a time when an adult who was not a member of the family had made a difference in their lives. Eighteen of the twenty adults who stood up to relate stories of significant incidents in their lives told about teachers who had said or done something that meant the difference between taking the road to self-destructive versus life-affirming behaviors. Probably none of the teachers ever realized the difference they made in the lives of those individuals. In our highly mobile society, most of us cannot even *find* our old teachers, even if we tried to go back twenty years later to let them know what they meant to us. In spite of the fact that teachers seldom hear of the long-term positive effects of their work with children, there is no doubt that teachers are an especially crucial part of that "whole village" it takes to raise a child.

Never doubt that the loving experiences and values you have given to a child through the years are permanent and form the core of that child's inner self. *But as long as you and the teenager are locked in a power struggle, it is almost impossible for a teenager to openly adopt your life style and value system.* To the extent the power struggle with the teenager has become a really bitter one, from the teenager's point of view *you* are seen as the enemy, *you* are the one who is preventing his or her growth into adulthood. Since no human being willingly adopts the values of an enemy, the teenager caught up in the power struggle looks elsewhere for a life style to copy. Unfortunately, as we have seen, there are many destructive alternative choices widely publicized in the media and on the internet.

What your teenager needs from you is help in stopping the power struggle that divides him or her from you and the family or school community. Once the power struggle is eliminated, your teenager will be free to make life style choices based on core values already deeply rooted in his or her inner self.

FIRST STEP: Let your teenager take charge of important areas of his or her life at home and at school

1. *When a teenager realizes she is perceived as a competent person able to manage her own life, the stairsteps on her staircase of emotional needs will strengthen and self-confidence will soar.* The power struggle will cease when your teenager believes you are helping her along the road to competent, respected adulthood by trusting her to make important decisions about her own life. The anger that fueled the aggression will fade, and the teenager will be freed to make responsible decisions about her life, based on what was learned in the past from you and other important adults. Giving up decision-making power over important areas of the teenager's life is difficult for many adults, but it is a necessary part of the process that can eventually sweep away the debris of past misunderstandings and reveal the solid bedrock of love and decency that forms the inner core of your teenager.

2. *Decide which areas you can let go of and give to your teenager to manage.* Sit down with other important adults in your child's life and make a list of all areas of your child's life, for example, schoolwork, friends, clothing, household chores, use of the car, use of electronic gadgets, church attendance, bedtime, diet, spending money, curfew, sports, hobbies, and work outside the home. If there are favorite teachers or other adults with whom your teenager has a positive relationship, invite them to attend this meeting to help you think about the decisions you are about to make. Which areas do you need to make the final decisions about, and which areas can belong to your child? Remember that to become a competent

adult your teenager's ultimate goal is to make *all* personal decisions.

Take a good look at your list. There are important areas of a teen's life that you won't want to give over to your teen. For example, use of the car is an area you no doubt want to keep under your control. Curfew and helping with household chores are two more areas in which most parents feel they must continue to have a say. Clothing, food, and hair style, on the other hand, are areas you can safely give to your teenager. Bizarre clothing and hair styles are often irritating to parents, but this is a difficult area for parents to enforce. It is easy for teenagers to keep forbidden food and clothing, even wigs, in their school locker to eat or wear the minute they get to school in the morning. A basic rule for deciding which areas to give over to your teenager is to ask yourself this question: "Am I infringing on my teenager's rights by keeping control of this behavior?" Both A and C-parents have trouble standing back and trusting that their children are competent enough to manage important areas of their lives.

Whether or not to try to keep control of your teenager's schoolwork is one of the biggest decisions a parent has to make. Schoolwork is an unmanageable task for some teenagers without the involvement of their parents. Other teenagers resent attempts by adults to monitor their work and only stiffen their resistance to schoolwork when parents try to get involved. As strange as it seems, the harder you push for good grades, the more it becomes impossible for some teens to oblige you. For many rebellious teenagers, becoming a good student means that their parents will win the schoolwork battle, and the teenagers will lose independence and self-respect. Not only does schoolwork suffer over the long term from this power struggle, but also the relationship between parent and child can become so adversarial that sometimes the wounds never heal.

Only you, the parent, can choose which of these two approaches is best for your child. If you have never tried monitoring your child's schoolwork in the way described here, it is well worth a try.

The first approach is for the teacher and parent, sometimes with the help of the school counselor, to work together to *monitor the teenager's schoolwork*. The teen schoolwork plan is scheduled on a weekly basis, using a modified form of the schoolwork plan for elementary school children presented at the end of Chapter Seven.

If you decide to try working with teachers to monitor your teenager's schoolwork, be sure you have first completed the process of letting your teen take charge of as many other areas of his or her life as you possibly can. The more areas you give to your teenager to manage, the more likely your child will respect your wishes in those areas for which you do need to stay involved. I am also assuming you have explored every possibility of adjusting your child's environment, and that you are by now certain your child is physically and mentally capable of doing the schoolwork assigned.

The main differences between the elementary school plan presented earlier in the book and this new middle and high school plan is that the middle and high school plan uses weekly reports and weekly consequences instead of day-by-day monitoring. The plan for older children ordinarily does not use secondary reinforcers. Middle and high school students are usually able to realize that the improved grades themselves, along with having access to certain privileges after their work is completed, is reward enough.

3. If you decide to monitor your teen's schoolwork, make a plan with your child's teacher and school counselor.

A. *Parent, teacher, or counselor can begin the process.* If you are a parent who is not sure just how to begin, call the school counselor and ask her about applying for a 504 plan for your child. The 504 plan is based on a federal regulation which enables a parent to be assisted by the school in creating a team of teachers who will help in creating and implementing a plan for raising achievement levels for a low achieving student. The school counselor is usually the person who will coordinate the schoolwork plan among your teen's many teachers. In one Seattle high school, however, a system of schoolwork monitoring is used on such a regular basis that every teacher knows the process and very little extra communication among staff members is required. For example, early in the first term, a ninth-grade social studies teacher contacts the parents of students who are not doing their schoolwork, either by email or a phone call, and offers to work with each parent in monitoring the student's schoolwork if things don't improve by the first grading period. This particular teacher carries out schoolwork plans with many of her students and insists it takes very little of her time.

B. *The parent's role is to tell his or her teenager about the plan, figure out what kind of a logical consequence would have some meaning for the teenager, and then make certain that the logical consequence occurs.*

The social studies teacher (in the above example) next asks the parent to figure out what kind of logical consequence would be appropriate for his or her student if the schoolwork is not completed for the week. She always emphasizes the importance of carrying out logical consequences in a matter-of-fact way, with no sabotaging. Parents may want to re-read Chapter Seven to refresh their memories about how to carry out a logical consequence. Parents often prefer a loss of privilege consequence. The loss of privilege consequence can work well without causing a power struggle *if it is perceived as reasonable.* Teenagers are very keen to sense if they are being treated unfairly. For example, losing the use of the car for the coming week is seen as a reasonable loss of privilege consequence because use of the car happens on a day-to-day basis, and can begin again as soon as the schoolwork is completed. On the other hand, not being allowed to go to the Junior/Senior prom is seen as an unreasonable consequence because obviously the prom is a once a year occurrence, and from your teen's point of view, it is a once in a life-time occurrence. *It is very important that each week your teen has the chance to try again with a clean slate.*

C. *The initiating teacher or the school counselor explains to the student that he or she is responsible for getting a schoolwork progress report every Friday from every teacher.*

After a parent has called our social studies teacher for help, the teacher asks the parent to buy a daily planner for their teenager, the kind you can buy at any school supply store, with plenty of room for writing on each calendar day. (Some Seattle schools have received grants for buying every student a daily planner.) In this particular school, all teachers are familiar with the Friday check-in system and very little extra communication on the part of the initiating teacher or school counselor is required. The student, not the teacher, is the one responsible for getting the Friday schoolwork notations.

If there are any complex written assignments for projects due, teachers staple them to the planner page. Our social studies teacher tries to be as describing as possible and mentions improvements: for example, "I'm really seeing an improvement in John's behavior" or "Only two out of four assignments were handed in this week" or "Schoolwork all complete this week!" It takes only a couple of minutes to make the notation, and, since this is a neutral time, she also gives the student a friendly smile plus any positive describing comments she can think of. If the parents request a weekly grade (either a letter grade or a pass/fail grade), she also includes that along with her one sentence notation, although she feels the one sentence notation is just as effective.

If your teenager comes home without the Friday notation from each teacher involved, it is the student's responsibility to get on the phone or email the teacher to get the assignment. If there are no notations from teachers and your student doesn't want to contact the teachers, then the parent assumes that the schoolwork was not done and the student loses the privilege for the following week.

D. *Try to convey the nonverbal message that there is nothing personal or spiteful about the consequence. There are no winners and no losers, this is just the way the world works.* Throughout this process, your teen needs the respect of both teacher and parent, as well as the recognition that he or she is a capable person on the verge of adulthood.

Example A

Laurel was a bright teenager who was rather reserved with adults but sociable with her peers. Laurel had no interest in school other than visiting with her circle of friends. As a freshman in high school, her grades began to spiral downward until she was getting all D's on her report card. After her concerned parents contacted Laurel's social studies teacher and were given the idea of the schoolwork plan, they decided that since their daughter spent almost all her time either chatting or visiting with friends, they would give her the loss of privilege consequence of no phone calls or email or internet chats, and no ordinary type social events like sleeping over at someone's house, nor ice skating and hanging out at the mall during the coming week. Laurel just shrugged her shoulders when her parents told her about the plan. She took her daily planner with her to school that Friday, and dutifully had five different teachers sign it. In every class, she had missing assignments.

When one of her friends called to ask her to go ice skating at the mall that Saturday, the parents tried hard to be matter of fact as they reminded her about the consequence, "Sure, as soon as all the schoolwork assignments are finished, you can go." Later that day, when Laurel's friends called to talk to her, the parents said they were sorry but Laurel couldn't talk on the phone right now, she had a lot of schoolwork to do. When they heard Laurel answering the phone in her own room and start talking with her friends, the parents took her phone and put it away, saying in a friendly way. "Just as soon as your work is done, you can plug the phone back in."

Laurel's family used only a telephone land line, but the same idea can be adopted for a mobile phone: "Just as soon as your work is finished you can have your cell phone back again."

The second week, Laurel "forgot" to go to each teacher for her schoolwork assignments. Again Laurel's parents stuck to their plan and saw to it that Laurel did not have a social life until she had called each teacher for the assignment and had finished her schoolwork. Laurel's parents were evidently very successful at not sabotaging themselves and in avoiding a power struggle, because by the third week Laurel began to do at least some of her schoolwork on a regular basis with the result that she had fewer schoolwork assignments to do each weekend before she could visit with her friends. By the end of the term, everyone involved was delighted that Laurel's grades had come up to straight B's. Laurel seemed to enjoy the extra bit of personal contact with her teachers the Friday check-in provided and she continued to use it voluntarily throughout her freshman year.

An interesting sidelight to this story is that Laurel's friend, Ginny, was in the same social studies class and, like Laurel, also received D's on her report card. The social studies teacher noticed that when Laurel's grades began to improve, Laurel urged Ginny to start her own Friday check-in system. Ginny carried out the program all year on her own, soon bringing her grades up to a C-plus average. The social studies teacher believed the reason for Ginny's improvement was not only the encouragement from Laurel and the extra attention from her teachers, but also the fact that, like so many young teens, Ginny had simply been overwhelmed about how to organize so many different schoolwork assignments.

Example B

Phil was a bright, fifteen-year-old freshman who was described by his mother as one of the "biggest computer, webmaster junkies alive, and lazy into the bargain." Where his computer was involved, Phil was definitely not lazy, but where school assignments were concerned, Phil's parents considered him a hopeless case. So naturally, they were delighted to hear that Phil's teachers were willing to participate in a schoolwork plan with him. It didn't take long for Phil's parents to figure out what the loss of privilege consequence should be for Phil.

They waited for a neutral time, pulled out a brand new daily planner, and explained to Phil about the new schoolwork plan. The logical consequence for not doing the weekly assignments was no use of the computer or other electronic connectors to the internet, for the following week.

Phil is an extremely articulate young man and he responded with every legal, rational argument at his command, "I'm going to be a computer programmer when I get out of school. I don't need all this other crap. What good is geometry? What good is social studies? None of that is going to help my career at all! Good computer people don't need fancy degrees."

Phil's parents remembered not to sabotage themselves by being baited into endless outer-reality arguments. They kept their mouths shut, listened carefully to their son, looked serious, and finally said, "No. We'll stick with the internet idea. It's the internet that takes so much of your time."

When logic didn't work, Phil tried bargaining with them, "How about just taking away some of my allowance?" "How about grounding me to the house for the weekend?"

Phil's parents stood firm. They knew what it was their son would be willing to work for. Next Phil sulked. He refused to talk to them for three days. Finally, on Thursday he said, "Okay, but only on one condition. I'm not going to use that stupid daily planner." His parents respected Phil's insistence on controlling at least this part of the plan and wisely agreed that any sheet of paper would do. Phil sat down at his computer and created his own form which he took around to his teachers each Friday. Such was Phil's passion for the computer, and his parents' skill at avoiding sabotaging themselves, that Phil's grade soon came up to a B average. Later in the term, Phil had the added satisfaction of seeing the school adopt his schoolwork form as an alternative to the daily planner idea.

4. *Give your teenager total responsibility for schoolwork.* If you feel you and your teen's teachers have tried monitoring his or her schoolwork, without sabotaging yourselves, and still things aren't better, it is time to try the second approach of giving all decisions about schoolwork to your teenager.

Many parents worry needlessly that teachers will think this second approach is an abdication of parental responsibility. Middle school and high school teachers can handle the idea that you are giving total responsibility for schoolwork to your child. Teachers understand that you can't keep pushing your child ahead of you through life forever. What middle and high school teachers do need from you is for you to clearly tell them about your decision to back out of the power struggle. If they know you and other teachers have tried the first approach and it hasn't worked, they will be in a much better position to switch to this new tactic.

Call every one of your child's teachers to tell them what you have decided to do and your reasons for doing it. Reassure your child's teachers that you want them to continue to set high standards for your teenager. Let teachers know that you will not interfere with any non-punitive, logical consequences they may impose for missing schoolwork, and that you will support them in their efforts to teach responsible behavior by making reasonable demands. Once most teachers realize that your goal and their goal for your child are the same, they will become your greatest ally. One of the reasons for writing this book is to provide a means through which parents and teachers can support one another in their efforts to achieve the shared goal of helping children grow into responsible, caring, confident, well-educated adults.

Example C

Even though Julie was bright and had good basic academic skills, by the beginning of the seventh grade she began to avoid completing schoolwork assignments. At school conferences, Julie's teachers expressed concern that this very capable girl was not living up to her potential. Consequently her parents, Ron and Mary, who were already very involved in Julie's life at school, began to get even more involved with overseeing her schoolwork. The teachers started to send home regular notes telling whether or not Julie had finished her work. It usually fell to Mary, who was an A-parent, to see that Julie did the missing schoolwork. But it seemed that the harder Mary tried, the worse things got. Not only did Julie's work habits continue to deteriorate, she became increasingly hostile, vacillating between being sullen and verbally abusive. She began to lie to both parents about her schoolwork. She also began to be secretive about her personal life, stopped sharing even the slightest information about her friends, frequently retreated to her room to listen to music which she knew her parents detested, and carried on mysterious conversations over the telephone. By the time Julie was nearing the end of the eighth grade, her grades had plummeted. Still, on achievement tests Julie continued to score in the top percentiles.

Desperate, Ron and Mary tried the intervention of allowing Julie to take total charge of her own schoolwork, even though it seemed extremely radical and scary. When Julie's thirteenth birthday came around towards the end of her eighth-grade year, Ron made a formal announcement to their daughter at the dinner table, "Happy thirteenth birthday, Julie! Your Mom and I have been talking about how you are now a teenager and before long you'll be an adult." Mary chimed in with, "Yes, and we think you're old enough now to manage your own schoolwork. I think sometimes we just get in the way anyhow. So, call on us if you need us for anything, but otherwise we'll just stay out of it." Julie stared at her parents but other than a guarded smile gave no indication she had even heard. Julie opened her presents, Ron took the family and one of Julie's friend to a movie. No one said anything more about it.

The following Monday, Mary called Julie's teachers and told them what she and Ron had decided to do. "From now on, we are going to let schoolwork be between Julie and you folks. Please continue to have high expectations of Julie and to apply appropriate consequences at school, but here at home we suspect we are just feeding a power struggle by constantly being on her case. We think she feels that if she gives in and does her schoolwork to please us, it means she has lost some kind of contest, and probably her independence and self-respect."

The last two months of the school year were not promising. Julie had occasional periods of enthusiasm about certain subjects but mostly just continued to ignore school assignments. Mary and Ron kept their word and avoided any talk of schoolwork. They instead concentrated on listening and talking with Julie about everything other than schoolwork, and gave her lots of positive attention at neutral times. They held firm on family rules like boundaries for use of electronic gadgets, household chores, and curfew, and did their best to avoid sabotaging themselves when conflicts arose over those issues. Julie's final report card was not an encouraging one: one B (in PE), one C (in music), and D's in all her academic subjects. Julie rather defiantly plunked her report card down in front of her parents and stood back, obviously waiting for the storm. But Ron and Mary kept good on their word. They were able to give Julie the ownership of her grades by saying, "Gosh, you must not feel very good about those D's." After that, Mary and Ron said no more about it. (At this point, both parents were plenty worried they might not have done the right thing, but they courageously kept on with their plan to respect their daughter's competency by allowing *her* to be the one to care, or not to care, about her grades.)

Next fall Julie entered ninth grade. Julie and Mary went on their accustomed fall shopping trip for new clothes and school supplies. Neither Mary nor Ron sabotaged by reminding Julie that the schoolwork was entirely on *her* shoulders now. Instead they continued to be interested in her school activities by asking, "What classes are you taking this year?" "What do you think of your teachers so far?" "Anything interesting happen today?" If Julie didn't want to talk about it, they changed the subject and told her about something *they* had done that day. If Julie wanted to talk about school, they just listened and neither parent sabotaged by giving outer-reality advice about anything to do with school. Ron and Mary could see that Julie was regularly taking books back and forth to school. Twice, Julie asked for a ride to the library to do some research, which Mary willingly gave her.

When Julie brought home her first report card, she had two A's, two B's and two C's. It was a decided improvement. Julie also decided not to play basketball, a sport she was not very good at but in which her father had always urged her to participate. Ron accepted her decision with good grace. Julie turned instead to becoming a member of her school drama club and a volunteer for the local hospital. All schoolwork problems evaporated. Julie became once more the open, vivacious girl she had been in her pre-puberty years, and she sailed through high school a self-motivated and involved student with many good friends.

5. *Listen to your teenager's inner reality and, if necessary, adjust his or her environment.* Giving your teenager control of more areas of his life will not alone instill a sense of being respected as a competent human being. You must also faithfully practice listening and accepting your teen's feelings and thoughts, even when they seem irrational. Try to listen to your teenager with no goal in mind other than to find out what is going on inside. Many parents have long conversations with their teenagers, but then sabotage the process every time by thinking these discussions are a failure unless some solution is found, some decision or judgment made. The expectation that some agreement has to be reached by the end of conversation fuels the power struggle, because teenagers then believe you were trying to manipulate them into agreeing with your point of view. In order to keep their self-respect and competency stairstep strong, they will fight back against any attempt to control their thoughts.

You and your teenager will need repeated sessions with nothing accomplished other than you listening to what your teen has to say. Doing nothing but listening will be hard at first, especially for an A-parent, because your teen is apt to accuse you of being the problem and may try to shift all blame to you. Remember that it took a long time for the power struggle to build to this point. Things aren't going to change in one week or even one month. But eventually, as your teen realizes you are actually hearing and considering what he has to say, your teen will feel safe in lowering his defense system. When that happens, you will be finally be able to talk and your teen will be able to listen. Once this point is reached, real problem-solving can begin. A word of caution: mothers sometimes expect that their sons should bare their souls and discuss their feelings at depth for these discussions to be a success. But the vast majority of boys and men are not hard-wired to enjoy taking part in lengthy emotional discussions. Let your son lead the way. Be content with any sincere verbal response, even if it is only five words long.

Many times, just listening is enough. There are times, however, as your teenager begins to share parts of her life that had been hidden from you, you may discover that a hostile or abusive situation exists for your child. In these cases your teenager desperately needs help from you to adjust the environment.

Example D

Here is the story of a father who considers himself to be a man of action with few communication skills. Yet he literally saved his daughter by learning to listen. Ralph and his wife, Margarie, divorced when their daughter, Becky, was ten years old. Margarie was soon promoted in her job and moved to the east coast, taking Becky with her. Becky visited her father in California for three months each summer and on alternate Christmases. In spite of the pain of the separation, Becky seemed to manage fairly well. She got excellent grades in school and made friends at her new school in Maryland as well as keeping up friendships with California friends each summer.

When Becky was thirteen, Margarie became involved with Carl, who eventually moved in with Margarie and Becky as a permanent fixture in the household. For the first six months of this arrangement, Becky seemed to handle the new situation well. Then Margarie began to complain to Ralph that Becky was becoming sulky, withdrawn, and that her grades were slipping. Becky's behavior continued to deteriorate until finally she was engaging in full-blown temper tantrums, kicking and slamming doors, spitting on the carpet, sneaking out at night, bringing home F's on her report card, and calling her mother a "stupid, fucking bitch." Every day was a war zone with constant verbal battles between Becky and Margarie. Carl sometimes took Becky's side in these disagreements but usually stayed on the sidelines saying it wasn't his place to get involved. By the time Becky was fourteen, she was smoking, both cigarettes and marijuana, and had started sneaking out to weekend beer parties with her questionable new friends. Margarie, now at her wits end, called Ralph and said, "You better take her. I can't handle her anymore."

After Becky went to live with Ralph in California, her negative behavior continued. She ignored her old friendships and gravitated to the same type of rebellious friends she had picked up in Maryland. What hurt Ralph most was that Becky was no longer the affection-ate girl who loved to be hugged. When he tried to give her a good night kiss on the cheek, which before had been their nightly ritual, she pushed him away and shouted, "Leave me alone, you creep!" She refused to do her chores or schoolwork and often skipped classes to disap-pear with her new friends until the wee hours of the night. Ralph tried every rational thing he could think of to get through to her. He tried asking her *why* she was acting this way. He tried telling her how her behavior was going to ruin her life. Every attempt to reason with her ended in Becky storming out of the house with long-suffering Ralph shouting commands that Becky never obeyed.

At this point, Ralph, who owned a small automotive repair business, confided his troubles to a woman whose car he was working on. They got to talking about the difficulty of raising teenagers in today's world and soon he was telling her the whole story. The woman had just finished one of the *Caring Discipline* parenting classes and still had the book in her car. On an impulse, she gave him the book, "Here, you take it. Maybe you'll find something in here that will help." Desperate, Ralph took the book home and read it until late into the night. When he woke up the next morning, Ralph decided the first thing he should try was listening. Becky's behavior must have something to do with the divorce, but he had no real idea why things had gotten so bad so fast. Maybe listening would give him a clue as to what was the matter. Believing he was not very quick with verbal responses, Ralph figured out ahead of time three things he could say and do when Becky got upset: first, "This is a really tough time for you;" second, "It's hard having to move back and forth between your mom and me;" and, third, he vowed to keep his mouth shut, look concerned, and just say "Hmm."

During the first week of Ralph's new listening program, Becky started responding with violent fits of sobbing and running from the room. This was distressing for Ralph but he figured it was better than tantrums and insults. Finally, late in the second week, Becky poured out the story of sexual abuse she had been experiencing from Carl for the past year: how at first the things he did were so gradual she didn't even realize what was going on, and later when he started coming into bed with her at night when her mother was on business trips, how she begged him to stop, and how ashamed she was to tell anyone.

What a relief to have her dad hold her in his arms while she cried, and hear him say, "That son-of-a-bitch! Don't you worry, your old Dad will take care of him. He'll never touch you again. That son-of-a-bitch!" At last, Ralph, the man of action, had a situation he knew how to handle. He immediately called Margarie and told her the story, which she at first refused to believe. "Just ask that son-of-a-bitch to tell you all about it. And tell him I'll be there on the first flight I can get out of here. Then he can tell me all about it, too. And if you stay with that son-of-a-bitch and if you want to see Becky again, you'll have to fly out here to do it." Next, he called a travel agent and got a ticket to Maryland for the next day. "I don't care what it costs. This can't wait for the cheap fares." By the time he walked into Margarie's house the following day, Carl had packed and left.

Three years later, the same woman who had given Ralph the original

Caring Discipline book brought her car into his shop and asked how his daughter was doing. "I'm sorry I never called you to thank you and tell you what happened. She's doing great." Ralph told her about using the listening approach and how he got rid of Carl. "We got Becky some counseling to be sure she understood it wasn't her fault; her mom apologized for being so stupid; and Becky just blossomed. She went back to her old friends, threw herself into her schoolwork and music, and ended up with a full four-year scholarship to Cornell University. I know it sounds too good to be true, but that's what happened."

The story of Becky illustrates how quickly even an older child can change negative behaviors when caring adults learn to listen and, if necessary, to protect their child from an abusive environment. When Ralph took charge of immediately protecting Becky from Carl, her weakened security stairstep was cemented back in place. When Ralph said he didn't care what it cost for an airplane ticket, Becky's stairstep of being an important and beloved person was strengthened. When her father believed her story without questions or accusations, when he let her see his anger at the man who had not respected her personal boundaries, Becky knew that she was respected as a competent human being who had a right to place boundaries on her own life. The fact that her mother apologized and that Becky was provided with a counselor who could reassure her that sexual abuse is never the child's fault, convinced Becky that she was a good person worthy of love and respect. And so Becky was free once more to move up the stairway towards self-esteem and becoming the best she could be.

By using both of these approaches—putting as many areas of your child's life as possible under your child's control, and listening to your child without expecting anything other than to hear what is going on in the inner self, and, if necessary, protecting your teen from a hostile or abusive environment—your teenager will eventually come to believe that you regard him or her as a beloved, competent human being. With that belief will come a strengthening of the being-love and competency/respect stairsteps, and your teen will be free to grow emotionally up the staircase of needs towards responsible and cooperative behaviors.

Example E

A woman who is now a grandmother tells this story about one of her sons. Robert was the younger of two brothers. His older brother loved to read, enjoyed academic life, and consequently did very well in school. Robert, however, even though he was very bright, had some kind of learning problem which caused him to reverse letters and have a hard time remembering things in sequence. He didn't learn to read easily until he was in the fourth grade. Spelling was an especially frustrating subject for him. His parents worked with him almost every evening on his schoolwork and tried to keep it pleasant. Even though Robert struggled with academics throughout his years in grade school, he managed to keep his sunny disposition. By the time he was twelve or thirteen, things changed for the worse. He began to withdraw from the rest of the family, spending most of his time alone in his bedroom. He stopped sharing anything about his personal life with his parents and no longer accepted their help with his schoolwork. In the first year of high school, his grades were mostly C's and D's. His clothing and his hair got scruffier and dirtier. By the beginning of his sophomore year he got his first F. At conferences with several of his teachers, the parents were told that Robert always behaved himself in class, but stubbornly refused to participate or complete schoolwork. Robert's sunny disposition had disappeared to reveal a sullen, depressed stranger. Robert refused to meet his parents' eyes. His only response to their attempts to find out what was bothering him was a sullen, "I don't know, I don't know." He continued to have friends, but they were friends who seemed to have even more problems at school than Robert. Robert's dad found a marijuana garden and a grow light in Robert's closet. After a short but intense shouting match, Robert's father elicited a grudging promise from his son never to bring marijuana into the house again

In his sophomore year, the parents felt a ray of hope when they found out about the possibility that Robert might have a learning disability which was then a new concept. They had Robert tested but the examiner found no traces of a learning disability. As often happens when a child's neurological system matures, Robert had apparently outgrown his learning disability. He now had the ability to do the schoolwork, but not the confidence or the will to do it. In the meantime, his older brother had became a national merit scholar and gone on to college.

Robert's high school mailed out report cards four times a year. At the second reporting period during his sophomore year, Robert's report card did not arrive. Robert's mother finally called the school to inquire and was told the cards had been mailed out two weeks earlier. No wonder Robert had thrown away his report card. The card showed not only straight F's, it also showed that for thirty-five days, Robert had not attended school. Robert was perceived to be such a hopeless case by his teachers that not one adult at the school had bothered to call Robert or his parents to question why there were so many absences.

For the first time, both parents stopped advising and lecturing Robert and instead expressed their deepest worries and concerns for him. "We are so worried about you. What can we do to help?" "Can you tell us what it is about school that you hate so much?"

When Robert realized the depth of their love and concern for him, he started to tell them some of the feelings and thoughts he had been hiding. He told them he had pretended to go off to school each day but would actually go off into the woods nearby where he would smoke marijuana and wait for both parents to leave for work. Then he would sneak back home and hide until it was time for his parents to return. Twenty years later, Robert's mother has tears in her eyes as she tells us Robert's answer to her question, "Can you tell us what it is about school that you hate so much?" His answer to her sincere question was short but painfully clear, "I don't know. But every morning when I have to walk in through the front door of the school, I get sick to my stomach."

This was the turning point for both Robert and his parents. The parents started researching alternative schools. Robert finally chose the local community college program to work for a two-year associate degree in machine technology and earn his GED at the same time. Robert was not quite sixteen and technically too young for the community college program, but after several meetings with community college staff members, Robert was finally accepted into the machine technology program. It developed that Robert had tremendous spatial skills. He could easily read blueprints and could put together the most complicated structures. His competency/respect level soared. After graduation from the community college program, he worked as a machinist for several years. Then for four years he served in the Air Force where he successfully enrolled in a few academic classes. After the Air Force, he got a maintenance job working outdoors in the landscaping department for the county in which he lived.

For years after the Air Force experience he was continually involved in bailing out a couple of his old high school friends who had chronic alcohol and drug problems by loaning them money and giving them a place to live. Finally Robert decided there was nothing more he could do to help them. It was then that he moved on to form other friendships. He joined the Civil Air Patrol working as a volunteer with young people, and got his private pilot's license. Finally, at the age of thirty-five, he announced to his family that he was quitting his full-time job and going to college to become a mechanical engineer. As a college student, he experienced increasing success. Robert recently graduated and now has a job working for a small manufacturing firm.

Robert's mother is very clear about why she was so happy with his decision. "It isn't the *college* part that's so wonderful. It's knowing that he finally felt confident enough about himself to go ahead and try it!" The best part of this story is the fact that once Robert's parents made the decision to let him quit his regular high school program, the relationship with their son steadily improved. When Robert was away in the Air Force, he often called them and would sign off by saying he loved them. Robert and his wife stop by to see his parents every week or so. They occasionally play tennis together, and each year they all spend some vacation time together with the older son and his family who now live in Canada. The parents consider Robert to be not only a beloved son, but one of their very best friends.

I included this story because it illustrates so well the considerable amount of time it sometimes takes for a young person to regain a sense of competency and self-respect. It also illustrates the precious long-term reward in store for any parent who is willing and able to listen to and respect the needs of their teenager.

Example F

Doug was the oldest child of three children. His father, Al, was a loving, concerned A-type parent. Like so many parents of firstborn sons, Al had high expectations for Doug. It seemed to Doug that no matter what he did, his father never thought it was good enough. Al acted out of the best intentions. He was only trying to teach Doug to be even better at whatever he was doing, whether building a block tower, or throwing a ball. Unfortunately, without meaning to, Al's constant advice and suggestions discouraged Doug to the point where he gave up trying to achieve in any area.

When he was eleven years old, Doug left the small elementary school where he was known and liked by many of his teachers and where he had two good friends. He entered Marshall Middle School, a large school of over one thousand students. Doug had never been good at taking tests so it was not surprising that on his seventh-grade placement test, Doug totally froze. He scored in the lowest tenth percentile of the population and was placed in the lower ability classes. Because of the lower placement, he seldom saw his two old friends from elementary school and they drifted apart. It was obvious to his mother, Ellen, that Doug was becoming depressed. He refused to go out for any extracurricular activity and seemed to have no social life. Al increased the pressure on Doug to get good grades, taking television privileges away and confining him to the house for weeks at a time whenever the parents got a bad schoolwork report from school. Ellen quietly refused to back Al on carrying through with many of these consequences because she felt they were too severe. Because of Doug's low test scores and because of his passive and noncommunicative behavior, some of his teachers even suggested that he be tested for placement in the mentally challenged class.

Ellen was a C-type parent. She tried to encourage Doug by giving him lots of outer-reality information about his high intelligence and capabilities, all of which was true, but this discouraged Doug even more. She continually protected and rescued him by bringing his books to school when he left them at home, and by taking his side against teachers who wanted to give him firm consequences for avoiding his schoolwork. But Ellen also knew how to listen to her son, and so she was aware of his smoldering anger at his father. Ellen could see that because Doug did not dare to confront his powerful father, he was passively resisting by failing at everything his father held dear. Ellen tried explaining to her husband how he was inadvertently the source of Doug's academic failure and deepening depression, but Al responded with anger and denials. The more Ellen talked about it, the more critical Al became of Doug and of Ellen's refusal to back him on his attempts at disciplining Doug.

Both parents agreed that Doug was just as smart as his high achieving younger brother and sister. They knew Doug definitely did not belong in a mentally-challenged class. Finally, Doug's English teacher gave Ellen and Al hope by saying, "You've got to get Doug out of here. He's bright but he's so shy, he'll never fit into any big school. Why don't you try a smaller school? How about Pine Lodge? They're expensive but they also give lots of scholarships every year." This was all it took to galvanize Ellen into action. She applied to the Pine Lodge School. Doug took the entrance test but, as usual, scored low, too low to be accepted. Then one day Ellen found a book Doug had been reading hidden under his bed, *War and Peace*, by the Russian novelist, Tolstoi. Ellen found the courage to confront the principal of Pine Lodge School. She carried the book into the principal's office, stuck it under his nose and said, "I thought you people prided yourself on taking kids who didn't fit into the regular school system. Well, this is a book Doug is reading. I found it hidden under the bed. Doug is smart! He just freezes up when he takes written tests. That's why Marshall Middle School has him in all the low ability classes!" The principal was convinced. After several of the school staff held interviews with Doug, he was finally accepted into the new school.

Nothing changed at first. Doug continued to be withdrawn and passively resisted doing his school lessons. Al continued to be critical, although Ellen could see he was trying to at least hold his tongue. The first conference period, in which Ellen and Al spent an hour with two teachers and the principal, was a revelation for them both. The school staff recognized that Ellen was a protective parent who had a terrible time setting limits and allowing Doug to experience the consequences of his behavior. They asked her to stand back and stop helping Doug do his schoolwork. Let Doug experience the logical consequences of his behavior. Stop finding his papers for him when he loses assignments. Stop bringing him his coat or his lunch when forgets them. Ellen's rescuing, protective behaviors were sending powerful messages to Doug that he was not a capable, respected person. For the first time, Ellen realized that she, too, was deeply involved as a source of her son's problems. Al, on the other hand, was delighted that someone had finally recognized that *he* was not the only parent doing things wrong. He subsequently became much more open to changing his own critical behaviors with Doug.

Ellen never forgot the principal's final advice, "Trust that Doug is a capable person. It will take at least two years to convince him of that. Change takes time. In the meanwhile, try to relax a little. You have to trust your own son."

The principal was right. Change came slowly, but it did come. Report cards at Pine Lodge were written and descriptive. The opening statements were always positive messages about Doug. One especially powerful message from a male teacher was, "I like this young man very much." Negative messages were straightforward and descriptive, "Doug turned in three out of five reports." Every student at Pine Lodge was expected to participate in the low-key sports program. Doug became involved first with lacrosse, a rough and tumble sport that provided an outlet for his normal male boisterousness which until now he had suppressed. He also learned to love playing soccer with his teammates. Pine Lodge was a small school that enabled Doug to know and be known by all the teachers and students. The principal took a personal interest in Doug. They occasionally ate lunch together to discuss books they were both reading. Doug's teacher applied for a summer Outward Bound scholarship for Doug, a program that provides a month of rigorous outdoor experience for a small group of teenagers. The month Doug spent with the Outward Bound program was probably the turning point in permanently raising his sense of competency and self-esteem. By now he was forming firm friendships with other students in spite of the great differences in income levels between his family and most of the other students' families. His grades came up to a respectable level. Family relationships improved. His younger brother and sister became openly proud of their older brother. In the last term of his senior year he "never got around" to finishing a final report for his Social Studies class. The principal dealt with this by matter-of-factly telling Doug he could graduate with his class with a blank diploma. The real diploma would be his once he completed a summer class in Social Studies. Doug cheerfully attended the summer school class with no complaints. It was as though he had been trying them out for one last time.

Doug's situation is a perfect example of how important teachers are, especially male teachers, in helping male teenagers through the often rough transition into adulthood. Boys need admired males in their lives. This is especially true for boys with fathers who have physically or emotionally abandoned their sons. In his book, *The Wonder of Boys*, Michael Gurian quotes a juvenile detention officer as saying, "I don't even read the profiles anymore—in ninety percent of my cases, the male delinquent comes from a single parent home." The primary caregiver to one-third of American boys in the 1990s was a single mother. Some of these boys were lucky enough to have fathers, male pastors, coaches, uncles, grandfathers, and male neighbors who were willing to spend time with the boy and act as mentors who initiate him into male society. It is still the case today that many boys have no respected adult men to pattern themselves after other than those they see on television, or in video games, or at school. If they don't connect with someone at school or in the community, these boys often pattern themselves after television and movie role models, or after respected male teenage peers, who are usually equally confused about how to become a man. Both male and female teachers can be that special person who helps a boy build his stairsteps to self-esteem and competency by using the approach outlined in this book. Yet only a male can provide a boy with the male role model he needs, in order to learn how to become a competent and respected man.

Unfortunately, our culture fails to support single mothers in pro-viding a network of male companions who can give their sons a sense of belonging to the world of responsible, caring, adult males. Most single mothers are well aware that their sons need male role models. If you are a male elementary school teacher, you know from experience that single mothers often request that their sons be placed in your classes. The result is that you end up with a disproportionate number of boisterous boys in your room each year. This is a lot to ask of all you male teachers, and yet you are the only responsible male role model many single mothers can turn to for help in saving their sons.

The fact is that boys are different than girls. They tend to take up more space, have more abrupt and larger physical movements, and need to have all that testosterone-driven energy channeled in ways that girls do not as often require. The anthropologist Victor Turner has noticed that many African tribes treat boys differently from girls in initiation experiences leading to adulthood. Boys are initiated through physical activities with large groups of boys and men, whereas girls are taken by individual elder women and initiated more intimately and individually. It is interesting that this different treatment is consistent with what we are now learning about the difference between men's and women's brains. Neuropsychologist Raquel Gur says, "Male and female brains do the same things, but they do them differently." Some of these differences include the female's tendency to have a higher comfort zone in dealing with emotional issues in small groups, and with her greater ability to express herself verbally. Men seem to be better at focusing on one thing at a time, and tend to be more comfortable with physical action rather than verbal tactics when confronted with a problem. This is one reason why participation in sports is so important for boys and is a powerful argument for doing away with the present system in our schools that allows only a few boys to participate as a member of an elite team. The sports program practiced at Doug's Pine Lodge School, for example, in which *every* child is expected to play on a team in an intramural system, is far superior to the ordinary high school sports program because it provides a chance for every child, boys especially, to experience a sense of competence and of belonging to the male "tribe." Doug was additionally blessed by being able to participate in an Outward Bound program which allowed him to discover the power of his own inner resources at the same time he learned to be a valuable member of his male group.

Male teachers cannot of course be expected to fill every boy's need for a male role model, nor can they be expected to commit hundreds of after school hours spending their free time with fatherless boys. Just by being who he is, an adult male who carries out his duties responsibly and with fairness, the male teacher has tremendous power as a role model for the young men in his classes. The positive influence of a male teacher who takes the time to give an occasional smile and friendly eye contact at neutral times, especially to those boys hovering on the edge of the school community, cannot be overestimated. Male teachers who learn how to avoid power struggles with their students are especially influential, because, by avoiding power struggles, they have transformed themselves from one of the enemy to a respected male elder of the tribe, a man a boy can look up to and pattern himself after.

SECOND STEP: Find the right therapist or family counselor

If you have tried all of the above and nothing has worked so far, it is time to look for outside help. Trust your intuition. If you are lying awake night after night feeling frightened about your teen's behavior, you need help from someone who knows what they are doing. If you are a person who finds it hard to share your private affairs with others, this first step will be difficult, but it is absolutely crucial for your child, for yourself, and for the community, that you be honest about your need for help. You may even discover it is a relief to finally be talking openly about the problem.

1. *Network with friends and acquaintances to find the right therapist or family counselor.* Some pastors and school counselors have the right training to lead a family meeting, but many do not. Inexperienced family counselors sometimes unwittingly sabotage a family meeting by taking sides, and by giving lots of outer-reality advice. You need someone who will not place blame on any individual member of the family. You need someone who can teach your family how to listen and how to problem-solve. You need someone who can help you network to find adults who are willing to be mentors and role models for your teenager. You also need

someone who is skilled at recognizing whether your teen is exhibiting signs of depression.

Pick up the phone and start networking. Ask people if they have personal knowledge of a good family therapist. Ask your school counselor, pastor, child's teacher, doctor, or perhaps a friend or acquaintance who has experience in this area. It is unfortunate that the cost of going to a therapist is a real problem for many families. Maybe one of your child's grandparents can afford to pay the cost. Many medical insurance policies provide short-term counseling help. Local service organizations like the Lions will sometimes subsidize a family in this way. Some excellent private therapists charge a reasonable sliding fee scale based on your family income, so do not just assume that you can't afford this kind of help.

When you find a family therapist, before you make an appointment, talk to the therapist on the telephone. Be honest about your difficulties with your child. Ask what their experience and training is for this kind of situation. Is this situation something they are comfortable with or would he or she rather refer you to someone else? No reputable therapist or counselor will object to these kinds of questions. When you are satisfied that this is the right person, make an appointment.

2. *The process you use to get your teenager to go to the first meeting needs to be planned ahead of time.* Wait for a neutral time and use describing language to tell your teenager about the family meeting with the counselor. Here is an example of what you can say, "I can see you're unhappy with me and with the school. I know I can't always be telling you how to live your life. After all, you're almost an adult. But I'm worried about you. I don't know how to make things better, and I guess you don't either. So I made an appointment with a person who teaches families how to solve the everyday problems of living together."

If you're afraid you can't say this in describing language and will sabotage yourself by placing blame, say these same things by writing your teen a short, describing note. Don't forget to sign it, "I love you."

Be very clear you are not taking your teen to this meeting to have him or her "fixed," or insinuate in any way that your teen is the problem. This meeting is taking place so that every member of the family can learn some new ways of living together. Every member of the family should attend the meeting. Ask your teen if there is a special adult they would like to invite. Including this person in the meeting will convince your child that at least one adult there will be on his or her side. If your child has a special relationship with an adult in the school (past or present), or a neighbor, count it as a great blessing. *There is nothing wrong with asking for help from other people who know your child. It is a great fault of our society that parents are expected to raise their children all by themselves.*

Tell your teenager the time and date and ask if that is an okay time. If your teen says it's a terrible time, pick up the phone, dial the therapist's number and hand it to your child, saying, "Let's set up a time right now that's good for us both."

If your teen refuses to respond or says "no way!" treat it as a self-indulgent behavior; be a solid, immovable moss-covered rock and say, "I'll be at school to pick you up at 2:00 p.m." *Let your nonverbal message be, this is the way things are. Nothing can be done to change it.*

Your teen is going to resist going to this meeting. His or her idea of a meeting is having several adults sit and stare at him while they scold, blame, question, and advise. If you can't get your teen to the meeting on your own, ask the school or therapist to send someone to help you get him or her there.

Do not expect any great ideas to surface at this first meeting. It will be enough if each family member feels listened to and respected. At the next meeting, your teen will be much more willing to attend because now he or she understands that the meeting is for solving problems, not for placing blame.

THIRD STEP: Keep involved with any outside agency—schools or the courts—who are working with your teenager

1. *Do not give up on your teenager.* Your child may already have committed some aggressive act that has brought him or her into the court or police system. No matter how much you may be tempted to walk away from your teenager, he or she needs the security of knowing you are still hang-

ing in there. Also, other adults are more likely to not give up on your son or daughter if they see that you have not given up. Try to work with the social worker and take every opportunity to have input into any consequence plans that are worked up for your child. Because of the knowledge gained from studying this book, you may be the only adult working with your teen who understands the difference between logical consequences and punishment. Punishment will only intensify the power struggle. Be sure you make it clear to whomever is in charge of overseeing your child's behavior that you would like to be involved on a regular basis.

Many schools expel the aggressive teen as a form of time-out. Expulsion is a powerful negative script that sends a message to the child that the school has totally given up on him. Expulsion not only sends the message that this person is beyond help, it also further isolates someone who has already been pushed to the outer fringes of the school community, thereby further tearing down an already fragile staircase of needs. Expulsion also shifts total responsibility to the parent, who by now has run out of ideas on how to improve things. *When the offense is one that does not seriously harm another person, in-school detention is much more effective than expulsion.* It provides firmness and fairness for the offending teenager, while at the same time it protects other people from his or her unacceptable behavior. Temporary in-school detention also has the benefit of sending a powerful positive message that this school and this staff care, and will not give up on this teenager.

If, however, the aggressive behavior crosses the line into actual or threatened violence, expulsion is the only immediate tool a school community can use in order to maintain a safe climate for teachers and students. The sixteen-year-old boy, for example, who continually used sexual innuendos in the presence of his teacher, and who finally tried to rape her, is an example of the type of aggressive behavior that must result in expulsion as well as a report of the incident to the police.

2. If it is apparent that your teen is not able to operate in a regular high school setting, do everything you can to see that he or she is enrolled in a good alternative school program. If your child is already in the juvenile court system, be aware that many judges are open to giving the teenager a choice between going to a locked juvenile detention facility or attending an alternative school. All large school districts run some kind of alternative school. There are dozens of alternative schools, public and private, that claim to hold the key to saving troubled teens. At first glance, it is puzzling why some work and some don't. But when these programs are evaluated in light of what we know about the emotional staircase of needs, it is easy to see what makes a successful alternative school.

No matter if the basic format of the alternative school involves working on a ranch, climbing mountains, training for a job, repairing houses for senior citizens, or participating in an inner-city basketball program, *the successful programs all strengthen the emotional needs staircase for the teen.* Physical needs like safe living environments free of drugs and violence, dental care and teeth straightening, clothing, and nourishing food are provided. Successful alternative programs engender emotional security for the teen by having clear rules, respect for each individual, and by ensuring that consequences for misbehavior are consistent, logical, predictable, and non-punitive. Successful alternative schools have small populations with fewer students per teacher. Here, every teen can be personally known by each staff member as a unique individual. In the best of situations, opportunities exist for boys to bond with adult males and girls with admired women. A small community means that teens have a better chance of practicing solid relationship skills with peers so they have a better chance of having their needs for belonging and being-love met. Successful alternative schools also meet competency/respect needs by giving opportunities for useful work, and setting high standards for learning and behavior. They also offer plenty of chances for regular family and classroom meetings so that students can explore and share values, listen to feelings, and problem-solve with peers and caring adults. All these experiences help the teenager to eventually realize that he or she can be a competent and respected member of society.

A juvenile detention center or prison is obviously the time-out of last resort. Effective logical consequence programs are extremely rare in American prisons because our society does not understand that it is possible to have firm, predictable consequences for aggressive behavior and still help aggressive individuals in prison to strengthen their staircase of needs. This is unfortunate because it is clear that strengthening the emotional staircase of needs brings about improved behavior, while weakening the staircase brings about a worsening of behavior. The result of a prison system geared primarily to punish the aggressive offender is an increasingly violent power struggle between the prisoner and society.

An example of a prison system based on rehabilitation rather than punishment is the Norwegian prison system. Norwegian prisons combine the logical consequence of incarceration with a focus on strengthening each inmate's staircase of needs so they will be able to leave the prison with increased ability to become a contributing member of society. The result is that far fewer of their prisoners ever return to prison. Arne Nilsen, warden of a high security Norwegian prison with a low recidivism rate of only 17%, says, "If we treat people like animals ... they are likely to behave like animals. Here we pay attention to (them) as human beings."

Standing in sharp contrast with Norway's overall recidivism rate of 20%, the recidivism rate in the United States is 60-70%. It is my hope that one day the Norwegian approach to dealing with prisoners will be the norm here in America. Until then, parents, families, teachers, and other caring members of the community can refuse to give up on their disruptive teens, and continue to take Rudolph Dreikurs's advice to, "Do what you can do."

For specific ideas on what adults can do to make the transition into adulthood a more rewarding process for all teens, three excellent books describe the problem, focus on the emotional needs of our sons and daughters, and offer solutions at school, family, and societal levels. They are important reading for all teachers, parents, and anyone who works with teenagers: *Lost Boys: Why Our Sons Turn Violent and How We Can Save Them*, by James Garbarino; *Reviving Ophelia: Saving the Selves of Adolescent Girls*, by Mary Pipher; and *The Wonder of Boys: What Parents, Mentors and Educators Can Do to Shape Boys into Exceptional Men*, by Michael Gurian.

REVIEW: Helping the Aggressive and Self-Destructive Teenager

FIRST STEP: Let the teenager take charge of important areas of his or her life, at home and at school

1. **When a teenager realizes she is perceived as a competent person able to manage her own life, the stairsteps on her staircase of emotional needs will strengthen and self-confidence will soar.**

2. **Decide which areas you can let go of and give to your teenager to manage.** The more areas you give to your teenager to manage the more likely he or she will respect your wishes in those areas in which you do need to stay involved. Sit down with other concerned adults and make a list.

3. **If you decide to monitor your teen's schoolwork, make a plan with your child's teacher.**

   A. Parent, teacher, or counselor can begin the process.

   B. The parent's role is to tell their teenager about the plan, figure out what kind of a logical consequence would have some meaning for their teenager, and then make certain that the logical consequence occurs.

   C. The initiating teacher or the school counselor explains to the student that he or she is responsible for getting a schoolwork progress report every Friday from every teacher.

   D. Try to convey the nonverbal message there is nothing personal or spiteful about the consequence. There are no winners and no losers, this is just the way the world works.

4. **Alternatively, you can choose to give your teenager total responsibility for schoolwork.**

5. **Listen to your teenager's inner reality and, if necessary, adjust any hostile or abusive environment you may discover.**

from *Caring Discipline: Practical Tools for Nurturing Happy Families & Classrooms*

SECOND STEP: Find the right therapist or family counselor

1. **Network with friends and acquaintances** to find the right therapist or family counselor. The therapist should be able to help your family learn to problem-solve and to listen to one another, and also know how to help you establish a network of people willing to be mentors/role models for your child.

2. The process you use to get your teenager to go to the first meeting needs to be **planned out ahead of time**. A basic understanding of the information in chapters Two, Three, Four, Five and Eleven on how to communicate with your child is essential for making this step work.

THIRD STEP: Keep involved with any outside agency—schools or the courts—who are working with your teenager

1. **Do not give up on your teenager.**

2. If your teenager cannot adapt to a regular high school or is already in the court system, explore the possibilities of an **alternative school.**

Chapter 12 Discussion: THE AGGRESSIVE AND SELF-DESTRUCTIVE TEENAGER

1. List all the important areas of your teenager's life you can think of. In which areas do you feel you must keep some control? In which areas can you step back and let your child take charge? Discuss your list and ask for ideas from the group.

2. Go back to the discussion ideas at the end of Chapter Five. Do the exercise of listening to inner and outer reality, this time role-playing the part of your own teenager. Choose a situation to role-play that is now a part of the power struggle between you.

3. Did the role-play give you any special insights into the power struggle with your teen?

4. Tell about a time an adult who was not a part of the family helped you grow successfully up your own staircase of needs.

5. List all the people you know of who might be interested in helping you by acting as a mentor and role model for your teenager. Discuss your list and ask for ideas from other members of the group.

Chapter THIRTEEN

Finding Solutions For Specific Problems

The *Caring Discipline* parenting philosophy is most effective when you use it as a unified, organic whole. In the same way an automobile needs all its various parts functioning together before it can operate, or a football team needs each member playing his individual position before the entire team can win a game, or each ingredient of a cake recipe needs to be mixed together for the cake to be edible, each part of the *Caring Discipline* approach to parenting needs to be used in the context of the entire philosophy. A basic concept to keep in mind as you apply these ideas is this: *To bring about positive, long-term change for a child you cannot use only one idea, like the broken-record or the time-out correction, and ignore everything else.*

For example, one mother found that the broken-record correction worked so well at first, she thought she had discovered a magic charm. But after a couple of weeks, her daughter not only started ignoring her again, she began to mimic her mother using the broken-record correction. The broken record stopped being effective because this mother did not understand that the broken-record technique needed the support of all other parts of the *Caring Discipline* philosophy. It is easy at first to use just one or two ideas, especially if they seem to be working, but in the long run, without a unified approach, things will fall apart.

One of the best ways to integrate the totality of the *Caring Discipline* philosophy into daily life is to schedule regular monthly problem-solving sessions with at least one other adult. At these ongoing meetings ask each other for ideas regarding a specific problem and a specific child. Ideally, you should include at least one person not directly involved with the day-to-day care of the child, someone who is able to keep some emotional distance from the problem. If this is not possible, go ahead with whomever shows an interest. (*Never ask a child to participate in this type of problem-solving session.*) The most important criteria is that the other adult be familiar with the *Caring Discipline* philosophy.

These ongoing problem-solving sessions use the same three steps of problem-solving you are familiar with from the chapter on The Family and Classroom Meetings: Step 1: Describe the problem; Step 2: Brainstorm for possible solutions; and Step 3: Attempt to choose a solution. The *Caring Discipline Overview* chart illustrates all major concepts presented in this book. Keep the chart handy during your problem-solving sessions to refer to for ideas.

Here are examples of three problem-solving sessions that will give you ideas on how to run your own meetings.

Problem-Solving Session A

This session took place in a parenting class:

STEP 1: Describe the problem. Molly told the other parents in the class about an incident with her three-year-old boy, Brent, who had a long-standing pattern of not-minding and of self-indulgent behavior. It was bedtime and she wanted him to take his bath. She gave him ten minutes lead time but he still ignored her when she told him, "Now it's time to take your bath." Molly physically assisted him into the bathroom and started taking off his clothes. Brent resisted the physical assist by stiffening his body, stomping his feet, hitting at his mother, and screaming, "I hate you!" Molly then gave him an either-or choice, either stop his behavior or go have a time-out. He continued with the obnoxious behavior. Molly gave him another physical assist to get him into the time-out; things eventually escalated to rage control. Molly ended up totally distraught and the father had to take over bathtime. Molly told this story to the class and ended by saying "Help!"

Several class members wanted to know just which specific behavior bothered Molly the most. "I hate it when he yells and whines. And I really get mad when he hits at me. It isn't actual hitting I guess. He mostly just flails his arms around, but I never would have got away with that kind of stuff when I was a kid!"

STEP 2: Brainstorm for possible solutions. As the class participants began to suggest possible solutions, the parenting leader wrote them on the flip chart.

Suggestion 1: "The basic correction for self-indulgent behavior is to ignore the behavior. How long were you able to ignore?" Molly said she couldn't ignore it more than a minute or so. "Maybe next time, if you could manage to ignore it longer, things wouldn't escalate. How about setting a goal for at least ten minutes of ignoring, maybe even until the end of the bath?"

Suggestion 2: "Were you able to remember not to sabotage by talking or scolding at him about the behavior?" The class laughed sympathetically when Molly emphatically shook her head NO.

Suggestion 3: "1 wondered why you used the time-out since you are only supposed to use that for really aggressive or out-of-control behaviors. Was he that aggressive?" Molly said that no, it was just that she was so mad at him, it was the only thing she could think of at the time.

"It sounds like he's having a good old-fashioned, self-indulgent tantrum. Next time could you think of yourself as a force of nature, like a rock, or a mountain? And if ignoring doesn't work, you could say, 'You can either stop this behavior and give yourself a bath, or keep on and I will have to give you the bath.' That would be an either-or choice that would allow him to learn self-control. If he stops being obnoxious, he can bathe himself. Putting the time-out in there really escalates the power struggle and then it's no longer an either-or choice."

Suggestion 4: "If your husband is better at ignoring, maybe he should give the bath." (Much laughter at this.)

Suggestion 5: "Do you have a routine for bedtime? Little kids thrive on routine, kind of like the idea that the sun goes up and the sun goes down. It's part of the natural order and nothing can change it."

Suggestion 6: "I was just thinking about some of the other areas on the *Caring Discipline* chart. Do you think he's getting enough attention at positive and neutral times? Is there something going on that makes him feel left out?" Molly then shared with the group how hard it was to give her son attention at positive and neutral times. Brent started whining and being pesky the minute she got home from work. Both she and her husband worked long hours during the day and there was very little time to spend with their son in the evening. By the time dinner was done, it was time for his bedtime.

Suggestion 7: "He must really miss you during the day. He probably needs to be just soaked in loving attention the minute you see him. Maybe you could schedule the first half hour when you get home just to be with him. You know, just sit and hold him and talk and laugh and cuddle. Maybe you and your husband could even take turns, you one night while he fixes dinner, and your husband the next while you fix dinner. And then maybe your son could help you set the table after your half hour is up. That would be good for his competency step." (The mother making this suggestion gave a small smile as she added, "I only wish I had a husband around to help me do the same with my two kids.")

STEP 3: Attempt to choose a solution. At this point the group stopped making suggestions and the parenting leader turned to the list of suggestions she had been making on the flip chart. "Okay, Molly. Tell us which of these ideas you might like to try."

Molly took each suggestion in turn. "As for those first suggestions: I know I didn't ignore long enough. I also sabotaged like crazy. I ended up yelling at him and slamming dishes around while my husband gave him the bath. And I totally forgot that the time-out wasn't an either-or choice. What a disaster! I'm so tired by the time I get home and I get so angry at him when he acts like that I can't think.

"As for the suggestion about the routines. That's not a problem. We have a pretty good bedtime routine. We have a bath and a little snack and then we put him in bed and read him a story.

"But those suggestions you gave me for paying attention to him the minute we get home ... well, you really hit a nerve. I sat here feeling like crying. I guess we haven't been paying enough attention to him for just being his sweet little self. We're always racing around, getting dinner, doing housework, and answering the phone. Maybe he has to act up to get enough attention from us. Yes, I'll try that. I'm sure my husband will too."

At this point someone made *Suggestion number* 8: "It sounds like you need to provide for your own unmet needs with some time for yourself. Maybe you could look on the cuddle time with Brent as a respite for yourself, too. Let voice mail answer the phone. The phone can wait for half an hour, and so can the housework."

The parenting leader tore off the sheet from the flip chart for Molly to take home.

The following week, Molly reported much improved behavior. Brent's self-indulgent behavior happened only once during that week. This time Molly was able to successfully ignore it and did not sabotage herself. An added benefit was that both Molly and her husband looked forward to the half hour cuddle-time and decided that a half hour to unwind at the end of the day was helping to meet their own emotional needs as well.

The major cause for the change in Brent's behavior was that the basic steps on his emotional needs staircase (physical touching needs, security needs, belonging and being-love needs) were strengthened when mother or dad gave him their total attention during a neutral time. Focusing on the neutral time when the family first arrived home was crucial because Brent had been isolated from his parents all day. The ignoring and physical assist corrections, although still important, were a relatively minor part of stopping the self-indulgent behavior, and seldom had to be used. Using describing praise during positive behaviors (setting the table) was helping to build his competency stairstep. A clue that something in Molly's past childhood was involved in her extreme anger towards Brent's self-indulgent behavior came when Molly said, "I would never have gotten away with that when I was a kid." Finding a way to provide for Molly to meet her own emotional needs was an important part of this solution. It took all of these ideas, working together, to bring about change for Brent.

Problem-Solving Session B

In which a group of parents discuss a problem with a teenager:

STEP 1: Describe the problem. The mother, Claire, asked two of her friends, Diane and Greta, for ideas about dealing with her fourteen-year-old daughter, Rebecca, who had lied to her. First, they got out the *Caring Discipline Overview* chart. Then the two friends tried to clarify and learn more specifics about the problem.

Question 1: "How often does she lie to you?" Claire said it didn't happen very often but it seemed to her the lying was becoming more frequent.

Question 2: "Can you describe a specific situation in which she lied to you?" Claire said: "Well, take last Saturday for example. We were getting ready to go to the zoo. I told the kids to be sure to make a sandwich and have some fruit before we went. They know we can't afford to be spending a lot of money on food at the zoo, the entrance fee is expensive enough. So just before we left the house, I asked Rebecca if she had had a sandwich. She said yes, a turkey sandwich, but when I went to the refrigerator to make a sandwich myself, I could see the turkey meat package from the deli hadn't even been opened. No one but me had made a turkey sandwich. I confronted her. I told her it was obvious she was lying. She insisted she had eaten a turkey sandwich. I finally told her that she could choose between telling the truth or not going to the zoo with the rest of the family. She wouldn't admit the truth so we went to the zoo without her."

STEP 2: Brainstorm for possible solutions. At this point, Diane and Greta began offering suggestions.

Suggestion 1: "It seems like you were trying to treat the lying as a routine not-minding behavior when you gave her the consequence of staying home. If she's lying often, I agree it makes sense to classify it as a routine not-minding behavior, but the consequence you gave was really a punishment, don't you think? Instead, couldn't you give her the logical consequence of just letting her go hungry at the zoo and not buying her anything to eat if she asked? Then the consequence would be directly related to her not eating."

Suggestion 2: "You said she doesn't lie very often. Maybe she lies to protect herself. In this case, she probably felt she had the right to lie because it's her body and she wasn't hungry. When we were taking the parenting class, we learned that kids will start a power struggle if they feel their sense of competency and self-respect is threatened. Knowing you are in control of your own life is so important for the competency stairstep, especially for a teenager. Why not just give control of what she eats to Rebecca? If she gets hungry once or twice, she will learn pretty quick that it's smarter to eat before she goes out. Just let nature's consequences be her teacher. That way, there would be no need for her to lie or get into a power struggle with you."

Suggestion 3: "The whole issue of providing food for our kids is such an important one because it involves our concept of ourselves as nurturing parents. Maybe that's why it's so hard for you to let Rebecca decide when to eat. Would you feel like you're not a good parent if you let her go hungry at the zoo? I know it's hard to tell a hungry kid she'll have to wait until you get home, but maybe just knowing you earlier offered nourishing food for her would help ease your mind." Claire answered that it would be awfully hard to let any child of hers go hungry. She wasn't sure she could do it.

Suggestion 4: "Maybe the reason it's so hard to allow Rebecca to be in charge of her own eating choices has something to do with that bottom section of the *Caring Discipline Overview* chart, your own emotional needs. Is there anything from your own childhood, anything about food, that triggers something for you?"

At this point, Claire protested, "Wait a minute. Somehow we've switched from Rebecca's lying to my childhood!"

"Okay," Diane said. "We'll shut up for awhile. You do the talking.

Did any of those other ideas we suggested make sense to you?"

STEP 3: Attempt to choose a solution. Claire: "Well, I agree that going hungry would be a better consequence than not going to the zoo if we're talking about not-minding, but it was the lying I was so upset about. And one thing I was successful at that you didn't mention was in not sabotaging. I didn't lecture and scold her about it. The other suggestions that somehow I backed Rebecca into a corner where she had to lie to protect her sense of being a competent person in control of her own life, or that it's her own business if she eats or not, I just never thought of it that way. Food really is an important thing to me. Providing a good diet for my family is a big part of what I do as a mother. Maybe it is all tied up with something from my past and my own emotional needs. I don't know. But I'll certainly think about it."

With the help of her two friends, Claire was gradually able to modify her own deep-felt need to control her children's eating patterns. Claire had a hard time realizing that control over body functions, such as how much and what to eat, is an area of a child's life that can be safely given over to the child from birth. The adult's role is, of course, an important one of providing regular mealtimes and keeping junk food out of the house. The younger the child, of course, the smaller the portion and the more often they need to eat. By keeping the house free of junk food, the parent provides an environment in which the child can safely eat what, and as much, as the child needs. Claire was fortunate to have sensitive friends who were able to be frank in pointing Claire toward the stumbling block of her own hidden unmet needs, while still respecting the fact that changes in that area come slowly.

Claire also began to realize that she needed to let Rebecca make other personal decisions about her own body, especially in the area of clothing and hair styles. Claire's attempts to control how her daughter looked was another factor fueling the power struggle between them. As Claire was able to step back and in this way demonstrate to Rebecca that she respected her daughter as a competent person capable of making her own choices, the power struggle with her daughter lessened and the lying faded away.

Problem-Solving Session C

This situation occurred in a high security detention center:

Nineteen-year-old Clayton has committed a violent crime and will be imprisoned for many years. At age twenty-one, Clayton will go into the state penitentiary for adults. Until then, he has an opportunity to go to school at a small detention facility where teachers conduct classes in basic reading, English, and math skills. Teachers are told to report all infractions of the rules to the prison guards. The guards take away a privilege such as television viewing, or a late bedtime, as a punishment for negative behavior. This problem-solving session involves a teacher, Loma, who has been teaching at the detention facility for only a short time, and Gill and Rosie, two other teachers on the staff.

STEP 1: Describe the problem. Loma said, "Yesterday when I walked over to help Clayton with his math, he deliberately began to scrawl with his pencil back and forth across the title page of the math book. I told him, 'Clayton, you know that's against the rules. That's defacing public property.' He just looked at me as bold as could be, kept right on scrawling across the page and said, 'I like it better this way.'

"Of course the other students in the room were watching all this, too. I knew very well they were all checking me out to see if I was someone they could push around. So I told him, 'I'll have to report you for breaking the rule against defacing public property.'

"So Clayton says, 'Well, I've got it all erased now.' And he did erase it. But I reported him anyhow. I felt it was some sort of a test of my strength and I had better not back down.

"The guard and Clayton had a meeting which I was expected to attend. The guard gave Clayton a long lecture on how to get along by following the rules and then he took away Clayton's television privileges until Clayton 'shaped up.' So then Clayton started complaining about how no one ever gives him a break, and no one ever gives him credit for anything. Clayton is very articulate and all the time he is talking he is looking daggers at me. He often complains about how nobody ever appreciates anything he does. So I reminded him how I had praised him for his good test scores and his improvement in his writing skills. I *have* been doing my best for him. But Clayton just sat there looking like a thundercloud, and if looks could kill, I wouldn't be alive today!

"At this point, my problem is I'm almost scared to go back on Monday. Today's Friday and he's got all weekend to brood about it. I don't want this to keep escalating until he pushes a homemade knife into my ribs. I've got to have some kind of a plan for Monday morning."

STEP 2: Brainstorm for possible solutions. Gill studied the *Caring Discipline Overview* chart and said, "Looking at the emotional needs staircase, it seems like the only needs met for this guy are the basic needs of a place to eat and a place to sleep. At the competency level, he can't even control when he goes to bed. I guess he compensates by trying to control people around him. I can see why you had to report him, even after he erased the marks. He was testing you to see who would be in charge, you or him."

Rosie agreed. "Besides that, every staff member is obligated to keep things consistent by enforcing the rules equally, otherwise this place would be in chaos."

Gill said, "Right now, Clayton probably feels justified in blaming you for his loss of television privileges, partly because you sabotaged by telling him all the good things you've done for him. I suspect what angered him was not so much the fact you reported him—he knows the rules and he knew he would get a punishment—what probably really bothered him was that the guard lectured him during the process. And then you gave him more outer-reality information, which aggravated him even more, though he knows you're right."

Loma said she didn't see how she could listen to Clayton's inner reality when she couldn't agree with anything he was saying.

Suggestion 1: Gill said, "Of course you can't agree with him, but do you think you could just listen? If you look at the *Caring Discipline Overview* chart under negative behavior, you can see that listening to inner reality is the recommended approach when the person has a problem with negative feelings, and that seems to be Clayton's problem, even though he tries to blame it all on you. Maybe he would respond if you waited until some neutral time and said something like, 'It must be hard to follow all these rules they have in here!' Just say this in a low-key way and then don't say anymore. If he launches into a tirade, don't say anything. Just look thoughtful and say, 'Hmm' or 'Gosh.' Let him do the talking.

"If you had listened to his inner reality, it might have made a big difference. But maybe not. It sounds like the guard was doing plenty of sabotaging and since you were there to witness it, you might have caught Clayton's rage anyhow. But it's worth trying at some neutral time, if you can find one."

Suggestion 2: Rosie said, "I think Clayton tries to manipulate people with a lot of self-indulgent behavior. I agree with you that it's important to do inner-reality listening when he's really hurting, but don't buy in to his everyday grumbling. Treat the usual complaints as self-indulgent behavior and ignore them, unless, as in this case, you feel it is a sincere problem for him. Of course, the tricky part of ignoring is to be sure to pay plenty of attention to him at neutral times with eye contact and smiles."

Suggestion 3: Gill had one more idea. "Another thing that might help is to give him describing praise instead of evaluating praise when he does well at his schoolwork. That should help build his sense of being a competent person in control of at least the academic part of his life. All these guys, no matter what they have done in the past, still respond to having as many of their emotional needs met as possible."

STEP 3: Attempt to choose a solution. Loma decided to try all the suggestions given by her colleagues. On Monday morning, Loma managed to catch Clayton's eyes as he came into the room. She smiled and said, "Hi." The response from Clayton was zero, no expression at all. Determined, Loma later stopped by Clayton's desk at independent study time to check his math and said, "It must be hard, Clayton, to have to follow all the rules we have in here."

Clayton suddenly looked up at her, really looked at her for the first time all day. "You better believe it," was all he said.

Since then, Clayton has launched into an angry tirade about being misunderstood only once. This time Loma managed to listen without making judgments about whether he was right or wrong. She just said

"Hmm" a few times and nodded her head sympathetically. She ignores his complaints whenever she judges them to be self-indulgent behavior. She is also trying to remember to give him eye contact and smiles at neutral times, plus describing praise at positive times. Loma says at first she had the feeling he was studying her, trying to figure her out. But he is increasingly cooperative now and hasn't tried to provoke any major power struggles with her. Loma believes they are at last developing a workable student/teacher relationship.

Loma is also using Gill and Rosie's suggestions with her other students. She is convinced that by applying these ideas, Clayton and the other students are learning more, feeling better about themselves, and in the process perhaps even reducing some of the rage they feel at the world.

With the knowledge you have gained from studying this book, you can use these three situations as a guide to begin holding your own problem-solving meetings. If, after a few sessions, you feel stuck and unable to bring about the changes you want, look for an additional person who can bring your group a fresh point of view. Remember that each situation is different because each individual is unique, but the basic principles outlined on the *Caring Discipline Overview* chart can be applied to every behavior problem that arises in your family or classroom.

REVIEW: Finding Solutions For Specific Problems

Parents and teachers familiar with the *Caring Discipline* philosophy can schedule regular monthly meetings to help each other problem-solve specific discipline problems as they arise. (*The child should never be involved in these meetings.*)

How to Problem-Solve and Look for Possible Solutions

1. Ask one person to keep written notes.

2. Keep a *Caring Discipline Overview* chart handy for everyone to refer to if needed.

3. Follow the Problem-Solving Process:

First Step: Describe the problem. It must be a real problem and not a hypothetical one. Ask the teacher or parent with the discipline problem to describe the specific situation. Members of the group should feel free to ask questions about the problem to be sure everyone understands exactly what the problem is. When the person with the problem agrees that the problem has been stated correctly, write it down.

Second Step: Brainstorm for possible solutions. Each person in the group gives suggestions for a solution. All suggestions should be written down, even apparently silly ones. (Have some fun with this.) Ask the person who is having the problem solved for her to please hold her comments about the ideas during the brainstorming session.

Third Step: Attempt to choose a solution. Remember that only the person with the problem can choose, or not choose, a solution. As the parent or teacher with the problem talks about each suggestion, keep track of her comments on the list of written ideas.

After the problem-solving session is over, whether or not a solution has been found, give the person with the problem the notes. He or she will find that a written reminder is helpful in thinking later about the discussion. (Some people are better visual than auditory learners. It is also hard for any of us to remember what we hear during times of emotional stress.)

from *Caring Discipline: Practical Tools for Nurturing Happy Families & Classrooms*

Epilogue

How will you know when you have integrated the *Caring Discipline* philosophy into your life? Here are some typical stories told by parents and teachers who have learned to apply the *Caring Discipline* principles in their relationships with children.

Donna, parent: "I was trying to get the kids ready for a doctor appointment, the telephone kept ringing, and we were going to be late. The more I hurried, the more my four-year-old Jason whined and complained. Finally, as we were getting into the car, he bumped his head and started to cry, way out of proportion to how hard he hit himself. I was so aggravated with him, I didn't trust myself to say anything so I just tried to ignore him. That's when Nita, my seven-year-old daughter, came to the rescue. She put her arm around his shoulder and said, 'It really hurts when you bump your head, doesn't it, Jason?' Jason stopped crying, sniffled a little bit, nodded his head, sat down and buckled his seat belt, and seemed perfectly happy for the rest of the morning. Nita did a better job of listening to Jason's inner reality than I could have done at that moment because I was so irritated. I realized then that I am no longer the only one who understands how to do some nurturing in this family!"

Jeanne, teacher: "I used to have such a hard time communicating with parents, especially if I was having a problem with their child. Parents used to get so defensive with me. Now I use a little inner-reality listening with every parent. I also always have a copy of the *Caring Discipline Overview* chart when I meet with them. I start the conversation by telling them first about the positive behaviors of their child before I mention any behaviors I am concerned about. After that, I share with them the problem behavior and what I have been trying to do to make things better.

"It helps to have the chart there to illustrate as I talk. One thing I've learned in this business is that many people, both adults and children, can't learn from just hearing something, they also need something visual to look at. If it seems appropriate, and if we have time, I also explain Maslow's emotional needs staircase and how it affects behavior. The librarian bought a few extra books for me to loan to those parents interested in learning more. Once parents actually read the material, we have a common vocabulary to use when we talk about their kids. The A and C-parent concept helps a lot, because usually at least one of the parents is a C. I tell them I'm an A-parent and I stress the fact that we're both okay. We can laugh about it and it clears the air.

"The ideas of self-sabotage and paying attention at neutral times are especially good in helping me get across some ideas of how to help their child. I don't know how many parents end up understanding the totality of the *Caring Discipline* system, but I do, and it's been a great help to me in establishing a more constructive partnership relationship with them."

Jim, parent: "It isn't that I never have conflicts or problems with my kids anymore. We don't have as many problems, but we still do have them. I guess that's just human nature. But the thing is that now we get over them so fast and can move on to living together and enjoying each other's company. For one thing, more often I just know what to do when a problem comes up, and for the times I don't have a clue what to do, I keep much calmer than I used to because I know I have the tools to figure out a plan to try tomorrow."

Anatole, teacher: "I teach history classes for seniors and juniors. I am considered a pretty tough teacher because I think kids are here to work and to learn. I have 150 different students each day. It's difficult to get to know very many of them personally.

"I've started having a class meeting every two weeks on Fridays during regular classroom time. I operate the meeting according to the *Caring Discipline* philosophy. Topics often deal with broader societal problems which affect the students personal lives, like drug use, the value of going to college over getting a job, whether or not to smoke, and, of course, the big one, dating practices. I've noticed how quickly the students are copying my listening behavior. More and more of them are actually beginning to listen to their peers' inner reality instead of leaping right away into an argument. They're taking turns running the meetings now and doing a wonderful job. We know each other better as individuals and things go more smoothly when we're doing the academic work. I really believe that for the first time I have found a way to meet some of their emotional needs at the same time I insist on keeping academic standards high."

Carlotta, parent: "My sister's little girl, Carmen, is three years old and I often take care of her. Carmen idolizes my youngest son, Ricky. She constantly tags after him and wants to do everything he is doing. One day, Carmen and my two kids (Ricky is five and Manuel, seven) were playing with some toys in the living room. I was in the kitchen but I could hear what was going on. Ricky was playing with a little car and Carmen tried to grab it from him. Ricky ignored her and kept the toy just out of her reach. So Carmen started to cry and scream. Ricky kept on ignoring her. Finally, Manuel couldn't stand it anymore and said to Carmen, 'You have to use words and tell Ricky what you want.'

"Carmen stopped crying and said, 'I want a turn with the car.'

"Ricky said, 'No way.'

"Manuel turned to Carmen, 'Use words and ask Ricky when you can have a turn.'

"Carmen asked, but Ricky only said, 'Tomorrow.'

"Manuel immediately said, 'That's too long, Ricky. Think of another idea.'

"Ricky gave a little smile and said, 'Okay. In two minutes you can have a turn.'

"In a little while he actually did give her a turn. The problem was solved and without any intervention from me. I was amazed, and so glad I had stayed out of it. It made me realize I have actually taught Manuel how to solve problems and now he is teaching his brother and cousin."

Jillian, parent: "Ever since I married Lisa's father, Lisa and I have been in a power struggle. I've been her stepmother for seven years now, and no matter what I did, it was wrong. I always thought Lisa hated me. Lisa was the one child that the *Caring Discipline* philosophy didn't seem to help. Lisa's mother is a drug addict, but of course Lisa loves her mother, and I always did my best to respect their relationship. I hung in there for years listening to Lisa's inner reality, paying attention at neutral times, trying to be a force of nature, carrying out logical consequences, and trying to ignore her constant self-indulgent behavior.

"Lisa is nineteen years old now and has moved out of the house. The other day she came over for dinner. In fact, I've been puzzled that she seems to enjoy coming over now to visit us. Then, when we were doing the dishes, she told me, 'I've always been afraid I will love you better than my own mother.'

"All that time I thought she hated me, she was loving me. No wonder she had to fight me so hard. What loyalty that little girl had to her crazy, screwed-up mother. But now, at last, I think we are actually going to be friends. Thank God I never gave up on her. It was worthwhile after all."

May all your dedicated efforts at learning to apply the *Caring Discipline* philosophy be rewarded by results similar to the ones these parents and teachers have described. In the process, you should realize an increased sense of calmness and confidence about your parenting and teaching; experience fewer power struggles; watch each child's sense of self-discipline and self-esteem strengthen; notice an increasing number of incidents in which the children themselves, using you as a role model, are able to apply the *Caring Discipline* philosophy to their own relationships; and finally, and perhaps best of all, you will discover that the relationship with your children becomes ever more compassionate and loving as they grow toward adulthood.

Epilogue Discussion: INTEGRATING THE *CARING DISCIPLINE* PHILOSOPHY INTO YOUR LIFE

1. Do any members of the group want to continue meeting for the purpose of helping one another problem-solve specific situations that arise in the future? If yes, decide if there are any changes you want to make in the way the group is organized and how often and where you will meet. Would people prefer to meet on-line or in a local library or church?

2. At the end of this book is a list of resources you may want to explore. Each offers insights into how to provide kids with loving discipline. The ideas in these materials will reinforce the concepts you have learned in this book.

3 Enjoy the journey, and Happy Parenting!

Caring Discipline Overview

CHILD'S STAIRCASE OF NEEDS *

Self-actualization

As the staircase strengthens, behavior improves.

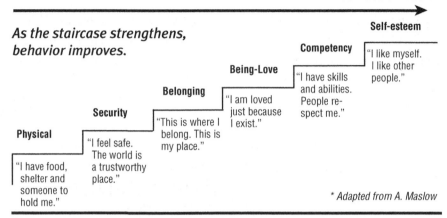

Self-esteem
"I like myself. I like other people."

Competency
"I have skills and abilities. People respect me."

Being-Love
"I am loved just because I exist."

Belonging
"This is where I belong. This is my place."

Security
"I feel safe. The world is a trustworthy place."

Physical
"I have food, shelter and someone to hold me."

* Adapted from A. Maslow

CHILD'S BEHAVIORS: Behaviors You Give Emotional Attention to Will Continue

Positive	Neutral	Negative
1. Adult gives nonverbal attention (eye contact, touching, smiles) 2. Adult gives verbal attention (describing praise)	1. Adult gives nonverbal attention (eye contact, touching, smiles)	1. Not-minding (Physical assist, broken record) 2. Self-indulgent (Ignore and either-or choice) 3. Routine not-minding (Choices and consequences) 4. Aggressive (Time-out)
Pleases you—a joy for you	Child doing his or her own thing—not a problem for you	Angers or irritates you —a problem for you

THE FOUR SELF-SABOTAGES

1. Procrastination

2. Talking and talking about the misbehavior. Act, don't talk. Carry out the correction and do not mention it again.

3. Forgetting to give 4–1 attention (4 parts positive to 1 part negative)

4. Negative scripting

Child Has Problem

Adult helps by:
1. Adjusting the environment
2. Teaching problem-solving and assertiveness skills
3. Listening and accepting the child's inner reality

ANGER

Hidden Unmet Needs of the Adult ⟶ Primary Feelings ⟶ Shame
Helplessness
Inadequacy

from *Caring Discipline: Practical Tools for Nurturing Happy Families & Classrooms*

Resources

Beattie, Melody. *Codependent No More & Beyond Codependency.* **Hazelden, 1997.**

A straightforward and personal explanation of how hidden unmet needs contribute to unhealthy, codependent relationships. The author gives hope and encouragement to all those trying to learn how to value and take care of themselves.

Bradshaw, John. *Healing the Shame that Binds You.* **Health Communications, Inc., 2005.**

Discusses the hidden unmet needs of the adult. Needs that were unmet as a child leave "gaping holes" which can cause rage directed at our own children. Bradshaw describes the dysfunctional family patterns which give rise to the problem and discusses ways these wounds can be healed. Bradshaw's video tapes may also be available from your public library.

Crook, William G., M.D. *The Yeast Connection Handbook.* **Professional Books, Inc., 2007.**

A good introduction to the idea that many children's behavior problems are caused by yeast infections. Dr. Crook explains the connection between antibiotic use, modern diet, and the resulting overgrowth of candida in the body. Chapter eight focuses specifically on children's behavior/health problems and gives detailed directions for how to reduce the negative effects when your child must take antibiotics. The book is also a wealth of information on where to go for more help.

Dreikurs, Rudolf and Loren Grey. *Discipline Without Tears.* **Plume, 1991.**

Influenced by the great Austrian psychotherapist Alfred Adler, Dreikurs was the first and best known popular advocate of using logical consequences to deal with misbehaviors. This book has numerous case histories. Dreikurs also emphasized the idea that parents should act instead of talking so much.

Elkind, David. *The Hurried Child: Growing Up Too Fast, Too Soon.* Da Capo Press, 1986.

> Shares concerns about children growing up too fast, too soon. Both schools and families demand things of children before they are ready to do them. Hurried children are stressed by the fear of failure—of not achieving fast enough or high enough.

Faber, Adele and Elaine Mazlish. *How to Talk So Kids Will Listen and How to Listen So Kids Will Talk.* Norton, 2012. *Siblings Without Rivalry: How to Help Your Children Live Together So You Can Live Too.* Norton, 2012.

> Both books are easy reading. *How to Talk So Kids Will Listen* focuses on communication skills, for example, how to give commands, how to use describing words for praise and sharing how you feel, and how to listen to feelings. Tells how to avoid power struggles. *Siblings Without Rivalry* has good tips on how to deal with the new baby, fighting, and ways to promote cooperation between children.

Fay, Jim and David Funk. *Teaching With Love and Logic: Taking Control of the Classroom,* (also audio CD available). Love and Logic Press, 1998. Fay, Jim et al. *Parenting With Love and Logic: Teaching Children Responsibility,* (also audio CD available). Love and Logic Press, 2006.

> Excellent ideas for logical consequence planning. The talks on the CD are highly entertaining and informative, but watch out for possible self-sabotage in the speaker's tone of voice.

Fraiberg, Selma. *The Magic Years: Understanding and Handling the Problems of Early Childhood.* Scribner, 1996.

> Explores the age of magical thinking when children believe their thoughts can cause things to happen, for example, when they take responsibility for a divorce or even a death in the family.

Garbarino, James. *Lost Boys: Why Our Sons Turn Violent and How We Can Save Them.* Free Press, 2000.

> An impressively well-researched and thoughtful study about why some American boys become violent, and what can be done to prevent such behavior and how to help when preventive efforts fail. Twenty-five years as a psychologist working with boys has convinced Dr. Garbarino that boys really are angrier and more violent than before. He outlines the steps par-

ents, teachers, and public officials can take to keep all children safer. One of his recommendations for ways to help violent boys is to place them in institutions more akin to monasteries than the boot camps that seem to be so popular today.

Gardner, Richard A. *The Boys and Girls Book About Divorce.* **Turtleback, 1992.**

Excellent book for elementary and middle school children whose parents are going through a divorce. Also good for a parent and younger child to read and discuss together.

Gurian, Michael. *The Wonder of Boys: What Parents, Mentors, and Educators Can Do to Shape Boys into Exceptional Men.* **J.P. Tarcher, 2006.**

A therapist and educator shares his thought-provoking ideas about raising boys. Gurian says that biological and neurological differences between boys and girls need to be accounted for in order to raise healthy, happy boys. He argues that boys do best when they are included in a "tribe" of men who teach by example how to become a fully functioning, responsible male member of society. A must-read for anyone who has a son or works with boys.

Hartmann, Thom. *Thom Hartmann's Complete Guide to ADHD: Help for Your Family at Home, School, and Work.* **Underwood Books, 2000.**

A former therapist who himself was diagnosed with ADD and expelled from school when he was in his teens, Thom proposes an up-beat explanation of ADHD/ADD involving the idea that there are two basic brain styles which he calls the Hunter and the Farmer brain. He emphasizes that there is nothing wrong with either kind of brain: the ADHD child does not have a defective brain. The ADHD child only looks like a problem because our schools are set up to teach to the Farmer child brain. This book is a treasure chest of ideas for anyone living with ADHD/ADD.

Hartmann, Thom. *The Edison Gene: ADHD and the Gift of the Hunter Child.* **Underwood Books, 2010.**

In this second edition of the *Complete Guide*, Thom expands on his earlier ideas and discusses how evolution culminated in the development of what is called the Edison Gene (Edison being one of the many creative people who had ADD). The Edison Gene is another helpful and up-beat presentation of ideas to help parents and teachers nurture the potential of the ADHD child.

Hayden, Torey L. *One Child: The True Story of a Tormented Six-year-old and the Brilliant Teacher Who Reached Out.* **William Morrow, 2016.**

Reads like a novel. A true story of one teacher's work with an emotionally disturbed child. Illustrates how discipline can be healing for children when, at the same time, it also helps build their emotional needs staircase. The teacher uses strategies like time-out, physical restraint, routines, ignoring, giving choices, paying attention at positive and neutral times, listening to feelings, and many others you will find familiar.

James, Muriel, and Dorothy Jongewar. *Born To Win: Transactional Analyses with Gestalt Experiments.* **Perseus Press, 1996.**

Based on the ideas of Transactional Analysis which were presented earlier by Eric Berne in *Games People Play*, this book is easier to read and is valuable for any group focused on exploring their own hidden, unmet needs. Contains many usable exercises and discussion topics at the end of each chapter. Chapter four is especially good for its comprehensive explanation of how children are unwittingly scripted for certain types of behavior.

Keirsey, David and Marilyn Bates. *Please Understand Me II: Temperament, Character and Intelligence.* **Prometheus, 1998.**

An explanation of the basic four personality types and their combinations, based on the writings of Jung, the Myers-Briggs Type Indicator test, and the authors' considerable experience. Includes a self-test. This book would be helpful for any discussion/support group to use as a way of gaining more understanding and respect for one another's basic personalities. It also offers insights into the difficulties involved when the adult's personality type clashes with that of the child.

Liedloff, Jean. *The Continuum Concept: In Search of Happiness Lost.* **Perseus Press, 1986.**

A look at the way the Tauripan Indians of South America raise their children. The Tauripan people keep young children close to an adult's body, even when sleeping, until the child no longer wants to be there. Logical and natural consequences are widely used with no scolding or other talking about the misbehavior. Punishment is unheard of and young children receive much nurturing from adults. The author is convinced these child-rearing practices must be the reason she saw so many happy, confident people in this society.

Masarie, Kathy, Kathy Keller Jones, et al. *Face to Face: Cultivating Kids' Social Lives in Today's Digital World.* **Family Empowerment Network, 2014, www.family-empower.com.**

Authored by a team of pediatricians and educators, *Face to Face* explores many important topics related to raising children. One of its key focuses is how to keep digital technology from influencing children's lives to the detriment of their social and emotional development. The award-winning book features many specific and useful ideas for parents and teachers who are trying to navigate and establish boundaries related to ever-increasing screen use by kids.

Maslow, Abraham. *Toward A Psychology of Being,* **3rd ed. John Wiley and Sons, 1998.**

Not especially easy reading, but well worth the effort for a look at Maslow's original concept of a hierarchy of needs which has been adapted in this book as a stairway of needs. An optimistic and caring look at the enormous potential of human beings.

Mayer, Mercer. *At the Beach With Dad.* **Inchworm Press, 1998.** *Just a Snowy Day.* **Golden Press, 2006.**

These two titles are only a sampling from this prolific author. Many of Mayer's stories tell about Henry, the rascally critter who is frequently getting into trouble and is lovable all the same. Conveys the message to young children that they are not bad persons even if they sometimes need to go sit in a quiet corner.

Miller, Alice and Hildegarde Hannum. *For Your Own Good: Hidden Cruelty in Child-rearing and the Roots of Violence,* **3rd ed. Noonday Press, 2002.**

Makes a convincing case that emotional and physical child abuse causes violence in later life and illustrates how cruel child-rearing tactics caused the destructiveness of an Adolph Hitler.

Nordling, JoAnne. *Taking Charge/Caring Discipline Classes,* **1997. Available for viewing on www.YouTube.com. Six video parenting sessions led by JoAnne Nordling.**

Tualatin Valley Community Access TV, 1998, produced and filmed by Dawn LaGrosa. Family Meeting session: Community Television of Lane County, Eugene, Oregon, 2000, produced and filmed by Sarah Lauer, Robert Mueller, and volunteers at CTLC. A series of six videos available for viewing on www.YouTube.com (enter "Parent Support Center" in the search window), filmed at Trillium Hollow, a co-housing community in Portland, Oregon. The teacher for these sessions is JoAnne Nordling, author of the *Caring Discipline* program. The first four sessions present the basic *Caring Discipline* approach, the fifth session is a problem-solving session with a group of adults, and the sixth session features two actual family meetings with both kids and parents participating.

Pipher, Mary Bray. *Reviving Ophelia: Saving the Selves of Adolescent Girls.* **Putnam, 1994.**

A counselor of adolescent girls talks about the myriad problems facing young women growing up in our hypersexualized culture, what one reviewer called "a girl-poisoning, junk culture." Pipher offers insight into the dilemmas parents face in trying to help our daughters through the cultural minefield of adolescence and offers ways to counteract the negative scripting that infiltrates our homes through the media. The book is filled with stories of Pipher's teenage clients and their struggle towards adulthood. This is a must read book for parents and teachers of adolescent girls.

Pollack, William and Mary Pipher. *Real Boys: Rescuing Our Sons from the Myths of Boyhood.* **Owl Books, 1999.**

A psychologist and counselor explore the unspoken "boy code" that teaches boys they should hide their feelings, be tough and independent. Pollack makes the case that being taught to cover up their emotions results in boys with fragile self-esteem, academic and emotional difficulties, school violence, sometimes culminating in suicide. The author gives advice on ways for parents and teachers to help boys learn to accept and express feelings.

Rapp, Doris, M.D. *Is This Your Child?: Discovering and Treating Unrecognized Allergies in Children and Adults.* **Morrow, 1991.**

A well-known pediatrician and children's allergist explains how to recognize whether your child has a behavioral or physical problem because of an allergy. She also helps you decide which form of therapy is best for your child. Practical and specific information.

Sax, Leonard. *The Collapse of Parenting: How We Hurt Our Kids When We treat Them Like Grown-Ups.* **Basic Books, 2016.**

A physician and psychologist with a long career of working with parents and kids, Dr. Sax observes that many parents are stunting their children's character development because of their fear of seeming too dictatorial. These parents end up not being able to set limits for their kids, an abdication of authority that allows a child become increasingly reliant on peers and the media for guidance on how to conduct themselves in relationships with others rather than getting such guidance at home; a problem made worse if the child has unlimited access to digital technology. The author dislikes the increasing practice of prescribing dangerous drugs to change the behavior of misbehaving kids, rather than strengthening the parental role to improve the child's behavior.

Trelease, Jim. *The Read-Aloud Handbook,* **6th ed. Penguin Books, 2006.**

This is an invaluable resource for any parent or teacher who wants their kids to love reading. The author tells you not only "why" we should read aloud to our children, but "how" to read and discuss books with children at various ages. An added bonus is the excellent chapter on how to control the use of television in your home. Includes an extensive list of recommended books.

Weil, Andrew, M.D. *Natural Health, Natural Medicine: The Complete Guide to Wellness and Self-Care for Optimum Health.* **Houghton-Mifflin Co., 2004.**

Dr. Weil is a Harvard educated M.D. who decided to incorporate natural therapies into his standard medical practice. He believes in a team approach to health care, and that the most important member of the team is you.

Parent Support Center

The *Caring Discipline* approach provides guidelines and tools for teaching practical ways to take charge of the adult/child relationship so that both adult and child feel respected, secure, and loved.

You can register for one of several types of *Caring Discipline* classes by clicking on our website link www.parentsupportcenter.org: 1) Those living in the Portland metropolitan area can register for a five-week course, with sliding scale and scholarship options available; 2) No matter where you live, you can register for a six-week online course; 3) You can also access free videos of six class sessions by going to Youtube.com and typing "Parent Support Center" into the search box; 4) Lastly, you can go to our website to download a free audio discussion of *Caring Discipline* by the author, JoAnne Nordling and Nancy Smorch, former director of the North American Parenting Institute.

 Parent Support Center teachers and board members send their best wishes that relationships with the children in your care become ever more joyous and loving as you help them grow towards the very best they are capable of becoming.

About the Author

JoAnne Nordling, M.S. M.Ed., began her career as a classroom teacher and then served as an elementary school counselor for many years. Her extensive experience working with children, parents and educators resulted in a parenting approach that gives adults the tools enabling them to establish loving relationships with their children, and set firm limits without creating power struggles, ensuring that their children will grow up happy, responsible, and confident.

She is director of Parent Support Center in Portland, Oregon and is active in organizing parenting and educator classes and workshops for Portland area communities.

Ms. Nordling and her husband, George, have four sons, three daughters-in-law, five grandchildren, and six great-grandchildren.

Index

Comments from those who have experience applying the *Caring Discipline* principles

"**I feel so blessed** ... Not only has the material been excellent ... and applicable to our family ... I think parents often find themselves feeling alone or isolated in raising children and dealing with problems and discipline ... this book almost gives you a hug in letting you know you're not alone ."
   — *Heather Creighton, mother*

"*Caring Discipline* **has been foundational** to my parenting and my classroom management as a teacher."
   — *Andrew Oldham, teacher and administrator, Maris High School, Eugene, OR*

"**Every parent and teacher should read it** ... this stuff works!! Nordling captures the basics and turns them into reality in this book of utilizing parenting skills at any age or stage ... it's a must have ... "
   — *Review from confirmed purchaser on Amazon.com*

"**It does work!** When my husband and I agreed to take on our troubled 14-year-old granddaughter for the three months of her summer vacation, we were worried ... because she was known for being hyperactive, undisciplined and uncooperative. A friend recommended the book *Caring Discipline*. We both read it and agreed that we'd follow the book's advice on handling children. The summer was a greater success than either of us had dared to hope for. After several weeks ... our granddaughter settled into a comfortable routine. She obeyed with few complaints and became a secure, happy, cooperative person. She even gained pride and self-esteem in her accomplishments. I would recommend the book to any parent or guardian."
   — *Jan McFadden, grandmother, Issaquah, Washington*

"... **The inner and outer reality information is amazing**. Understandably, our adopted child has a lot of anger and we have not known how to deal with that effectively. I can see that just listening to her and acknowledging her feelings may go a long way to helping her overcome the issues she still wrestles with. There are many such solutions for issues we face every day in the book, I literally take notes so I can remember them and put them into practice ... thank you ..."
   — *Sue Hawes, Parent*

"**I am convinced** after teaching over twenty-seven years in the grade school classroom and physical education that her positive, practical approach to discipline is the 'only way to fly!' "
— *Paul E. Voeller, physical education teacher*

"**I was given a copy** of *Caring Discipline* upon the birth of my daughter, 12 years ago. It is the most intelligent and clearly written book on children's behavior that I have ever read. Now, as director of a preschool, I require that all of our teachers and parents read JoAnne Nordling's book. This book has become a powerful and intelligent guide for dialoguing about our children's behavior and development. One of the most important parts of early childhood development is the social peace that happens when children are learning how to be with each other. When conflicts arise between children, we employ the problem-solving techniques that Ms. Nordling so clearly describes. It isn't long before our children are empowered to negotiate their own conflicts independent of the adults. When that happens, we know that these children are beginning to learn what it means to care about and live in this world with other people.
— *Michele R. Miller, M. Ed., Director of The Garden's Noise Preschool, Portland, Oregon*

"**I teach a course on Parenting,** Partnering and Resolving Marital Conflict. In preparing the course, I read every book I could find on positive parenting and discipline ... *Caring Discipline* is the best ..."
— *Steven Allen Smith, Family Law Attorney, Portland, Oregon*

"**I must tell you, and thank you, for your book again.** My daughter was here one day, fit to be tied, she was having so much trouble with her six-year-old. That was three months ago. What a nice change has taken place in their relationship. I wanted you to know it's working in North Dakota!"
— *Phyllis Jesson, grandmother, Beach, North Dakota*

"**Your presence here in Lake County has made a difference** ... Know that none of us who participated in your workshop will think the same (about parenting) anymore."
— *Audrey Ward, Coordinator for Home Peace, Lake County, California*

"**In the six years that I have been a parent,** I have read and learned a lot of information about parenting. This book has been more help to me than anything else. It really works!"
— *Darlene R. Weverka, mother*

"**My husband and I were living in Costa Rica** sixteen years ago when we formed our first *Caring Discipline* parenting group. While there were distinct differences in parenting styles and practices, the material crossed these boundaries and was effective in both cultures ... the material works its magic with preschoolers as well as it does with teenagers. I had read other parenting books and tried to apply the techniques but nothing ever stuck. I don't know what we would have done if we hadn't found *Caring Discipline* ... My husband and I feel that because of *Caring Discipline* we have built a wonderful relationship with our children. The techniques are so much a part of our children's lives that they have naturally incorporated them into their interactions with others.
— *Sarah Lauer, teacher and parent, Eugene, Oregon*

"**I came to Foster Parenting** with almost no real parenting experience, but with a huge desire to be a supportive person for teens separated from their families because of their involvement with the juvenile justice system ... Luckily for me, I was led to the work of JoAnne Nordling and her organization Parent Support Center by a friend. Suddenly I had guidance and understanding for why behaviors were happening with my youth, and my reactions to them. JoAnne's book gave me methods and tools to shift that behavior, and more importantly a new mind-frame that totally transformed the way I was parenting so that misbehaviors occurred less frequently ... Five years and more than 80 boys later ... who they (the boys) are with me is often 180 degrees different than who they are at school or with the other agency staff ..."
— *Erin Middleton, Foster Mom of more than 80 teenage boys*

"**This material is outstanding as a resource** for teachers and parents. The concepts are understandable and easy to put into practice. But best of all, they work!"
— *Sue Rowland, elementary school teacher*

"**I have been struck by the excitement** parents experience after using the *Caring Discipline* approach. Parents consistently come back to report an increased calmness in dealing with their children's misbehaviors and a feeling that they can build positive relationships."
— *Karen Bissonnette, M.A., child development specialist*

"*Caring Discipline* **is the most practical guide** to disciplining children that I have found. I share it regularly with family, friends, and clients."
— *Sharon C. Firsich, R.N., M.S.*

"**Coming from a home** with a lack of self-discipline and consistent discipline, I found *Caring Discipline* an organized but gentle way of providing discipline for my children and for myself. A must as a workbook and constant reference!"
— *Paulette Wheeler, parent*

"**This jewel of a parenting guide** fills in the gaps left by yesterday's 'authorities' on parenting. Of special importance to today's parents is Ms. Nordling's concept on correcting children's self-indulgent behavior. She writes with authority and love."
— *Mary Lansing, LMFT Family and Group Therapist, author of Loving Your Child, Past, Present and Future*

"**Not only does it give practical suggestions** for dealing with specific behaviors but it helps parents and teachers to understand the root causes of children's behaviors. I highly recommend this book to parents, teachers, child care providers, teen parents, and anyone who works with children."
— *Dr. Dorothy Anker, Ph. D., Erikson Institute*

"**When I first read the material** I was skeptical about whether it would work with the group I've had most of my previous experience with. Let me say that all my skepticism has disappeared ... never before did I feel I had really changed the way parents are dealing with their children. I do now. Parents tell me over and over again how much difference knowing this material has made to their relationship with their children. It also provides a framework that parents can go back to and use again and again. I cannot praise it enough!"
— *Lorraine Heller, Head Start Teacher (retired), parenting class teacher, and co-founder of Parent Support Center*

"The book by JoAnne Nordling is one of the best resources I have found for parents. We have used it as the primary curriculum for our parenting classes and have found it to be both solid in theory as well as practical in guidance for the daily trials of raising a child in today's world. The insights you will find herein will benefit you and your children for years to come ... Parents who put the principles of *Caring Discipline* into practice will find parenting to be the true joy it should be for all."
> — *Rev. Daniel E.H. Bryant, D. Min., Senior Minister,*
> *First Christian Church, Eugene, Oregon*

"One single mother told me that going to the *Caring Discipline* parenting class was her favorite evening of the week, and we have seen positive changes in her child at school. She also felt very comfortable in the class which is an important consideration."
> — *Sally Krebs, M.A., Elementary School Counselor*

"This book is an invaluable guide for single parents."
> — *Betty Daggett, M.S.W., L.C.S.W., Director,*
> *SOLO Center, A Resource for Single Adults*

"As a teacher of parenting classes sponsored by the Washington County Community Action Organization, I found the *Caring Discipline* information to be of tremendous value ... my students reported positive results with excitement. They were especially happy they were able to make positive changes without resorting to yelling or spanking."
> — *Derene Meuresse, parenting teacher*

"The book is so easy to understand, concise, and concrete."
> — *Elsa Jane Weeslogel, Good Samaritan Ministries*

"In a volunteer capacity, I teach Parenting Workshops for the Division of Children and Family Services, Department of Social Services, in Vancouver, Washington. The clients are parents who often fall into the high risk category for psychological and/or physical abuse of their children through aggression or abandonment behaviors. This book answers major needs for this population. With clear simplicity, it addresses complicated problems. *Caring*

Discipline successfully presents the tools that children (and adults) need to develop self-esteem and personal courage ... and with a few fundamental steps, teaches parents how to amend misbehavior and move toward a more successful family."
— *Victoria Shenk, parenting teacher*

"**I would like to express my enthusiasm** for JoAnne Nordling's book *Caring Discipline*. I have found the ideas and suggestions in the book to be very helpful to me in working with the parents I see in both my private practice, and my work as a clinician at Solano County Mental Health ... The numerous vignettes presented by Ms. Nordling from her work with parents over the years offers parents a humorous, non-threatening way of examining their interactions with their children ... interventions are well defined in relation to identified behaviors, and are presented in an easy to understand fashion ... "
— *Marie O'Meara, M.S.W, L.C.S.W.*

"**The Caring Discipline model has had a significant impact** on the women and children in residence at our shelter. The women are able to understand the concepts and utilize the training in the short time they are in residence (four to six weeks.) I've found the book to be invaluable in work in the shelter, and in my own family with my four-year-old daughter."
— *Marilyn May, former executive director of the Domestic Violence Resource Center in Hillsboro, Oregon*

"**As a parent who loves her child** and as a teacher who cares about her pupils-the true concern is that all youth maintain self-esteem ... this book teaches that ... right to the point, without a lot of psych terms or technical language. It is straight-forward, practical advice which eliminates anger or defensiveness in either adult or child."
— *Julie Hitchman, teacher and mother of two*

"**I really enjoyed getting concrete** and specific corrections for common, everyday behavior problems in JoAnne's book ... . I use the information from her book every day in my classroom!"
— *Cheryl Watson, elementary school teacher*

"**Caring Discipline has made a lasting,** good impression on me … you have brought so much common sense and experience to the subject … the book is a wonderful service to parents and teachers and deserves to be widely read, at home, and in schools … you have chosen a subject basic to happiness all over the world! Bless you!"
— *Charlotte Tompkins, grandmother*

"**What a thrill to open your book** for the first time! It's a book that will create needed changes in families to become more respectful to each other's feelings. Many blessings will come from your love and insights given to others through this expression of yourself … "
— *Jean Lawrence, past Director of Fanno Creek Children's Center, Portland, Oregon*

"**I have taught parenting classes for four years** now using *Caring Discipline* and the best recommendation for JoAnne Nordling's book are the comments of the parents. They enthusiastically recommend the book and class to everyone they know! Not only have I been able to help other parents with the dilemmas they face, I have learned how to work more effectively with my own family."
— *Dennis Adams, teacher, West Linn School District, Oregon*

"**The stories in the book are wonderful examples** … I have learned so much and have applied these concepts over and over with my three children, and they work!"
— *Marietta McCaha, mother*

"*Taking Charge* (*Caring Discipline*) **is a well-designed guide** to setting healthy limits and putting yourself back in charge without undermining the child's sense of security and self-worth."
— *The Bloomsbury Review*

"**This book has wonderful insights** into the way parents think which lead to in-effective ways of discipline. But I've been able to rethink my reasons for disciplining and found more effective ways of intervention. Great book. Time well spent."
— *Donna Gould, mother*

"**As an older parent of a five-year-old**, I thought I knew everything necessary to be a great parent. We used time-outs in the traditional manner when discipline was needed. But this book is much more sophisticated and much better in its recommended approach. The time-out is a last resort in this book and is only suggested for aggressive behavior problems. Many good ideas for fostering cooperation and harmony in a respectful way. I wish I had read it years earlier. Get this book for a new parent you know and make their life—and their child's—easier and happier!"

    — *Victor, Parent*

Made in the USA
Las Vegas, NV
08 September 2022

54913160R00203